Lecture Notes of the Institute for Computer Sciences, Social Informatics and Telecommunications Engineering 261

More information about this series at http://www.springer.com/series/8197

Ingrid Moerman · Johann Marquez-Barja
Adnan Shahid · Wei Liu
Spilios Giannoulis · Xianjun Jiao (Eds.)

Cognitive Radio Oriented Wireless Networks

13th EAI International Conference, CROWNCOM 2018
Ghent, Belgium, September 18–20, 2018
Proceedings

 Springer

Editors
Ingrid Moerman 🄳
Ghent University
Ghent, Belgium

Wei Liu
Ghent University
Zwijnaarde, Belgium

Johann Marquez-Barja
University of Antwerp
Antwerpen, Belgium

Spilios Giannoulis 🄳
Ghent University
Zwijnaarde, Belgium

Adnan Shahid 🄳
Ghent University
Zwijnaarde, Belgium

Xianjun Jiao
Ghent University
Zwijnaarde, Belgium

ISSN 1867-8211   ISSN 1867-822X   (electronic)
Lecture Notes of the Institute for Computer Sciences, Social Informatics
and Telecommunications Engineering
ISBN 978-3-030-05489-2   ISBN 978-3-030-05490-8   (eBook)
https://doi.org/10.1007/978-3-030-05490-8

Library of Congress Control Number: 2018963585

This Springer imprint is published by the registered company Springer Nature Switzerland AG
The registered company address is: Gewerbestrasse 11, 6330 Cham, Switzerland

Preface

We are delighted to introduce the proceedings of the second edition of the 2018 European Alliance for Innovation (EAI) International Conference on Cognitive Radio-Oriented Wireless Networks (CROWNCOM). This conference has brought together researchers from around the world from academia, industry, standards, and policy to present their new solutions of how cognitive radio systems will help deliver the required stringent requirements of future 5G and beyond 5G networks.

The technical program of CROWNCOM 2018 consisted of 19 full papers, divided into three tracks. The tracks were: Track 1, Experimental; Track 2, Licensed Shared Access and Dynamic Spectrum Access; and Track 3, PHY and Sensing. Aside from the high-quality technical paper presentations, the technical program also featured four keynote speeches, two discussion panels, two technical workshops, and four tutorials.

The four keynote speakers were Prof. Jens Zander from KTH, Sweden, Dr. Haris Gacanin from Nokia Bell labs, Belgium, Prof. Danijela Cabric from UCLA, USA, and Dr. Domenico Giustiniano from IMDEA, Spain. The two discussion panels were focused on issues regarding "5G and Beyond" and also on the "Struggle for Spectrum." The two workshops organized were the Orchestration and Reconfiguration of Networked Software-Defined Radios (ORCA) and the Open Radio Platforms for 5G Research and Beyond. The ORCA workshop aimed to present advanced SDR capabilities and how these capabilities can be used by wireless innovators from academia and industry to increase spectrum efficiency and end-to-end performance in verticals that have to cope with extreme and diverging communication needs. The second workshop aimed to present the latest developments on existing platforms (both in the hardware and software domains) for 5G research and beyond, with a special focus on open source developments, as the latter facilitate innovation in the mobile networks ecosystem. The four tutorials were: Unlicensed Spectrum Technologies: From Wi-Fi to 5G and Beyond; NOMA for Next-Generation Wireless Networks: State of the Art, Research Challenges, and Future Trends; Wireless Link Virtualization and Network Function Virtualization in Cognitive Radio Networks: Theories, Use-Cases, and Hands-On Experiments; and Transceiver Design for Spectrum Sharing Full Duplex Radio.

Coordination with the steering chair Imrich Chlamtac and the rest of the Steering Committee members was essential for the success of the conference. We sincerely appreciate their constant support and guidance. It was also a great pleasure to work with such an excellent Organizing Committee team, they truly gave their best in organizing and supporting the conference. In particular, we thank the Technical Program Committee, led by our TPC co-chairs, Dominique Noguet, Johann Marquez-Barja, Xianjun Jiao, Miquel Payaro, Pierluigi Gallo, and Andres Garcia Saavedra, who completed the peer-review process of technical papers and compiled a high-quality technical program. We are also grateful to our conference manager,

Andrea Piekova, and the EAI team for their support and all the authors who submitted their papers to the CROWNCOM 2018 conference and workshops.

We strongly believe that CROWNCOM conference provides a good forum for all researchers interested in wireless communications to discuss all science and technology aspects that are relevant to cognitive radios and new immersing wireless technologies applicable to 5G and beyond. We also expect that CROWNCOM will continue to be a successful and stimulating conference, as indicated by the contributions presented in this volume and the challenges that still arise in front of us in the wireless research domain.

November 2018   Ingrid Moerman

Organization

Steering Committee

Chair

Imrich Chlamtac   Bruno Kessler Professor, University of Trento, Italy

Members

Thomas Hou	Virginia Tech, USA
Abdur Rahim Biswas	CREATE-NET, Italy
Tao Chen	VTT – Technical Research Centre of Finland, Finland
Tinku Rasheed	CREATE-NET, Italy
Dominique Noguet	CEA-LETI, France

Organizing Committee

General Chair

Ingrid Moerman   IMEC – Ghent University, Belgium

TPC Chair and Co-chairs

Dominique Noguet	CEA-LETI, France
Johann Marquez-Barja	IMEC – University of Antwerp, Belgium
Xianjun Jiao	IMEC – Ghent University, Belgium
Pierluigi Gallo	CNIT, Italy
Miquel Payaro	CTTC, Spain
Andres Garcia Saavedra	NEC Laboratories Europe, Germany

Sponsorship and Exhibit Chair

Steven Latré   IMEC – University of Antwerp, Belgium

Local Co-chairs

Karen Van Landegem	IMEC – Ghent University, Belgium
Muhammad Aslam	IMEC – Ghent University, Belgium

Workshops Chair

Wei Liu   IMEC – Ghent University, Belgium

Publicity and Social Media Co-chairs

Margherita Trestini	Martel Innovate, Switzerland
Adnan Shahid	IMEC – Ghent University, Belgium

Publications Chair

Spilios Giannoulis   IMEC – Ghent University, Belgium

Posters and PhD Track Chair

Felipe Augusto Pereira de   IMEC – Ghent University, Belgium
   Figueiredo

Panels Chair

Jorge Pereira   European Commission, Belgium

Demos Co-chairs

Sofie Pollin   KU Leuven, Belgium
Ivan Seskar   Rutgers University, USA

Tutorials Chair

Hamed Ahmadi   University of Essex, UK

Technical Program Committee

Youping Zhao	Beijing Jiaotong University, China
Chung Shue Chen	Nokia Bell Labs, Paris, France
Rahman Doost-Mohammady	Rice University, USA
Mubashir Husain Rehmani	Waterford Institute of Technology (WIT), Ireland
Keith Nolan	Intel, Ireland
Syed Ali Hassan	National University of Sciences and Technology, Pakistan
Shahriar Shahabuddin	Centre for Wireless Communications, University of Oulu, Finland
Tanguy Risset	INSA-Lyon, France
Takeo Fujii	The University of Electro-Communications, Japan
Ludovic Apvrille	Telecom ParisTech, France
Henning Sanneck	Nokia Bell Labs, Research, Munich, Germany
Yue Gao	Queen Mary University of London, UK
Vincent Le Nir	Royal Military Academy, Belgium
Adrian Kliks	Poznan University of Technology, Poland
Fernando Velez	IT-DEM, Universidade da Beira Interior, Portugal
Bernd Bochow	Fraunhofer FOKUS, Germany
Zexian Li	Nokia Bell Labs, Finland
Michael Gundlach	Nokia Networks, Munich, Germany
Seppo Yrjölä	Nokia
Angelos Antonopoulos	CTTC, Spain

Pawel Kryszkiewicz	Poznan University of Technology, Poland
Pravir Chawdhry	European Commission Joint Research Centre, Italy
Olivier Sentieys	IRISA/Inria, France
Hans-Jürgen Zepernick	Blekinge Institute of Technology, Sweden
Igor Radusinovic	University of Montenegro, Montenegro
Dionysia Triantafyllopoulou	University of Surrey, UK
Hamed Ahmadi	University College Dublin, Ireland
Luca De Nardis	Sapienza University of Rome, Italy
Adnan Aijaz	Toshiba Research Europe, UK
Marco Di Felice	University of Bologna, Italy
Anwer Al-Dulaimi	EXFO Inc., Toronto, Canada
Marc Emmelmann	Technical University of Berlin, Germany
Paulo Marques	IT, Portugal
Mika Kasslin	Nokia Bell Labs, Finland
Antonio De Domenico	CAE Leti, France
Allen MacKenzie	Virginia Tech, USA
Carlos Caicedo	Syracuse University, USA
Serhat Erkucuk	Kadir Has University, Turkey
Samson Lasaulce	CNRS, France
Paweł Kaniewski	Military Communication Institute, Poland
Matthieu Gautier	Université de Rennes 1, IRISA, Inria, France
William Lehr	MIT, USA
Kimon Kontovasilis	NCSR Demokritos, Greece
Martin Weiss	University of Pittsburgh, USA
Heikki Kokkinen	Fairspectrum, Finland
Doug Brake	ITIF, USA
Stefan Aust	NEC Communication Systems, Ltd., Japan
Seong-Lyun Kim	Yonsei University, Japan
Dominique Noguet	CEA-LETI, France
Milica Pejanovic Djurisic	University of Montenegro, Montenegro
Ozgur Ergul	Koc University, Turkey
Jean-Baptiste Doré	CEA-LETI, France
Fabio Giust	NEC Laboratories Europe, Germany
Ozgur Akan	Koc University, Turkey
Markus Mueck	Intel Mobile Communications, Germany
Rogerio Dionisio	Instituto Politecnico de Castelo Branco, Portugal
Cristina Cano	Universitat Oberta de Catalunya, Spain
Klaus Moessner	University of Surrey, UK
Vincenzo Sciancalepore	NEC Laboratories Europe GmbH, Germany
Marco Gramaglia	Universidad Carlos III de Madrid, spain
Karthick Parashar	IMEC, Belgium
Mohammad Hossein Anisi	University of Essex, UK
Victor Valls	Trinity College Dublin, Ireland
Rahman Doost-Mohammady	Rice University, USA

Luis Diez	University of Cantabria, Italy
Paul Patras	The University of Edinburgh, UK
Yuanjie Li	UCLA, USA
Dan Lubar	RelayServices, USA
Carlos Donato	imec, Univeristy of Antwerp, Belgium
Gerhard Wunder	Fu Berlin, Germany

Contents

PHY and Sensing

Experimental

Experimental Analysis of 5 GHz WiFi and UHF-TVWS Hybrid Wireless Mesh Network Back-Haul Links

Richard Maliwatu$^{(\boxtimes)}$, Natasha Zlobinsky, Magdeline Lamola,
Augustine Takyi, David L. Johnson, and Melissa Densmore

University of Cape Town (UCT), Cape Town, South Africa
{rmaliwatu,mdensmore}@cs.uct.ac.za

Abstract. This paper reports on the experimental analysis of hybrid back-haul links comprising WiFi operating in the 5 GHz and Ultra High Frequency Television White Space bands. Possible link permutations are highlighted. Performance results show that overall network optimisation requires a combination of frequency division and time division duplexing.

Keywords: Multi-radio · Dynamic spectrum access
TV white space · Wireless mesh network · 5 GHz WiFi

1 Introduction

Alternative network deployments [1] such as community wireless networks [2] are said to hold the most hope in meeting the goal of extending connectivity services to rural and unconnected communities. However, as currently deployed, realising the required scale has been hampered primarily by WiFi's operating frequency propagation characteristics. The clear line-of-sight required by 2.4/5 GHz bands limits its use cases. Furthermore, the limited transmission radius at the access layer results in prohibitive costs when attempting to provide ubiquitous coverage.

This paper builds on the foundation laid in prior related work [3] for optimal use of Television White Space (TVWS) and 2.4/5 GHz industrial, scientific and medical (ISM) bands for back-haul Wireless Mesh Networks (WMNs) across rural and urban areas, and the region in between. We conducted performance measurements of 5 GHz and Ultra High Frequency (UHF) TVWS links to study the performance of hybrid links in different environmental settings. Prior related work on hybrid links (*see Sect.* 2) has been in the context of infrastructure-mode cellular networks where a client simply connects/disconnects from the base station or access point, which is much more straight forward whereas, for multi-point-to-multi-point multi-radio ad-hoc type networks, the connectivity decision is a non-trivial task in that the choice of connectivity has to be synchronised on both ends of a link. The main contributions of this paper are as follows: (i)

© ICST Institute for Computer Sciences, Social Informatics and Telecommunications Engineering 2019
Published by Springer Nature Switzerland AG 2019. All Rights Reserved
I. Moerman et al. (Eds.): CROWNCOM 2018, LNICST 261, pp. 3–14, 2019.
https://doi.org/10.1007/978-3-030-05490-8_1

Report on the performance of UHF-TVWS and 5 GHz WiFi links in different deployment scenarios using different transmitter/receiver parameter settings; (ii) insight into UHF-TVWS based network deployment; and (iii) a new perspective on multi-radio enabled nodes' link configuration.

2   Background and Related Work

Network capacity and performance can be improved by using multiple channels simultaneously, which requires multiple transceivers. Basic multi-channel capable nodes can be built using one of the following architectures: (i) *Multiple hardware platform* where two or more single-radio nodes are connected via Ethernet to form one logical multi-radio mesh router; (ii) *Single hardware platform* where a single node has multiple transceivers fitted; or (iii) *Single-chip multi-transceivers* where multiple transceivers are integrated into one wireless chipset on a router [4]. This study focuses on nodes fitted with 5 GHz and UHF-TVWS transceivers to realise multi-band-multi-radio nodes. The ISM band is suitable for densely populated urban areas, whereas UHF-TVWS is ideal for sparsely populated rural areas, which also happen to have significantly more TVWS compared to urban communities.

When confronted with diverse population densities, there exists a grey region (sometimes referred to as peri-urban) that is characteristically a cross between rural and urban regions from a spectrum requirement standpoint as shown in Fig. 1. Combining ISM and TVWS bands is appropriate in this region of intersection. Research [3] has shown that in such scenario, the gains of using a combination of the two bands are much larger compared to using either spectrum band by itself.

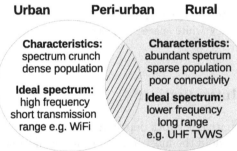

Fig. 1. Spectrum requirements by region.

Applications of WiFi can be categorised coarsely into *access-tier* and *back-haul-tier* network architectural components. The problem of optimal use of TVWS and ISM bands for back-haul connectivity amid diverse population densities is highlighted in WhiteMesh [3]. Other researchers have proposed combining TVWS with 5G infrastructure for rural coverage where traditional cellular coverage models are less economically viable due to low user density and subsequent revenue [5]. The work on TVWS with 5G considers the cost and analyses the feasibility of using TVWS for rural Internet access in 5G, but does not provide any test results of TVWS performance for the proposed architecture.

Regarding the performance of WiFi-like access points operating in TVWS, the benefits of larger coverage area and better obstacle penetration are challenged when inter-access point interference is considered [6]. The lower operating frequency of TVWS results in larger cell sizes and the overlap in contention domains among interfering access points significantly reduces the link data-rate. Therefore, it may be said that the wider coverage range provided by TVWS is considered best suited to rural settings because degradation due to inter-access point interference is minimal because of low access point density. However, a few judiciously well placed TVWS radios spaced far apart in urban areas can offer lower data-rate coverage filling and better building penetration, which is useful in bridging the gaps among clusters of radios operating in the 2.4/5 GHz band.

3   Network Architecture

One of the biggest challenges in rural communities is the extension of connectivity from the nearest point-of-presence (POP) to the houses. These areas are typically characterised by sparse population and rugged terrain, which makes it economically and technically impractical to lay down copper or optical fibre cables. Moreover, vegetation and other obstacles along the signal propagation path results in obstructed line-of-sight.

Owing to the known advantages and drawbacks of *high* and *low* operating radio frequencies, this work considers using a combination of 5 GHz and TVWS for *first-mile* connectivity. We define "first-mile" as the stretch from the location of the remotest user to the closest POP. Figure 2 illustrates the envisioned application scenario. The architecture comprises nodes with radios operating in the 2.4 GHz, 5 GHz and UHF-TVWS bands strategically deployed at key community sites such as schools, clinics, libraries,

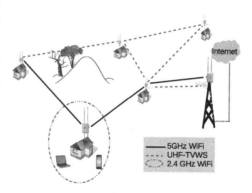

Fig. 2. TVWS, 2.4 and 5 GHz combined to extend broadband connectivity.

office parks and houses. The 2.4 GHz radio serves the access-tier whereas the 5 GHz and UHF-TVWS radios interconnect the nodes in mesh mode to form the back-haul-tier.

4   Problem Description and Formalisation

Given the combination of radios described in Sect. 2, there are nine possible link configurations as the Alice & Bob topology illustrates in Fig. 3.

To generalise, we first consider two wireless devices, node A and node B. Each of these devices has a number of wireless interfaces, which can form connections between the two devices in a variety of configurations and permutations. Consider the different options of technology and band that can be used, and possible combinations of these links with parallel links and link aggregation as shown in Fig. 3. Each individual interface-to-interface link is modelled as a directed edge

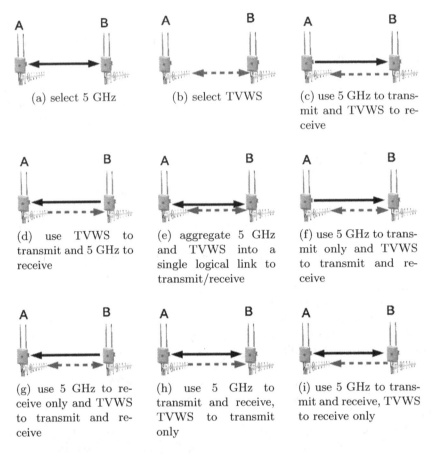

(a) select 5 GHz

(b) select TVWS

(c) use 5 GHz to transmit and TVWS to receive

(d) use TVWS to transmit and 5 GHz to receive

(e) aggregate 5 GHz and TVWS into a single logical link to transmit/receive

(f) use 5 GHz to transmit only and TVWS to transmit and receive

(g) use 5 GHz to receive only and TVWS to transmit and receive

(h) use 5 GHz to transmit and receive, TVWS to transmit only

(i) use 5 GHz to transmit and receive, TVWS to receive only

Fig. 3. Possible options when using 5 GHz and UHF-TVWS hybrid links. The black solid line and blue dashed line respectively represent 5 GHz and UHF-TVWS radio links. (Color figure online)

E in the graph model. An edge can be in one of a number of states, for example we may define the possible states as incident or transmitted. If we assume the wireless devices have a uniform number of radio interfaces, the total number of possible link configurations n is given by

$$n = (p^r - 1)^k \quad \text{for } p, r, k \in \mathbb{N}$$

where p is the number of possible edge states, k is the number of nodes and r is the number of wireless interfaces. The "-1" term is to remove the empty set, which is not a valid link configuration.

The system aims to find the set of link configurations:

$$S = \{S_j\} := \{y_{ji}\} \mapsto \min_i z_{ji}(x)$$

$$\text{where } j = 1, 2, ..., N - 1 \text{ and } i = 1, 2, ..., n \tag{1}$$

where x = amount of data to be served, y = link, z = transmission time, which depends on interference, congestion, etc. and is handled by the MAC protocol, and n = number of possible links, which is dependant on the number of radios per node.

4.1   Single Point-to-Point

It is very easy to determine the optimal link in one of two extreme deployment scenarios: (i) in an area where there is no TVWS available, 5 GHz remains the only option; (ii) when the node spacing is beyond 5 GHz transmission distance capability, TVWS becomes the only option because UHF-TVWS attenuates less compared to 5 GHz as explained by Friis path-loss model [7]. The focus of this paper is on a typical scenario where both 5 GHz and TVWS radios are operable with performance subject to prevailing spatial/temporal spectral and environmental conditions.

For a one-hop scenario i.e. two wireless radio devices communicating only with each other (local optima), the link selection scheme chooses a link configuration y_i from the set of possible link configurations of size n to transmit a data package of size x in the minimum possible time. The time taken for that package transmission on that specific link configuration is $z_i(x)$.

$$y_i \mapsto \min_i z_i(x) : \quad i \in 1, 2, ..., n$$

For a multi-hop system of N identical radio devices, the link selection method chooses a link configuration for each hop S_j, $j \in \{1, 2, ..., N-1\}$ such that the total transmission time is minimised. The total link selection set is denoted

$$S = \{S_1, S_2, ..., S_{N-1}\}$$
$$S_j \in S := y_{ji} \mapsto \min_i z_{ji}(x) : \quad j, i \in \mathbb{N}$$

In Sect. 6 we show that performance depends highly on the combination of parameter settings such as channel, transmission power (txpower), channel width, modulation and coding scheme (MCS), and environmental factors.

4.2   Point-to-Multi-Point

Suppose there are three nodes A, B and C connected as shown in Fig. 4.

When node A has a queue of data destined for node B and another queue for node C, it can aggregate the links, send to node B and thereafter send to node C. Alternatively, node A can split i.e. send to node B on one interface and send to node C on the other interface. We choose a set of link options $\{S_j\}$ where, in this case, $j = 1, 2, ..., N-1$ for N−1 nodes connected to a single node.

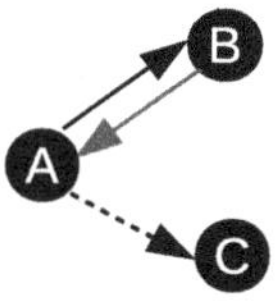

Fig. 4. Transmission options for a point-to-multi-point link.

$$S_j := y_j \mapsto \min_i z_{ji} + \tau \qquad (2)$$

where τ = delay associated with media contention.

5   Experimental Setup

The objective of the study was to investigate the performance of the different 5 GHz and UHF-TVWS radio settings, namely channel, channel-width, and txpower under different environmental conditions such as trees/vegetation, building structures and landscape that tend to affect line-of-sight. Figure 5 shows the node specifications and physical setup. The measurement process involved setting up the nodes on two ends of a site to set the environmental variable. Performance was measured using *iperf* and *ping* tools for different combinations of channel, txpower and channel width settings. The process was controlled from a laptop (not visible in the picture) connected to the node over a dedicated 2.4 GHz WiFi access connection. We also conducted performance measurements using an indoor setup to establish baseline performance prior to setting up the experiment outdoors. The indoor setup comprised nodes set up inside the lab such that node A and node B were 21 m apart, and 1 m, 0.9 m and 4.5 m away from the wall sides while the TVWS antenna stood at 0.36 m below the ceiling.

5 GHz radio:

- i) System board: Mikrotik RB435G
- ii) Operating system: OpenWRT
- iii) WNIC: Atheros-based 802.11 a/b/g mini PCI adapters.
- iv) Driver: Ath5k
- v) Antenna: Brand: made/distributed by scoop (www.scoop.co.za); Model: ANT-P523; Gain: 23 dBi; Frequency: 5150 - 5850 MHz; Cable type and length: coax, 1 m.

TVWS radio:

- i) System board: Mikrotik RB435G
- ii) Operating system: OpenWRT
- iii) WNIC: Doodle labs DL509-78 Broadband Radio Transceiver for the 470-784 MHz TV band.
- iv) Driver: Ath5k
- v) Antenna: Brand/Model: Maxview, MXR0053 TV Aerial -10 element Forward Gain: 8 dB; Front to back ratio: 10-20 dB; Acceptance angle: 25; Frequency range: 470-860 MHz; channel 21-69; Cable type and length: coax, 1.55m.

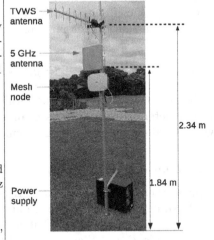

Fig. 5. Node specifications and physical setup.

6   Results and Discussion

6.1   Indoor Performance

Figure 6 shows the relationship between throughput and transmit power observed from the indoor setup. For the 5 GHz WiFi radio, throughput slightly increases with transmit power. We would expect in an outdoor real-world setup there would be a more marked increase in throughput owing to the expected increase in SNR but we suspect that the reduced distance between the nodes reduces the possible range of throughput values. Very surprisingly and counter-intuitively, once the trans-

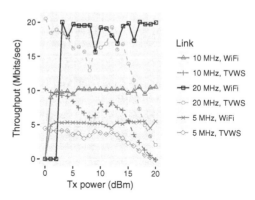

Fig. 6. Throughput vs txpower.

mit power surpasses 10 dBm for TVWS, the throughput in fact decreases rapidly, which completely contradicts Shannon's Law. This is owing to the input signal level at the receiver being well above its recommended range, causing saturation of the electronics and distortion of the signal. The DL509-78 transceiver is quoted to have a recommended input signal strength range of −40 to −80 dBm, while on the TVWS interface the input signal levels were measured to reach above −30 dBm, even climbing to +9 dBm in one measurement and above −20 dBm for a transmit power of 20 dBm in several measurements. Such high input power values cause the signal responses of the RF receiver front-end electronics to become distorted. The operational amplifiers cannot output a voltage above their supply voltage in response to a higher input power - i.e. they saturate at such high input signal levels - so they are unable to reflect the variations in the received signal accurately, causing signal distortion and inability of the system to decode the signal correctly. On the other hand, for the same transmit power values, the receiver-side 5 GHz WiFi card showed lower input signal strength measurements, all falling below −40dBm, so saturation and the resulting decreased throughput was not observed in the experiments on the 5 GHz radio under the same conditions. This observation underscores the point that considering signal strength alone can be misleading when assessing link quality or determining optimal operating parameters as it clearly fails to reflect possible link failure/deterioration due to phenomena such as power saturation.

6.2   Outdoor Performance: Clear Line-of-Sight

Figures 7c and d show the link performance at the University of Cape Town rugby field for the channels tested. Figure 7b shows the TVWS channel mapping to UHF. Performance difference between TVWS channels was due to frequencies mapped to channel 1 & 11 being busier than channel 4 as Fig. 7a shows.

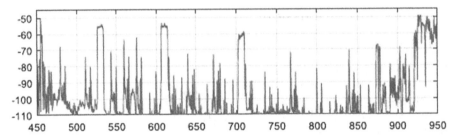

(a) TVWS band spectrum scan. Vertical axis: uncalibrated signal strength; horizontal axis: frequency in MHz.

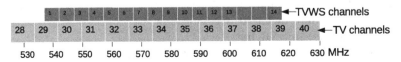

(b) Down-converted WiFi mapping to UHF-TVWS channels.

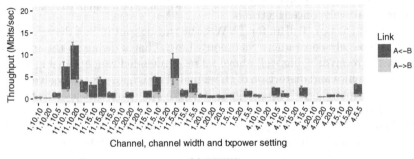

(c) TVWS

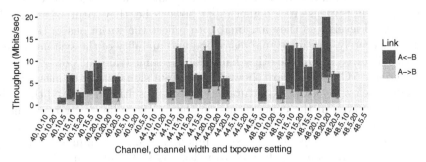

(d) 5 GHz

Fig. 7. Link performance for each of the channel, txpower and channel width settings at one location. The bars are labelled x.y.z where x, y and z respectively represent the channel, txpower (dBm) and channel width (MHz) settings. The absence of a bar at a point e.g, '44.5.20' implies that channel 44 was inoperable with channel width set to 5 MHz and txpower set to 20 dBm. The blue lines indicate the *standard error* calculated as $(standard\ deviation) \div \sqrt(sample\ size)$. (Color figure online)

6.3   Outdoor Performance: Line-of-Sight Obstructed by Trees

One node was fixed on one end while the other was positioned such that a tree obstructed the line-of-sight and repositioned such that there was an incremental number of trees in between. The site had pine trees with trunks typically 2 m in circumference and spaced as follows: 20 m, 28 m, 7 m, 9 m, 5 m, 18 m, 25 m.

Multiple data samples were collected for different combinations of settings. We considered the combination of channel, channel-width and txpower that gave the best results at the highest tree count and used that at all the other tree counts. The rationale is that it is better to have a low-throughput link that works end-to-end than a high-throughput link that breaks mid-way along the path. For the TWVS radio this turned out to be channel $= 7$, chanbw $= 5$ MHz, txpower $= 5$ dBm whereas for 5 GHz it

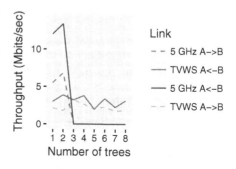

Fig. 8. TVWS and 5 GHz WiFi throughput through trees.

was channel $= 44$, chanbw $= 20$ MHz, txpower $= 20$ dBm. Figure 8 shows the average forward and reverse throughput. From the results it is evident that a 5 GHz WiFi link breaks completely as soon as the link is obstructed by more than two trees. On the other hand, a TVWS link is operable with as many as eight trees obstructing the line-of-sight.

6.4   Summary of Observations and Implications

(i) **Optimal operating parameters.** Each channel appears to perform differently with different settings as shown in Figs. 7c and d. The optimal setting is time and location dependent, and there seems to be an interesting interplay among channel quality, txpower and channel width settings. The task of determining optimal operating parameters is a complex and relevant problem. The immediate implication is that though throughput is generally directly proportional to txpower and channel width, keeping the txpower and channel width at its max does not always maximise performance. Some data points in Figs. 7c and d are missing throughput readings (e.g. TVWS channel $= 11$, chanbw $= 20$ MHz and txpower $= 10$ dBm) because the link became inoperable for that setting at that point in time, which underscores the importance of preceding channel selection with spectrum analysis.

(ii) **Effects of environmental factors.** Objects between or around the nodes affect performance in two ways: (i) obstructing the line-of-sight, thereby impinging on the Fresnel zone clearance, (ii) signal reflections off of objects around the node, which is more pronounced in TVWS compared to 5 GHz due to differences in antenna characteristics. This may account for some of the the performance variations between 5 GHz and TVWS radios.

(iii) **Txpower vs throughput.** At short distances with nodes in close proximity to walls, the 5 GHz link throughput is generally directly proportional to txpower, whereas the TVWS link throughput is inversely proportional to txpower as observed in Fig. 6. This discovery suggests that for indoor applications, the current TVWS state-of-the-art will require low txpower for optimal performance.

(iv) **Link asymmetry.** More often than not links are asymmetric as Figs. 7c and d show. This is caused by a combination of factors ranging from interference sources to imperfections in hardware. Routing protocols need to factor in this link characteristic.

(v) **Vertical vs horizontal polarization.** There were performance variations observed between vertical and horizontal polarization, which may be attributed to differences in channel quality subject to polarization due to other transmitters using a specific polarization. For example, a channel may be vertically occupied, but horizontally vacant or vice-versa. Besides channel quality, there is no statistical evidence to suggest a difference in obstacle penetration/circumvention capability between vertical and horizontally polarised radio antennas.

7   Multi-link Performance

Link aggregation was realised by distributing outbound frames over the 5 GHz and TVWS interfaces, while link splitting was implemented by alternating frame sending and receiving tasks between the two radios using Batman-advanced mesh protocol [8]. Batman-advanced was used because of its inherent support for multi-link optimisation. The data-rate was set by varying the channel width from the set of supported values, which are 20 MHz, 10 MHz, and 5 MHz.

When the radios' data-rates are approximately equal, aggregating provides the best performance in terms of throughput and round trip time (RTT) as shown in Figs. 9a and b. The increases in throughput when aggregated ranges 44.5–61.8 %. The benefit of splitting compared to selecting either radio is not immediately clear unless we consider throughput in the forward as well as reverse direction. The horizontal orange lines in Fig. 9a mark the throughput in the reverse direction. Splitting achieves optimal throughput consistently in either direction, whereas a single radio may have significantly lower throughput in one direction as shown in Fig. 9a.

For links with unequal data-rates, the resultant throughput when the 5 GHz and TVWS links are aggregated is higher than the throughput of the link with a lower data-rate, but less than that of the individual link with higher data-rate as shown in Fig. 9b. Therefore, layer-2 link aggregation is most beneficial when the radios have uniform data-rates. For radios with unequal data-rates, link splitting provides better performance as observed from the RTT in Fig. 9c. The poor performance of aggregation involving non-uniform data-rates is due to an increase in the number of frames arriving out of order, which exacerbates delays in fragment reassembly at the receiving end. On the other hand, when the uplink

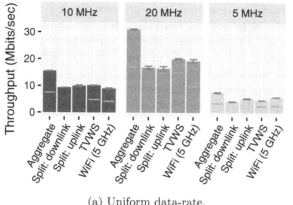

(a) Uniform data-rate.

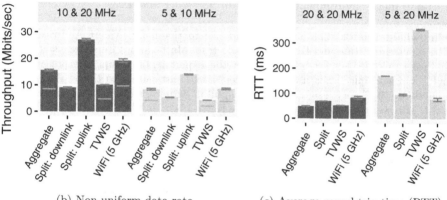

(b) Non-uniform data-rate   (c) Average round trip time (RTT).

Fig. 9. Performance of individual radios, aggregate and split link from the indoor setup. The orange horizontal lines in (a) and (b) mark the link's reverse direction or downlink throughput. To determine RTT, 500 packets were sent with a wait interval of one second and a packet size of 65507 bytes. The maximum transmission unit (MTU) on each interface was 1532 bytes.

and downlink are split between the two radios, there is a significant improvement in throughput relative to individual radio performance as shown in Fig. 9b. The improved performance of a split link sometimes going beyond theoretical expectation may be attributed to the minimised contention delay and subsequent efficiency in the store and forward mechanism, and the sending/receiving of acknowledgement packets.

8   Conclusion and Follow on Work

The results confirm the theoretical expectation, which is that high operating frequencies such as 5 GHz band are suitable for short to medium distance with clear line-of-sight whereas for medium to long distance and obstructed line-of-sight, lower operating frequencies such as UHF-TVWS band out-perform higher frequencies. The choice of spectrum could make or break a wireless link. Further work is needed to understand the intricate interplay among operating parameters, namely txpower, channel width, channel quality and how the surrounding environment influences the choice of optimal operating parameter -especially in a mesh network environment with interdependencies between links.

Future work will include an exploration into effects of weather conditions such as rainfall on link performance. In addition, an expansion of the test-bed is imminent for further investigation into the performance of aggregate and split links as the node count and subsequent traffic flows increase. Furthermore, the next node design iteration will include the following features: (i) Dynamic antenna polarization for efficient spectrum utilisation and clean/optimal channel selection; (ii) Inbuilt mechanism for auto-adjusting operating parameters such as txpower; and (iii) Auto-adjusting radio selection and operating parameter in a multi-hop mesh environment described in Sects. 4.1 and 4.2.

Acknowledgements. The authors would like to thank Dr. Albert A. Lysko from CSIR Meraka Institute and Dr. David Erwin from Mathematics Department at UCT. Dr. Lysko provided expert RF advice on the experimental setup, interpretation of results and multiple other useful resources, and logistical support. Dr. Erwin contributed Graph Theory insight that was helpful in deriving a generalised expression in Sect. 4. This work was funded in part by the Hasso Plattner Institute (HPI) scholarship award.

References

1. Saldana Ed. J., et al.: Alternative Network Deployments: Taxonomy, Characterization, Technologies, and Architectures (2016). https://www.rfc-editor.org/info/rfc7962
2. Cerdà-Alabern, L., Neumann, A., Escrich, P.: Experimental evaluation of a wireless community mesh network. In: Proceedings of the 16th ACM International Conference on Modeling, Analysis and Simulation of Wireless and Mobile Systems, MSWiM 2013, New York, NY, USA, pp. 23–30. ACM (2013)
3. Cui, P., Dong, Y., Liu, H., Rajan, D., Olinick, E., Camp, J.: WhiteMesh: leveraging white spaces in wireless mesh networks. In: 2016 14th International Symposium on Modeling and Optimization in Mobile, Ad Hoc, and Wireless Networks (WiOpt), pp. 1–7, May 2016
4. Akyildiz, I.F., Wang, X.: Wireless Mesh Networks, p. 74. Wiley, Chichester (2009)
5. Khalil, M., Qadir, J., Onireti, O., Imran, M.A., Younis, S.: Feasibility, architecture and cost considerations of using TVWS for rural internet access in 5G. In: 2017 20th Conference on Innovations in Clouds, Internet and Networks (ICIN), pp. 23–30, March 2017
6. Simić, L., Petrova, M., Mähönen, P.: Wi-Fi, but not on steroids: performance analysis of a Wi-Fi-like network operating in TVWS under realistic conditions. In: 2012 IEEE International Conference on Communications (ICC), pp. 1533–1538, June 2012
7. Friis, H.T.: A note on a simple transmission formula. Proc. IRE **34**, 254–256 (1946)
8. Open-Mesh: Multi-link Optimizations, January 2013. https://www.open-mesh.org/projects/batman-adv/wiki/Multi-link-optimize

High-Level and Compact Design of Cross-Channel LTE DownLink Channel Encoder

Jieming Xu and Miriam Leeser[✉] (iD)

Northeastern University, Boston, MA 02115, USA
xu.jiem@husky.neu.edu, mel@coe.neu.edu
https://www.northeastern.edu/rcl/

Abstract. Field Programmable Gate Arrays (FPGAs) provide great flexibility and speed in Software Defined Radio (SDR). However, as a mobile wireless protocol, the LTE system needs to maintain coding procedures for different channels, and the hardware's implementation is more complex than other wireless local area network (WLAN) specifications. Thus a compact and resource reusable LTE channel coder is needed as hardware resources and speed are the main pain points in SDR implementation. Traditional FPGA design and synthesis only focus on low levels of resource reuse, and IPs are independently designed without considering the whole system, which causes resource waste. In this paper, we describe a LTE downlink channel encoder processing chain implemented in FPGA hardware. Reuse in the whole system is done at a channel level and above, and scarce resources like BRAM are shared between processing units to maximize reuse. The system can efficiently process data and control channel signals at the same time using the same hardware. For the data channel, we use cross-component optimization to reduce the usage of BRAMs up to 25% for high volume data buffering. A novel rate matching design reduces the latency which improves the performance. By applying high-level reuse, the cross-component design can reduce resource usage while maintaining a good processing speed.

Keywords: LTE · DL-SCH · Reconfigurable hardware · SDR

1 Introduction

To keep up with the pace of updating standards, an SDR should have reconfigurability and software programmable hardware; FPGAs provide a good implementation platform that achieve these goals. The gap between wireless communications and hardware design requires developers to be proficient in both these areas. Libraries of Intellectual Property (IP) for wireless communications simplify hardware design for those proficient in SDR. However, without considering

© ICST Institute for Computer Sciences, Social Informatics and Telecommunications Engineering 2019
Published by Springer Nature Switzerland AG 2019. All Rights Reserved
I. Moerman et al. (Eds.): CROWNCOM 2018, LNICST 261, pp. 15–24, 2019.
https://doi.org/10.1007/978-3-030-05490-8_2

the whole processing chain and dependencies between different IPs, systems may suffer from resource waste and lower than optimal speed.

To implement the LTE system, many features can be efficiently implemented on a general purpose processor. Some blocks, such as Orthogonal Frequency-Division Multiplexing (OFDM), are best placed in hardware. Further, as massive MIMO and wideband OFDM will be applied in next generation systems, resources for baseband channel encoding will be quite limited. For the Downlink Shared Channel (DL-SCH) using QAM256 modulation, the maximum size of the transport block is 97896 bits and 105528 bits in releases 12 and 14 respectively. This requires the encoding system to be compact and efficient. In addition we design our system to accommodate processing for several different channels.

The contributions of this paper are: (1) We process both data and control channels using the same hardware, (2) we optimize rate matching to reduce latency, and (3) we optimize across the whole system to improve on-chip memory usage. In our implementation, reuse is considered across different channels and between IPs, which saves resources.

Previous research has focused on optimizing individual components for channel encoding independently. Researchers have investigated paralellizing the CRC and turbo encoder [3], and optimizing code block segmentation [5]. Santnanam et al. [8] examine choosing the FPGA Block RAM to achieve optimal power consumption and resource usage. Others have proposed a high speed architecture and a solution to reduce latency and resource usage in rate matching [2,4]. Fahmy et al. [7] introduces a method to improve resource sharing for DSP blocks, which can reduce the DSP consumption in OFDM systems. Hassan et al. [1] have designed a LTE downlink transceiver with synchronization and equalization; however, implementation details are missing. While excellent work has been done on each processing unit independently, to make the system work as a whole requires consideration of components' compatibility and resource usage.

2   Background

In LTE systems, information in the logical channel from the MAC layer are assigned to the transport channel in the physical layer for encoding. At the same time, control information is added for encoding which is irrelevant to the higher layer. The standard defines turbo encoding, tail biting convolutional coding, block coding etc. as coding schemes. For turbo and tail biting convolutional coding, each has its own rate matching scheme.

In the downlink, turbo coding is applied to DL-SCH, Paging Channel (PCH) and Multicast Channel (MCH). Tail biting convolutional coding is applied to Broadcast Channel (BCH) and Downlink Control Information (DCI). We refer to the DL-SCH, PCH and MCH as data channels and BCH and DCI as control channels. In each Transmission Time Interval (TTI), the CRC encoder receives data from the MAC layer and attaches parity bits to the transport block bit stream. The padded transport block is segmented into code blocks for turbo coding in predefined sizes. To align the size of padded transport block with different segmented code blocks, a number of F filler bits may be added to the

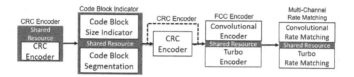

Fig. 1. Hardware architecture

head of the first code block as null bits. For data channel encoding, if the total number of segmented code blocks is larger than one, an additional CRC encoding process will be added to each code block before the turbo encoding process. For the control channel, the data will be sent directly to the convolutional encoder for processing. Next, each code block is processed by the turbo encoder, a Parallel Concatenated Convolutional Code (PCCC) with two 8-state constituent encoders with one (Quadratic Polynomial Permutation) QPP interleaver, and code rate 1/3. For control, The convolutional encoder first initializes its registers in the Shift Registers (SR) to the last 7 bits of each code block. Then the encoder encodes the data with these initialized SR with constraint length 7 at a coding rate of 1/3. Rate matching, which contains bit selection and pruning, is the last step of channel coding. It merges three bit streams (one information bit stream and two parity bit streams) generated by the turbo (or convolutional) encoder into one. After rate matching, the data will be send to the rest of the LTE physical layer processing.

3 Hardware Architecture

The processing chain for our hardware architecture, shown in Fig. 1, contains CRC encoder, code block indicator, Forward Correction Coder (FCC) encoder and multi-channel rate matching. To support encoding different channels' data using the same hardware, we merge different processing units by sharing hardware resources. The first CRC encoder is the same for different channels. To make the control channel's processing chain compatible with the data channel, we redefine the use of the code segmentation processing unit as code block size indicator without changing the hardware design. This redefinition scheme allows CRC encoded control information to be passed to the FCC encoder while using the same hardware architecture. The convolutional and turbo encoder are merged into one FCC encoder, and their rate matching is also merged into multi-channel rate matching with some resource sharing. In this design, the data and control information can be encoded using the same hardware. Optimized rate matching is also applied to improve the performance for both the data and control channels.

3.1 Rate Matching

The sub-block interleaver is based on matrix interleaving. Bit streams $d_k^{(0)}$, $d_k^{(1)}$ and $d_k^{(2)}$ of each code block are first reshaped into a $R \times 32$ matrix, where

$R = \lceil K/32 \rceil$, and K is the size of each code block after turbo encoding. The bit stream is stored in the matrix in row-wise order and N_D dummy bits padded to the head of each bit stream as null bits if K is less than K_Π (defined as $R \times 32$). Then a column-wise permutation is performed for the resized bit streams. For the convolutional encoder, all bit streams use the same permutation pattern. For turbo coding, the permutation is applied to bit streams $d_k^{(0)}$ and $d_k^{(1)}$ and bit stream $d_k^{(2)}$ uses the permutation pattern shown in Eq. 1.

$$\pi(k) = \left(P\left(\left\lfloor \frac{k}{R} \right\rfloor \right) + 32 \times (k \bmod R) + 1 \right) \bmod K_\Pi \tag{1}$$

where $\pi(k)$ is the index of the kth bit in $d_k^{(2)}$ after permutation.

In bit collection, the permuted bit streams v_k^0, v_k^1, v_k^2 are read out from the matrix in column-wise order and written into a circular buffer in interleaved order, where w_n is the nth data bit in the circular buffer:

$$w_k = v_k^0, \text{ for } k = 0, 1, 2..., K_\Pi \tag{2}$$

$$w_{K_\Pi + 2k} = v_k^1, \text{ for } k = 0, 1, 2..., K_\Pi \tag{3}$$

$$w_{K_\Pi + 2k + 1} = v_k^2, \text{ for } k = 0, 1, 2..., K_\Pi \tag{4}$$

In bit selection and pruning, data is read out from the circular buffer skipping the null bits until the data size reaches the capacity of a channel. The read starting point for turbo coding is chosen through the calculation of redundancy version (rv) and bits capacity for each code block (N_{cb}). For convolutional coding, the data is read from the first bit of v_k^0.

In DL-SCH processing, the rate matching process slows down the whole system's speed which needs to merge three bit streams into one. Researchers [4] have optimized this performance by implementing two RAM sets for sub-block interleaving and bit collection, directly following the process described in the LTE standard. In hardware, the interleaving process can be done by calculating the address while writing data bits to RAM; thus, the sub-block interleaving and bit collection can be done using only one RAM set. In this way, the RAM cost will be cut in an half. This work does not clearly describe how to design the FSM for bit selection, which needs to select information bits and skip dummy bits. Without proper optimization, at least one clock cycle is needed for skipping the dummy bits which results in extra latency. This latency is obvious when the code block is small. A patent [6] describes an approach to reduce this latency by calculating and storing the number of dummy bits before the information bits. However this approach cannot be efficiently implemented in hardware because storing the number of dummy bits before the information bits requires large amounts of RAM, and eliminates the ability for parallelization, which results in extra latency.

The proposed rate matching hardware architecture is shown in Fig. 2. Three RAMs are used for sub-block interleaving to mimic a circular buffer. Compared to [4], which uses two RAMs for each bit stream to do matrix resize and inter-column permutation in sub-block interleaving, we use only one RAM for each

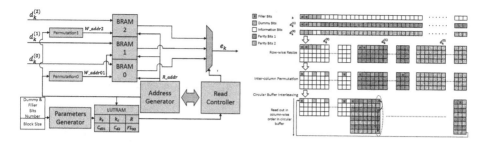

Fig. 2. Rate matching

Fig. 3. Rate matching circular buffer (Color figure online)

bit stream to finish interleaving. After address permutation, the data streams are written into BRAMs in interleaved order. By reading out the parameters from LUTRAM, the read controller controls the address read from the RAMs and selects the correct output from the three RAMs.

In bit selection and pruning, the processing unit should distinguish null (filler and dummy bits) bits that are scattered in valid bits (the information, parity bits0 and parity bit1, shown in Fig. 3). Solutions include using 2 bits to store valid and null bits or locating the address of null bits using Eq. 1 and the permutation table. However, the first solution doubles the cost of RAM and both solutions consume at least one clock cycle to read out or calculate whether a null bit is there. This reduces the performance of rate matching, especially when the code block is very small. The difficulty in skipping the null bits is how to locate these bits before the address generator reaches their addresses. To do this, we must have knowledge of where these null bits are. Because the null bits are always padded at the head of each bit stream, after inter-column permutation, these null bits will be located in the first several rows of each matrix (see Fig. 3). If we know how many null bits exist in each column, the address generator can preload this number and increase the address from that number in column-wise order, so the null bits will be skipped. After the address number reaches the last row, it moves to the next column and repeat this process.

As each bit stream is reshaped into a $R \times 32$ matrix, the number of null bits d_c for each column c is represented as:

$$d_c = \left\lfloor \frac{N}{32} \right\rfloor + J(c) \quad \left(J(c) = \begin{cases} 1, & \text{if } P^{-1}(c) < C_d \\ 0, & \text{if } P^{-1}(c) \geq C_d \end{cases} \right) \quad (5)$$

where $P^{-1}()$ is the inverse of the inter-column permutation function for different coding schemes, and C_d is the pattern of null bits calculated using:

$$C_d = \begin{cases} C_{d01} = (N_D + F) \bmod 32, \\ \text{(for } d_k^{(0)}, d_k^{(1)} \text{in turbo)} \\ \\ C_{d2} = N_D \bmod 32, \\ \text{(for } d_k^{(2)} \text{in turbo and } d_k^{(0)}, d_k^{(1)}, d_k^{(2)} \text{in convolutional)} \end{cases} \qquad (6)$$

In hardware implementation, term $\lfloor \frac{N}{32} \rfloor$ can easily be calculated by bit shifting. Permutations are parity permutation without overlap, which share the same pattern as their inverses. Therefore, for $d_k^{(0)}$ and $d_k^{(1)}$ streams in turbo code and all the bit streams in convolutional code, the function $P^{-1}(c)$ is the same as the permutation $P(c)$. Thus a 32×5 (LUT) can implement function $P^{-1}(c)$. However, the permutation of $d_k^{(2)}$ in turbo code involves the calculation of Eq. 1 whose inverse cannot be directly implemented as a small LUT. Looking at Eq. 1, we find it cyclic shifts the $d_k^{(1)}$ stream and then applies the sub-block interleaving using the same turbo permutation. Therefore, to implement function $P^{-1}(c)$ for that bit stream, we only need to add one to the LUT for permutation to represent the cyclic shift. In a real implementation, all the permutation LUTs should be left-cycle shifted by one; this helps the row address generator load the null bit number before the next column's read begins. To reduce latency, parameters calculated in Eqs. 5 and 6 are stored in LUTRAM as k_s and k_c for read starting point, R, C_{d01}, C_{d2} and FL_{32} for filler bits information (Fig. 2).

We use three BRAMs with control logic to mimic a circular buffer structure. However, the interleaving order shown in Eqs. 3 and 4 introduces another challenge to the control logic's implementation for the circular buffer. The problem is that the $d_k^{(2)}$ stream uses a different permutation and the null bits it contains are also different from the other two bit streams. This may result in the data not being read from BRAM1 and BRAM0 in sequential order. Sometimes, a number of data bits may need to be read from a single BRAM continuously, for example when the data is read from the column (red circle in Fig. 3). To solve this BRAM iteration problem, we use Algorithm 1 to decide which BRAM to select while comparing the row address of different BRAMs dynamically. Here, d_{c01} and d_{c2} are calculated as in Eq. 5. In this way, BRAM selecting can be easily done using a comparator.

3.2   High Level Resource Reuse

Xilinx Vivado provides IP including 3GGP Turbo Encoder and LTE DL Channel Encoder which provide ease of use but remove freedom for the designer. The LTE DL Channel Encoder includes the downlink channels in LTE. It is powerful however it consumes a lot of resource which restricts its usage in limited resource situations such as MIMO and OFDM transceiver. The independent 3GGP Turbo Encoder IP cannot be optimized with other packaged IPs when directly connect to them. We use a high level of resource reuse between blocks for more compact systems. We fully merge the CRC encoder for control and

---

Algorithm 1: Circular Buffer Interleaved Data Read Out with null Bits

---

if $row\_address1 == R$ & $row\_address2 == R$ **then**
  | $row\_address1 \leftarrow d_{c01}$;
  | $row\_address2 \leftarrow d_{c2}$;
else
  | **if** $row\_address1 < row\_address2$ **then**
  | | $row\_address1 \leftarrow row\_address1 + 1$;
  | | select BRAM1;
  | **else**
  | | $row\_address2 \leftarrow row\_address2 + 1$;
  | | select BRAM2;
  | **end**
end

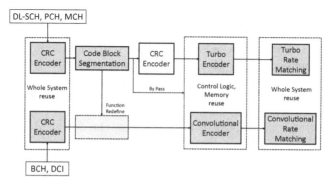

Fig. 4. High level resource reuse

data channels by simply using the same hardware, as shown in Fig. 4, because of their same options for the coding polynomial. Compared to the control channel, the data channel has additional code block segmentation and a CRC encoder. Code block segmentation divides a long code into small code blocks and outputs their sizes. The control channel also needs that code block size information for encoding; however no segmentation is needed. In the data channel's encoding, if there is only one code block in the TTI, this code block will be bypassed to the turbo encoder without a second CRC encoding. The control channel code blocks can also bypass the second CRC encoding. To apply this, the code block segmentation in the control channel's processing is redefined as a code block size indicator that segments the control information into a single code block to avoid the next CRC encoding. In this way, the encoding before the FCC encoder can share the same resources without changing the hardware architecture. The FCC is designed to use the same control logic and memory to finish these two coding schemes. The convolutional encoder shares one RAM with the turbo encoder for data buffering and register initialization. Independent design of the convolutional encoder alongside the turbo encoder costs resources. In multi-channel rate matching, we use the same hardware for the data channel by making some slight changes. Another permutation table for convolutional coding is added. The algorithm for the circular buffer data read works for both channels. As the code blocks in the control channel have no filler bits, the null bits pattern will be the same as C_{d2} in turbo rate matching. In this way, the bit collection and bit selection and pruning elements can also be applied to control data's rate matching using the same hardware.

3.3   Buffer Optimization

For the FPGA implementation, the largest code block size requires a 13-bit address. As a result, the 18 Kb BRAM is divided into two areas for code block storage and the 36 Kb BRAM is divided into four areas for data buffering. Therefore, a simple ping-pong buffer can be realized using one 18 Kb BRAM for the CRC while two 18 Kb BRAMs are need for turbo encoding as it uses two independent data streams. Maximum delay is achieved when the lowest code rate is chosen at 1/3 which requires the largest amount of data buffering. To reach this rate, the total number of code blocks is 6, and the output size is three times the input size. If the data ports timing strictly follows the timing diagram shown in Fig. 5, the rate matching can only process five continuous code blocks at a time with a 36 Kb BRAM for each bit stream. However, the output code block size may exceed the size shown in Fig. 5 because the output data size of each code block needs to match the modulation order, the number of bits coded into one modulated symbol. Consider that the system has some timing slack, more than four code blocks should be stored in RAM. Therefore, two 36 Kb BRAMs are needed per data stream. Because the rate matching process uses three data streams, a total of six 36 Kb BRAMs are needed. These are the BRAM resources needed if we independently implement the processing units. Turbo encoding triples the size of RAM needed for data buffering and rate matching because three bit streams are generated. However, if the system is optimized together, the buffer usage in rate matching can be greatly reduced. The buffers in CRC and turbo encoder can help rate matching to buffer data. A simple approach is to assign one code block to the turbo encoder processing unit and four code blocks to rate matching. When the rate matching processing finishes any code block's encoding, which frees the space for one code block's buffering, the turbo encoder can then transfer its buffered data to the rate matching processing unit. If the system is optimized as a whole, the rate matching processing unit needs only three 36 Kb BRAMs to buffer four code blocks. As a result, the whole system can buffers more code blocks while using fewer RAMs than if the processing units are implemented independently.

4   Results

We use Mathworks and Xilinx tools to support our design flow. Simulink is used with HDL Workflow Advisor to generate HDL code from Simulink blocks and

Matlab code. Xilinx Vivado 2016.4 is used for synthesis and implementation. Except for the LTE CRC and turbo encoder blocks provided by Mathworks, we formulate and implement the whole system in our design and run the results on a Zedboard. Resource usage on a Zedboard is shown in Table 1 along with the percentage reduction achieved compared to the design without resource sharing. BRAM usage is shown in Table 2. Note that the turbo encoder uses 5 18 Kb RAMs, two for data buffering and three for the QPP interleaver. Thus, the non-resource sharing design costs more resources, with 33% more BRAMs consumed. Although a single LTE downlink encoding system consumes very few resources, the LTE OFDM modulator requires a large amount of resources, which won't leave abundant resource for the encoder. As a result, the resource consumption should be kept as small as possible. In addition, MIMO requires multiple encoders to work together to achieve high throughput. When multiple encoders are implemented, the resources they save together can be considerable. Because the size of filler bits may vary from 0 to 31 randomly, we pick the mean of 16 bits for testing. Results show that optimized rate matching can reduce delay by 28.6% for small blocks when compared to non-optimized running at the same clock frequency. For very large blocks the optimized design has lower delay, but only 1% delay improvement.

Fig. 5. Data ports timing of rate matching

Table 1. Resource usage of downlink encoder (with resource sharing)

Resource	Utilization	Available	Utilization%	Utilization reduced%
LUT	1073	53200	2.02	27.34
LUTRAM	163	17400	0.94	18.97
Flip-Flop	1243	106400	1.17	22.00
BRAM	6	140	4.29	39.91

Table 2. BRAM usage

Items	Independent non-optimized		Cross-component optimized	
	18 Kb RAM	36 Kb RAM	18 Kb RAM	36 Kb RAM
CRC encoder	1	0	1	0
FCC encoder	5	0	5	0
Rate matching	0	6	0	3
Total usage	6	6	6	3

5   Conclusions and Future Work

We have shown that optimizing the data channel processing chain as a whole and high level resource reuse saves scarce resources in FPGA implementations such as BRAMs. In addition, we presented a novel architecture for a rate matching system with low latency. If multiple LTE downlink encoders are implemented for parallel processing in a MIMO system, the saved resources are considerable. The designs presented in this paper run at frequencies of 130 MHz on Zedboard. In the future, we plan to implement multi-channel resource reuse as a tool to facilitate research and realization of SDR designs. We also plan to investigate tools that optimize designs across blocks, and not just within individual blocks. If these tools can work with vendor tools such as Vivado HLS, it will simplify the design of SDR system and result in improved resource efficiency. Furthermore, we plan to investigate targeting the RFSoC chip from Xilinx for similar designs. The RFSoC included cores for FEC that can be used for turbo encoding.

Acknowlegdements. This research is funded in part with support from Mathworks.

References

1. Hassan, S.M., Zekry, A.: FPGA implementation of LTE downlink transceiver with synchronization and equalization. Commun. Appl. Electron. **2**(2) (2015)
2. He, S., Hu, Q., Zhang, H.: Implementation of rate matching with low latency and little memory for LTE turbo code. J. Inf. Comput. Sci. **10**(13), 4117–4125 (2013)
3. Hwang, S.Y., Kim, D.H., Jhang, K.S.: Implementation of an encoder based on parallel structure for LTE systems. In: IEEE Wireless Communication and Networking, April 2010
4. Lenzi, K.G., de Figueiredo, F.A., Figueiredo, F.L.: Optimized rate matching architecture for a LTE-advanced FPGA-based PHY. In: IEEE CAS (2013)
5. Lenzi, K.G., Figueiredo, F.A., Bianco Filho, J.A., Figueiredo, F.L.: Fully optimized code block segmentation algorithm for LTE-Advanced. Int. J. Parallel Prog. **43**(6), 988–1003 (2015)
6. Reinhardt, S.: Technique for rate matching in a data transmission system, US Patent 8,446,300, 21 May 2013
7. Ronak, B., Fahmy, S.A.: Improved resource sharing for FPGA DSP blocks. In: Field Programmable Logic (FPL), pp. 1–4. IEEE (2016)
8. Santhanam, V., Kabra, L.: Optimal low power and scalable memory architecture for turbo encoder. In: DASIP, October 2012

Detection of Different Wireless Protocols on an FPGA with the Same Analog/RF Front End

Suranga Handagala, Mohamed Mohamed, Jieming Xu, Marvin Onabajo[ID], and Miriam Leeser[(✉)][ID]

Northeastern University, Boston, MA 02115, USA
{handagala.s,mohamed.m,xu.jiem}@husky.neu.edu, {monabajo,mel}@ece.neu.edu
https://www.northeastern.edu/rcl/

Abstract. The surge in smart phones, tablets, and other wireless electronics has drastically increased data usage and wireless communication, creating massive traffic spectrum demand. Congestion is mainly due to inefficient use of spectrum, rather than spectrum scarcity. Spectrum coexistence schemes provide opportunities for efficient use of the spectrum. Furthermore, software-defined hardware reconfiguration after signal detection can be completed to reduce the power consumption of adaptive analog/RF front ends. In this paper, we propose a Wi-Fi and LTE protocol coexistence architecture, and present its implementation using a Xilinx evaluation board and ADI RF front end.

Keywords: Software defined radio · Wireless protocols · RF front end FPGA

1 Introduction

Wireless protocols are rapidly changing as more and more devices are interconnected wirelessly. These include both devices with high throughput and low latency requirements such as cell phones and tablets, and devices with low throughput communications such as is exhibited with many devices in the Internet of Things (IoT). At the same time, research efforts for 5G are examining higher flexibility and adaptability in implementations [10]. Researchers would like to easily prototype existing protocols and experiment with new concepts, while still being able to meet real time communications requirements. For many years FPGAs have been used for Software Define Radio to meet such needs. As requirements for wireless communications have become both more difficult to meet and more diverse, capabilities of FPGAs have grown as well.

Our research targets an environment where a single hardware platform can be used to support multiple different protocols. We envision a scenario where this hardware platform does not know *a priori* which protocol it will be supporting. It

ⓒ ICST Institute for Computer Sciences, Social Informatics and Telecommunications Engineering 2019
Published by Springer Nature Switzerland AG 2019. All Rights Reserved
I. Moerman et al. (Eds.): CROWNCOM 2018, LNICST 261, pp. 25–35, 2019.
https://doi.org/10.1007/978-3-030-05490-8_3

senses the environment, determines what packets it is receiving, and then loads the optimum processing for the rest of the receive and transmit chain. This paper focuses on the first step of this processing; namely, sensing the environment and choosing which protocol to support. We limit our discussion to 802.11a and LTE; however the model will be extended to other protocols in the near future.

The hardware platform we use is an Analog Devices ADI FMCOMMS3 board[1] connected to a Xilinx ZC706 Evaluation board. The FMComms3 board supports a relatively wide bandwidth range of 70 MHz–6 GHz and 2 × 2 MIMO. It connects to the FPGA board through an FMC connector. The Xilinx ZC706 board is an evaluation board with Xilinx Zynq XC7Z045 with embedded ARM processor as well as reconfigurable FPGA hardware resources. This represents very popular hardware setups for radio researchers working at the PHY layer [6,7].

The main contribution of this paper is a platform with common RF front end, settings and reconfigurable hardware that can accurately detect different wireless waveforms and thus be deployed in various different settings. The approach is flexible and extensible to waveforms of the future.

2 Background

2.1 Radio Technology and Hardware Trends

When observing analog/radio frequency (RF) front end design trends for software-defined radio (SDR) applications, reconfigurable analog integrated circuits help to reduce power consumption while improving performance [2,11]. Ongoing circuit and system design trends create a great need to co-design analog and mixed-signal circuits together with computing resources for the control of optimizations, particularly to support future reconfigurable and cognizant radios that will be realized as SDRs. FPGAs can play a key role in this process [4]. Integrated analog/RF transceiver circuits for Wi-Fi and LTE increasingly include signal processing and control methods to continuously tune components for high performance and reliable operation under varying conditions [1,8]. Hence, these digitally-assisted analog design and calibration approaches are significantly gaining importance to enhance the performance and reliability of low-power mixed-signal systems-on-a-chip in ubiquitous complementary metal-oxide-semiconductor (CMOS) technologies. Such calibrations can incorporate existing or dedicated analog-to-digital converter (ADC) and digital signal processor (DSP) resources for computation of corrective actions and automatic tuning with digital-to-analog converters (DACs). However, reconfigurable analog front-ends for SDRs require different settings and digital calibrations, depending on the mode of operation and the type of signal that is received at a given time. For example, Wi-Fi and LTE have different receiver sensitivity specifications, which leads to different requirements for the gain, noise figure, and linearity of the RF/analog frond end blocks in the receiver path. Similarly, the two standards have different requirements with regards to the suppression of interference

---

[1] https://wiki.analog.com/resources/eval/user-guides/ad-fmcomms3-ebz.

signals having specified power levels and offset frequencies relative to the channel of interest. This results in different baseband filtering requirements, which can also be changed through settings that reconfigure active filter circuits. A universal digital hardware implementation for all modes of operation would incur excessive power overhead in many applications. The signal detection research described in this paper is in part motivated by the need to extract information for real-time optimizations and power reductions of reconfigurable analog/RF front ends. An AD9361 Agile RF transceiver was employed in the experiments reported in this paper for a proof of concept, but it is envisioned that future reconfigurable application-specific integrated RF front ends will benefit through adaptive optimizations based on the information obtained through on-board FPGA processing.

2.2   Wi-Fi and LTE Waveforms

Wi-Fi is a wireless local area network (WLAN) protocol that allows devices such as smart phones, laptops, and tablets to communicate wirelessly. Long Term Evolution (LTE) was developed by 3GPP to enhance the performance of 3G systems in terms of data throughput, spectrum utilization, and user mobility, and works on the uplink (UL) and downlink (DL). The LTE DL channel uses an OFDMA interface, which supports multiple input multiple output (MIMO). Using OFDMA increases stability against multipath distortion, reduces latency, and allows for multiple data rates. The LTE radio frame is 10 ms long, consisting of ten 1 ms sub-frames. In frequency-division duplexing (FDD) operating mode, each sub-frame contains two 0.5 ms slots. Each slot contains 7 OFDM symbols for the normal cyclic prefix and 6 OFDM symbols for the extended cyclic prefix.

3   Coexistence Architecture

The goal of our approach is to use the same RF front end and FPGA based processing hardware to detect which waveform is being communicated with the

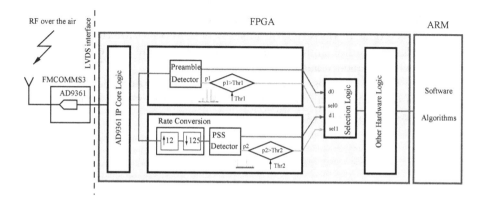

Fig. 1. Proposed coexistence setup

intent of later adjusting RF front end settings and downloading the appropriate processing to tune the transceiver to the current waveform. Jiao et al. [6] take a complementary approach by supporting multiple protocols on the same platform at the same time. While this is very similar to our goal, it is not extensible as the number of protocols continues to grow. Figure 1 shows our architecture, including the block diagram for each receiver. Note that these make use of a common RF front end and common sampling rate of 20 MHz. The receiver chains for each are described in this section, as well as steps taken to deal with different bandwidths.

3.1   802.11a Receiver Chain

All WiFi standards use a preamble for timing synchronization, frequency offset compensation and channel estimation. In an 802.11a frame, there are two types of preambles; a short training sequence consisting of 10 identical patterns each of which has 16 samples, and two identical long training sequences each of which has 64 samples. The short training sequence can be used to obtain a coarse estimate of the start of a frame while the long training sequence produces a more accurate estimate. We use a 64 tap, hardware friendly, matched filter for detecting the long preamble based on multiplier-free efficient implementation techniques [3].

3.2   LTE Receive Chain

In FDD operating mode, the Primary Synchronization Signal (PSS) is located in two locations in each 10 ms LTE radio frame. The first one is in the last OFDM symbol of the first time slot of the first subframe, where each subframe is 1 ms and each slot is 0.5 ms. The PSS is repeated in the last OFDM symbol in subframe 5. LTE uses a synchronization channel (SCH) inserted periodically in the DL LTE radio frame. The SCH is composed of a PSS and a Secondary Synchronization Signal (SSS). The PSS is generated from a 63-length frequency-domain Zafoff-Chu (ZC) sequence whose root index determines the sector identity. Detection of PSS in the TD is implemented by cross-correlating the TD signal with the three PSS coefficients in which one of the three correlation outputs will display two peaks, indicating both PSS locations within one LTE radio frame [9]. The cell search process is done by detecting the position of the PSS within the received DL signal in order to acquire timing information and determine the sector index by identifying which sequence has been transmitted out of the three ZC sequences. The received DL is then cross-correlated with each of the three ZC sequences in which one of the correlation outputs will demonstrate two peaks, indicating the successful detection of an LTE radio frame.

3.3   Adjusting Sampling Rate for LTE

In the 802.11a standard, the sampling rate is fixed at 20 MHz. For LTE, the sampling rate varies from 1.92 MHz to 30.72 MHz. However, the PSS signal is always located at the center frequency of the LTE transmission band regardless of the sampling frequency. This feature allows us to detect the PSS signal at a fixed frequency by applying filters to the received signal. The PSS signal only and always occupies the central 63 subcarries in the whole band. For the smallest sampling rate, which is 1.92 MHz, the IFFT size is 128 points. As a result, the received signal sampled at 20 MHz shall be downsampled to 1.92 MHz for matched filter processing. The resample ratio is:

$$\frac{1.92 \times 10^6 \text{Hz}}{20 \times 10^6 \text{Hz}} = \frac{12}{125} = \frac{2 \times 2 \times 3}{5 \times 5 \times 5} \tag{1}$$

The resample ratio shows that the 20 MHz signal should be downsampled by 125 and upsampled by 12 to achieve the 1.92 MHz sampling rate. Directly implementing the sampling rate conversion filter requires 3000 taps, which is almost impossible to implement in hardware. An optimized FIR design that factors the downsample and upsample ratio to $2 \times 2 \times 3$ and $5 \times 5 \times 5$ still requires a 405 tap filter. As a result, for symmetric FIRs, at least 200 DSP slices would be consumed by the sampling rate converter.

To reduce the consumption of DSP blocks on the FPGA, we replace the traditional FIR by a CIC filter. The CIC filter for sampling rate conversion was first introduced by Hogenauer in [5]. This multiplier free FIR filter can be implemented in an economical way for decimation and interpolation to reduce the usage of registers and adders. The goal is to keep the resampling filter small to be able to accommodate other processing, including OFDM demodulation and channel equalization which consume a large amount of resources.

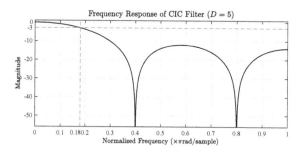

Fig. 2. CIC filter frequency response.

From Eq. 1, we can see that the downsample factor is larger than the upsample factor. Hence, only one low-pass filter for the downsampler is needed to implement the whole conversion system. In our design, we use three cascaded CIC filters with a factor of 5 for the low-pass filter. The frequency response of a downsampling CIC filter with a factor of 5 is shown in Fig. 2. This design can be used to detect the PSS in any LTE signal.

4 Results

The target hardware for this design consists of an ADI FMCOMMS3 RF front end and Xilinx Zynq ZC706 Evaluation Board. We detect both 802.11a and LTE signals using this setup. We present simulation results as well as results on running hardware. Transmission using an SMA cable between two boards was used to detect LTE signals, while over the air transmission using one board was used to detect Wi-Fi signals. The results on running hardware consist of both Built-In Self-Test (BIST) loopback as well as over-the-air experiments.

4.1 Software and Hardware Configuration

Our setup includes two processors, the embedded ARM processor that is part of the Xilinx Zynq XC7Z045 chip on the ZC706 board, and the host CPU in the computer attached to the platform. The ADI 9361 has its own device drivers that control all transmit/receive chain parameters of the AD9361 chip such as local oscillator frequency, bandwidth, sampling frequency, TX/RX path automatic gain control mode, and gains of analog front end blocks. In addition to including device drivers, a user needs the LibIIO framework installed for applications to communicate with ADI hardware. For simulation results, which do not include any FPGA hardware, we run Analog Devices IIO Oscilloscope on the host PC.

For experiments that involve the Zynq processor, we use Petalinux, a version of Linux supported by Xilinx, on the embedded ARM processor. The interaction between ARM and the AD9361 device is performed using two platform device drivers built into the kernel. There is also an AD9361 FPGA core driver for the

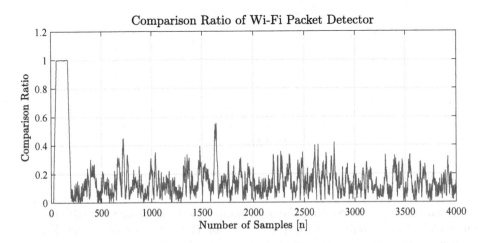

Fig. 3. Packet detector output of detected Wi-Fi signal.

FPGA fabric that provides the user with an option to correct IQ imbalances and DC offsets on the receiver side.

4.2 Simulation

Simulations, using MATLAB R2017a with the Signal Processing, Communication, and LTE System Toolbox have been performed based on the block diagram presented in Fig. 1, where signals are received using the AD9361 FMCOMMS3 at a sampling rate of 20 MHz. Each signal is passed through both the Wi-Fi and LTE paths in parallel and using peak-to-average ratio thresholds, the signal is determined to be either Wi-Fi or LTE. Figure 3 shows the packet detection of a Wi-Fi packet in discrete samples, where a comparison ratio of an autocorrelation of x[n] and x[n−16], where x[n] indicates the received samples and 16 is the length of the short training sequence, and the variance of x[n] for the received samples is displayed. In this figure, the falling edge position, located at sample 165, indicates the beginning of the Wi-Fi packet. The packet detection flag is asserted when the peak-to-average ratio threshold is met, indicating the presence of a Wi-Fi signal.

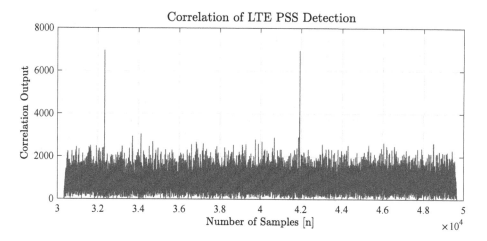

Fig. 4. LTE PSS correlation output.

The LTE PSS detection is performed using the cross-correlation of the received TD signal with the PSS coefficients. Since one LTE radio frame contains two PSS signals, two peaks indicating the positions of each one of the PSS signals are shown in Fig. 4. Another peak-to-average ratio threshold is used to indicate the received signal is indeed an LTE signal.

4.3 Hardware Experiments

Our hardware setup is shown in Fig. 5. Two antennas are used on the ZC706, one for transmit and one for receive. In experiments not depicted here, two separate

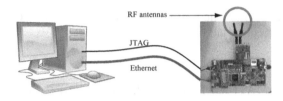

Fig. 5. Hardware setup and host PC interfacing over JTAG and ethernet connections

setups were used with one functioning as transmitter and one as receiver. We use pre-created 802.11a and LTE signals which are stored in a text file. We use a C program to read these complex I and Q samples, and send them through a DMA channel along the transmit chain. One set of experiments bypassed the RF section by using the BIST loopback feature available in the AD9361 chip, so that the accuracy of the received signal could be verified in the digital domain. Once the digital design had been verified, over the air experiments were undertaken.

The detection logic that was mapped to FPGA hardware for 802.11a and LTE receiver chains were designed using the Mathworks Simulink HDL code generation workflow (version 2017b) and implemented using Xilinx Vivado version 2016.4 with an FPGA clock frequency of 100 MHz. The PL also consists of AD9361 AXI IP core which provides the digital interface to the FMCOMMS3 card. For the receiver chain, this core has been configured to compensate for IQ imbalances and DC offsets.

The detection logic mapped onto the FPGA could be used to identify the presence of either 802.11a or LTE signals received via the common RF front end. Figure 6(a) corresponds to an 802.11a signal where the entire receive chain operates in real time. For LTE, the rate conversion takes place offline. This converted signal is passed through the LTE matched filter implemented in FPGA fabric, resulting the peaks in Fig. 6(b).

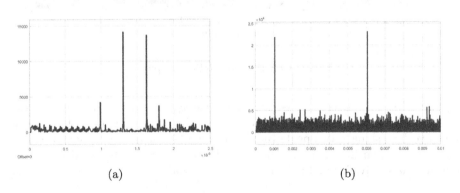

(a)   (b)

Fig. 6. (a) 802.11a (b) LTE hardware friendly matched filter outputs of two real world signals received with the common RF front-end

4.4   FPGA Utilization

Vivado post-implementation utilization figures (Table 1) revealed that a significant reduction in resources, especially for the DSPs, can be achieved by using hardware friendly matched filtering without compromising the detection capability. Had the conventional discrete FIR been used, the DSP resource count would have been four times the number of filter coefficients. Although this number can be reduced by 25% by using 3 DSP48s per complex multiplication, accommodating other complex logic could still be challenging because of high receiver complexity. Detection results in Fig. 6 show that the 802.11a preamble and LTE PSS can be successfully detected even at the expense of peak-to-average ratio. This reduction is quantified in Table 2.

Table 1. FPGA resource utilization statistics (percentages given are with respect to the total number of resources available in the device).

	Discrete FIR (802.11a)	Hardware friendly (802.11a)	Discrete FIR (LTE)	Hardware friendly (LTE)
LUT	8726 (3.99%)	4246 (1.94%)	15238 (6.97%)	7261 (3.32%)
FF	17004 (3.89%)	5905 (1.35%)	30135 (6.89%)	9844 (2.25%)
DSP48	258 (28.67%)	2 (0.22%)	514 (57.11%)	2 (0.22%)

Table 2. Peak to average ratio comparison for 802.11a and LTE matched filter outpus.

	802.11a	LTE
Discrete FIR	62	47.5
Hardware friendly	43	38

Through these experiments, it was possible to accommodate both detection algorithms on the same device, while consuming a small amount of FPGA resources, and more importantly keeping the detection accuracy intact. This resource saving can potentially be capitalized to accommodate multiple protocols on low end FPGAs as well.

5   Conclusions and Future Work

We have successfully demonstrated that a common hardware platform can be used to distinguish between 802.11 and LTE signals. The ADI RF front end receives samples at 20 MHz; which are downsampled to 1.92 MHz for LTE. The hardware design recognizes either the preambles in the 802.11 stream or the

Primary Synchronization Signal (PSS) in LTE with sufficient accuracy to determine which signal is being received. The RF front end uses common settings for parameters such as the automatic gain control mode.

In the future, we plan to take this base design into several different directions. Once the type of signal being received has been determined, we can download the receive chain for the rest of the processing onto the FPGA fabric. We plan to investigate using partial reconfiguration for this process. Our current implementation takes up a very small portion of the FPGA fabric, such that the first few steps for each receive chain could be included as part of the implementation without loss of data. In a typical coexistence scenario where multiple protocols work over the same channel, we plan to reuse the same components with different configurations in order to minimize resource utilization. It is our expectation that switching from one protocol to another should not create a negative impact on the receiver performance since FPGAs can be clocked at much higher rates than the baseband frequencies of such protocols. We also plan to investigate supporting other protocols, including 802.15.4 and Zigbee. The result will be an agile, flexible PHY layer platform that can support a variety of protocols, including some which have not yet been standardized.

Acknowlegdements. This research is funded in part with support from Mathworks.

References

1. Banerjee, A., Chatterjee, A.: Signature driven hierarchical post-manufacture tuning of RF systems. IEEE Trans. VLSI **23**(2), 342–355 (2015)
2. Bazrafshan, A., Taherzadeh-Sani, M., Nabki, F.: A 0.8–4-GHZ software-defined radio receiver with improved harmonic rejection. IEEE TCAS I **65**, 3186–195 (2018)
3. Dick, C., Harris, F.: FPGA implementation of an OFDM PHY. In: Asilomar Conference on Signals, Systems Computers, vol. 1 (2003)
4. Dinis, D.C., Cordeiro, R.F., Oliveira, A.S.R., Vieira, J., Silva, T.O.: A fully parallel architecture for designing frequency-agile and real-time reconfigurable FPGA-based RF digital transmitters. IEEE Trans. Microw. Theory Tech. **66**(3), 1489–1499 (2018)
5. Hogenauer, E.: An economical class of digital filters for decimation and interpolation. IEEE Trans. Acoust. Speech Signal Process. **29**(2), 155–162 (1981)
6. Jiao, X., Moerman, I., Liu, W., de Figueiredo, F.A.P.: Radio hardware virtualization for coping with dynamic heterogeneous wireless environments. In: Marques, P., Radwan, A., Mumtaz, S., Noguet, D., Rodriguez, J., Gundlach, M. (eds.) CrownCom 2017. LNICST, vol. 228, pp. 287–297. Springer, Cham (2018). https://doi.org/10.1007/978-3-319-76207-4_24
7. Machado, R.G., Wyglinski, A.M.: Software-defined radio: bridging the analog-digital divide. Proc. IEEE **103**(3), 409–423 (2015)
8. Onabajo, M., Silva-Martinez, J.: Analog Circuit Design for Process Variation-Resilient Systems-on-a-Chip. Springer, New York (2012). https://doi.org/10.1007/978-1-4614-2296-9
9. Setiawan, H., Ochi, H.: A low complexity physical-layer identity detection for 3GPP LTE. In: Advanced Communication Technology (ICACT). IEEE (2010)

10. Sexton, C., Kaminski, N.J., Marquez-Barja, J.M., Marchetti, N., DaSilva, L.A.: 5G: adaptable networks enabled by versatile radio access technologies. IEEE Commun. Surv. Tutor. **19**(2), 688–720 (2017)
11. Yksel, H., Yang, D., Boynton, Z., et al.: A wideband fully integrated software-defined transceiver for FDD and TDD operation. IEEE JSSC **52**(5), 1274–1285 (2017)

Demonstration of Shared Spectrum Access of Different User Groups

Topi Tuukkanen[1], Heikki Kokkinen[2(✉)], Seppo Yrjölä[3],
Jaakko Ojaniemi[2], Arto Kivinen[2], and Tero Jokela[4]

[1] Finnish Defence Research Agency, 11311 Riihimäki, Finland
[2] Fairspectrum Oy, Otakaari 5, 02150 Espoo, Finland
heikki.kokkinen@fairspectrum.com
[3] Nokia, Kaapelitie 4, 90650 Oulu, Finland
[4] Turku University of Applied Sciences,
Joukahaisenkatu 3, 20520 Turku, Finland

Abstract. Spectrum availability is challenged everyday as the consumer consumption of mobile data increases. At the same time, the public safety and military authorities have the need to secure spectrum access for their mandated tasks that may vary temporally and spatially. Current spectrum administration and management schemes do not facilitate such short-term changes in time and space. In this paper, we show that minor adjustments to the Licensed Shared Access (LSA) scheme, and introduction of a spectrum manager function may provide administrations the tools to adjust spectrum assignments in time and space, so that they provide Mobile Network Operators sufficient security of spectrum access to justify investments, and that they allow authorities to access spectrum when their legally mandated tasks so require.

Keywords: Cognitive radio · Homeland defense · Hybrid warfare
Licensed Shared Access · Military · Public safety · Scenarios
Spectrum manager · Spectrum sharing

1 Introduction

This paper demonstrates shared spectrum access between different types of user groups, which include commercial Mobile Network Operator (MNO), Public Protection and Disaster Recovery (PPDR), and Military (MIL). In the demonstration, the priority order between these user groups changes in time. The changes are managed through a User Interface (UI) of a National Regulatory Authority (NRA). In the standardized Dynamic Spectrum Access (DSA) systems, including Television White Space (TVWS) [1], Licensed Shared Access (LSA) [2], and Citizens Broadband Radio Service (CBRS) [3], the priority order is fixed. We demonstrate a scenario, where a frequency band allocated for a MNO can normally be used for practice by PPDR and MIL on secondary

The research described has been partly funded by the Finnish Defence Forces.

I. Moerman et al. (Eds.): CROWNCOM 2018, LNICST 261, pp. 36–45, 2019.
https://doi.org/10.1007/978-3-030-05490-8_4

basis, and during a rescue mission or hybrid war situation, PPDR or MIL can become the primary user locally and temporarily according to a pre-defined sharing agreement.

Conceptually, the spectrum sharing option space is depicted below in Fig. 1. Different options are placed along X-axis as a continuum that begins from *unlicensed*, unregulated, opportunistic common use to the other end, where the ultimate opposite is *licensed* exclusive use mode. In Y-axis, we have either *horizontal sharing* among similar actors and technologies as opposed to vertical sharing among different actors and different technologies. The third dimension is that of the *primary user* versus the *secondary user*.

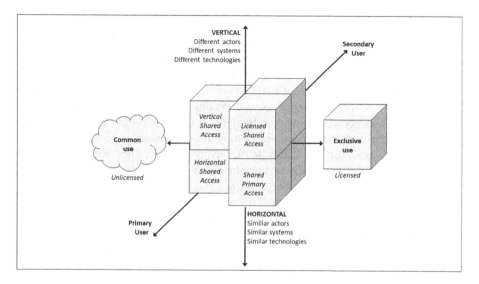

Fig. 1. Spectrum access option space adopted from [1].

Vertical shared access denotes technically regulated sharing between different types of actors or technologies that is exemplified by the unlicensed public use of the TVWS frequencies for broadband wireless data [4]. Horizontal shared access denotes technically regulated sharing between similar users or technologies, an example being wireless local area networking (802.11) within the ISM band. As the notion of primary or secondary user is somewhat ambiguous in this technically regulated sharing domain, the option space depicted to the left of the vertical axis in the Fig. 1 is more constrained. LSA in Fig. 1 denotes shared spectrum access concepts intended for different actors or technologies. Examples of such approaches are the LSA and the CBRS. Shared Primary Access, also known as co-primary sharing, refers to a case where two or more incumbents with equal access rights share their spectrum bands in a common pool. Currently, a generic homeland defence scenario does not provide military any operational incentive to relinquish exclusive access to spectrum. In fact, new spectrum may be needed to support activation of reserve forces or mobilisation. The quality and availability of commercial network and user equipment for LTE and 5G in the future and the possibility to use the same end user equipment both in commercial networks and military or public safety LTE networks may motivate military and public safety for spectrum sharing arrangements.

Tuukkanen et al. [5] observed that the armed forces' requirements for spectrum access vary greatly over time and location depending on the scenario. The same temporal-spatial variation of spectral needs applies also to public safety in scenarios like large-scale accidents or natural disasters. Therefore, one-off or location specific spectrum occupancy measurements cannot provide credible picture of such needs.

Contemporary standardized Shared Spectrum Access concepts, the LSA [6], LSA evolution [7, 8] and the CBRS [9], are based on the notion of providing secondary user an access to underutilized parts of spectrum. Besides, these concepts have already built-in mechanisms for the incumbent to inform the system on changes in the spectrum needs dynamically. Many nations already have legal provisions that would allow military to have a broader access to spectrum in war time. However, contemporary hybrid warfare homeland defence scenario seriously challenges this notion. Military access to spectrum, which normally is assigned to other use by the administrative application of legal norms, would not meet rapid reaction times needed. Furthermore, military would not be the sole user of spectrum in this scenario, as the scenario involves significant public safety operations amidst fighting units in populated urban combat areas. Future acquisitions and procurement may allow for shared secondary access in peace or normal time yet also allowing for temporally assigned local or regional priority access in disaster recovery or homeland and hybrid scenarios. Capabilities of local and regional prioritization should be pre-planned into the design of dynamic spectrum access systems.

In this paper, we demonstrate tools for dynamic spectrum access to support spectrum management and administration, which could also be expanded to cover the spectral domains of legacy systems. The paper suggests a system model and enabling technologies to support transition from, or an extension of, Licensed Shared Access to incorporate characteristics of Shared Primary Access. For the armed forces, partly also for public safety, already existing inventories of legacy systems have led to fixed, static, and exclusive use approaches to Spectrum Access regardless of location or temporal scope of actual need. We study the applicability and performance of different communication procedures between incumbents and licensees in changing priority sharing arrangement. We also demonstrate that different procedures can co-exist in a single dynamic spectrum sharing system. The key challenge in the work, which is demonstrated in this paper, is how an additional level of complexity, the changing priorities, can be introduced to previously piloted dynamic spectrum access frameworks like TVWS, LSA, or CBRS in a manageable and practical way.

The research questions in this paper are: *which spectrum management controls are applicable for each user group (MNO, PPDR, and MIL) in the selected sharing arrangement; what can be learnt from allowing different controls to be used in a single spectrum management system; how to implement the priority changes, which can be local, regional, national, and temporary; and which elements are important for NRA UI.*

The rest of this paper is organized as follows. The system model, demonstration setup, and method are discussed in Sect. 2. The results are presented in Sect. 3, and finally, conclusions are drawn in Sect. 4.

2   System Model, Demonstration System Setup, and Method

The research method used in this paper is a proof of concept demonstration. We implement a demonstration system of a sharing agreement between different user groups, depicted in Fig. 2. NRA has a user interface to control the priority order between the user groups locally, regionally, nationally, and temporally. MNO and PPDR are demonstrated with off-the-shelf Nokia 2.3 GHz eNodeBs and MIL with Program Making and Special Events (PMSE) wireless camera using DVB-T physical layer for transmission. The PMSE camera is manually operated, and it connects to the Spectrum Manager through a similar reservation system, which is used by the Radio Adminis-tration of the Netherlands [10]. The spectrum resource in the LTE TDD 3GPP band 42 (2300–2400 MHz) is managed by a Spectrum Manager. The demonstration uses two discrete 10 MHz channels, which are 2320–2330 MHz and 2330–2340 MHz. If all three user groups want to use the spectrum simultaneously, two highest priority ones get a 10 MHz channel, and the lowest priority one does not get a permission to transmit.

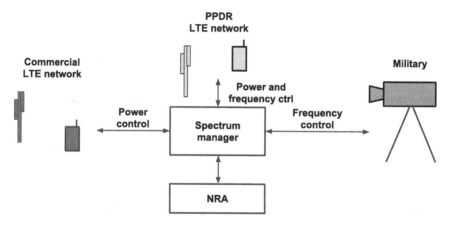

Fig. 2. The demonstration system.

Analyses of scenarios above led to the notional concept of changing the roles of user groups, and that such changes could have temporal and regional variation as depicted in Fig. 3. With three user groups and three priority levels there are 6 states, when all users groups have a different priority level. In case two or more user groups have the same priority level, there are further states in the system. For simplicity, Fig. 3 shows only three different priority orders and the changes between them. The tested concept incorporates changing the priority order. In LSA terminology, each spectrum user can be an incumbent or a licensee [2]. The status as an incumbent or a licensee depends on the temporal and local or regional priority order, which is determined by the alert level of the society. In the shared legacy military or public safety bands, military and public safety may relinquish the protection requirements to allow com-mercial operations in the specified parts of spectrum in peace time. On the shared bands, which are allocated to commercial operators, the protection requirements are relinquished in times of disaster recovery or homeland defense to allow military or public safety operations in the specified parts of spectrum. Through active, trusted operations of a dynamic spectrum management system, military or public safety authorities can be assigned access to spectrum in times and in locations as the scenario requires. Commercial operators can be assigned access to spectrum in peace time. The communication between the spectrum users is dynamic and automatized as far as possible. Commercial systems can implement dynamic changes in spectrum access in operationally relevant timeframes for military and public safety use (i.e., in minutes or at maximum in hours). Military and public safety systems are allowed more time to enforce changes in spectrum access, e.g., hours or days.

Peace	
Primary	Commercial
Secondary	PPDR
Tertiary	Military

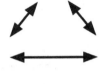

Disaster	
Primary	PPDR
Secondary	Commercial
Tertiary	Military

Hybrid war	
Primary	Military
Secondary	Commercial
Tertiary	PPDR

Fig. 3. Concept of changing access rights of different user communities in different scenarios.

The protocols for the communication between the Spectrum Manager and spectrum users are simplified from the ETSI LSA specification [6] using https protocol. In the case that the communication is initiated by the Spectrum Manager (Notification procedures), an intermediate connectivity layer is needed, just like in email app in the mobile phone. In this study, WebSocket was used. TCP/IP is carried over the physical and Medium Access Control (MAC) layers. Between TCP/IP and HTTPS there is a WebSocket in the Notification procedure communication. The LSA-1 protocol is encapsulated in JSON messages and carried over HTTPS.

A spectrum manager can generally control the permission to transmit, transmit power, transmitter center frequency, nominal bandwidth, and in the future, antenna patterns of the devices. The control capabilities may be limited by the sharing arrangement. For example, the original TVWS geolocation database in US was able to change the center frequency but not the power nor the bandwidth. The original LSA is able to control the power level, but not to change the center frequency or bandwidth. The commercial operating environment may also limit the management choices. Considering the demonstration system in this paper, we assume that the spectrum is shared between a MNO, PPDR, and military. The MNO has most likely been assigned the band through an auction or a beauty contest, and the MNO uses the full capacity of the band, when possible. It is not likely that the MNO would change the center frequency to a band of another MNO. The MNO network forms a large area coverage, and we assume here that the PPDR/MIL use is local or regional. Changing the bandwidth and center frequency even within the MNO assigned band, would probably cause unexpected errors at the border of LSA limited network area and unaffected parts of the MNO network. The MNO networks are wide area networks, where each basestation of a MNO has the same center frequency. If a single basestation or a small group of basestations of the MNO wide area network have a different center frequency, the mobile UEs would experience an untypical change in the traditional mobile network coverage. Due to this, at the moment we assume, that the MNO base station control is limited to permission to transmit and maximum allowed power level. PPDR and military are considered here as local networks, and they may have sharing agreements with all operators, whereby the control of PPDR/MIL networks may include also the center frequency and bandwidth changes.

We evaluated the spectrum management controls individually for each user group. Our system consisted of a mixed use of controls, and we evaluated the experiences gained during testing and demonstrations. Furthermore, applied spectrum prioritizations were verified by spectrum measurements using a spectrum analyzer. During the demonstrations, we operated the priorities through the implemented NRA UI. The possibility for local, regional, national, and temporary priority changes was incorporated to the NRA UI as well as to the Spectrum Manager. The key novelty of the system is that the changing priorities were tested with various state changes. These state changes included various arrival sequences and priority orders starting either from an unoccupied spectrum state or from a pre-occupied spectrum. During the demonstration, we monitored the radio signals with a spectrum analyzer, as illustrated in Fig. 4.

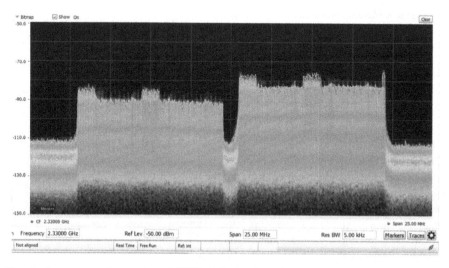

Fig. 4. Spectrum analyzer view of MNO (left signal) and PPDR (right signal) transmitting.

The priority order changes illustrated in Fig. 3 was tested in the demomstration. The conceptual schematic depicting the demonstration is presented in Fig. 5, and which is broken down to use cases, valid priority order, arrivals and spectrum occupancy. For simplicity, we present the highest priority order changes only from commercial MNO to MIL and from MIL to PPDR. In the first case the MNO arrives first, and they are allocated the lower one of the two available spectrum blocks. Next arrives PPDR, and they get the higher spectrum block. Last comes MIL, having the lowest priority. As there is no capacity available for MIL, the access to spectrum is denied. In the second case, MIL has the highest priority. The order of arrival is the same as in the previous case. MNO and PPDR get their spectrum blocks. When MIL with the highest priority arrives, MNO allocation is cleared, and MIL gets the lower spectrum block. The third case continues from the end state of the second case. MNO priority is increased to be higher than that of MIL. Consequently, MIL use is cleared, and the lower spectrum block is allocated to MNO.

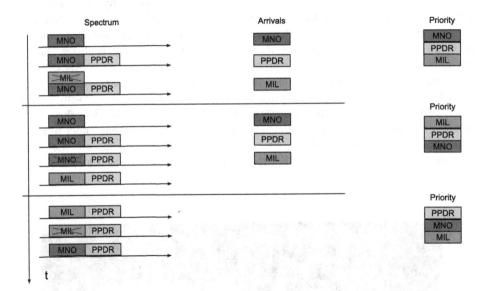

Fig. 5. Changes in the demonstration spectrum use.

3   Results

The main spectrum management controls are the transmit power, and its special case of permission to transmit, transmitter center frequency, and the nominal bandwidth of the transmitter in the demonstration. The MNO center frequency cannot be changed to another operator's frequency block and the change of center frequency within the operator's band would also cause deterioration of the mobility service. Narrowing the bandwidth could in theory be possible, but most likely it would cause unexpected behavior in the network and should be avoided. Thereby we assumed that wide area MNO networks are only controlled by transmission power by the Spectrum Manager.

The center frequency and bandwidth changes of MIL and PPDR are not as restricted as they are in the MNO networks. The mapping of the spectrum management controls and user groups are summarized in Table 1.

Table 1. Mapping spectrum management controls and user groups

Control	MNO	PPDR	MIL
Power level	Possible	Possible	Possible
Center frequency	Restricted	Possible	Possible
Bandwidth	Restricted	Possible	Possible

In the standard dynamic spectrum management, the controlled devices, such as White Space Devices (WSD), LSA Licensee, and Citizen's Broadband Radio Device (CBSD), are homogenous, and they have the same controls available. On the other hand, the systems employed by priority users are heterogenous, and the way how the protection requirements are derived from the priority users varies a lot. The main reason for this is that the incumbents are considered legacy systems. The secondary devices are new, and the same capabilities can be required from them. When the controlled secondary systems are legacy systems, a possibility for heterogenous controls are required. In this demonstration system, we have shown that a plurality of control mechanisms for secondary systems can co-exist and their capabilities can be defined in the rules and algorithms of the Spectrum Manager.

We demonstrated the feasibility to use priority profiles to implement a spectrum management system with changing priorities. The stakeholders of the sharing arrangement negotiate the possibility for priority changes, related spectrum ranges, and the authority to initiate the priority change in advance. By default, the mandate for priority changes is associated with the NRA, but it may also be given to the PPDR organizations. The PPDR has pre-defined rescue plans for a wide range of catastrophes. The plans may include area definitions and rescue times. Both areas and time periods can be included in the priority profiles or they can be left to be defined at the time of need. When a spectrum priority profile is taken into use, it defines the priority of different user groups, the frequency range, geographic area, and the period for the priority profile to be active. A country may have several priority profiles active simultaneously, and the profiles should also have a mutual priority order.

In this study, we develop a UI for NRA to create, manage, and operate the priority changes in a dynamic spectrum management system. The UI has a map interface to define the areas, as illustrated in Fig. 6. Separately defined region or municipality areas can also be used. The location definitions can be named and stored for later use. The spectrum priority order and the frequency range are stored and named. Finally, a period with begin and end time (or permanently) are bound together with the area, frequency range, and priority order definitions. The defined and active priority orders are presented as a list where the position in the list defines the priority order between the priority profiles.

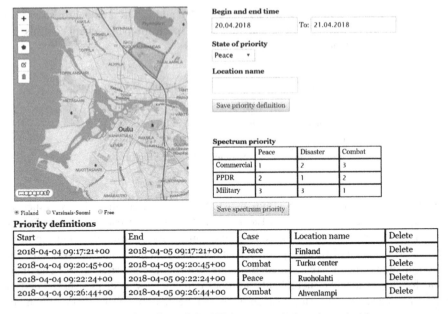

Begin and end time

20.04.2018   To: 21.04.2018

State of priority

Peace   ▾

Location name

Save priority definition

Spectrum priority

	Peace	Disaster	Combat
Commercial	1	2	3
PPDR	2	1	2
Military	3	3	1

Save spectrum priority

● Finland   ○ Varsinais-Suomi   ○ Free

Priority definitions

Start	End	Case	Location name	Delete
2018-04-04 09:17:21+00	2018-04-05 09:17:21+00	Peace	Finland	Delete
2018-04-04 09:20:45+00	2018-04-05 09:20:45+00	Combat	Turku center	Delete
2018-04-04 09:22:24+00	2018-04-05 09:22:24+00	Peace	Ruoholahti	Delete
2018-04-04 09:26:44+00	2018-04-05 09:26:44+00	Combat	Ahvenlampi	Delete

Fig. 6. User interface of the NRA to control changing priorities.

4   Conclusions

The standard dynamic spectrum management systems have fixed user groups as priority and secondary users and do not allow the priority order to be changed. Especially, PPDR and military users may have training and similar non-critical use, which could be carried out with secondary spectrum access. For obvious reasons, the critical use of PPDR and military should be prioritized when appropriate. In CBRS, this could be enabled by having the military and public safety as incumbent users and MNO as Priority Access License (PAL) user. The military and PPDR could enter the system also as General Authorized Access (GAA) users. Only at the time of critical missions, they would utilize their incumbent status. This arrangement would work for two different spectrum users in CBRS. When the system contains three or more different user groups, which should be able to change their relative priorities, a spectrum priority management system, introduced in this paper, would be required.

The introduced system and demonstration has various types of controlled systems and the capabilities to control them. In the standard systems, the incumbents are heterogenous, but the controlled devices are relatively unified. The demonstration shows that a dynamic spectrum management system can control simultaneously various types of devices and they may have differing capabilities and restrictions in spectrum use.

In this demonstration, we showed how the priority order can be defined locally, regionally, and temporally in addition to the nation-wide priority order. Furthermore, MNO and PPDR type of spectrum users can flexibly adapt to power level, center frequency, and bandwidth control. Only the power level of the eNodeBs of a nationwide MNO network should by default be controlled by the Spectrum Manager. If the commercial LTE network is a local private LTE network, there is freedom for center frequency and bandwidth changes within the private LTE frequency block. The pre-defined spectrum priority profiles support well the pre-planned disaster recovery of PPDR and military contingencies. Carrying out the negotiations between the sharing parties in advance, and allowing the electronic control of the spectrum management, improves the response times and communication capabilities at the time of critical missions. The NRA UI demonstrates how the priority profiles can be created and managed.

Interest towards dynamic spectrum access has increased. This demonstration shows that new capabilities could be introduced to the future spectrum management systems: changing priority order, geographically limited changes in priority order, and simultaneous control of heterogenous networks. As future work, we recommend to study how different procedures (request, notification, and reservation) impact the evacuation time, extending the mixture of different controls in this paper to include also the procedural dimension. We would also welcome studies about the impact of local center frequency change and local bandwidth change in a nation-wide MNO network.

References

1. Ofcom: Statement on Implementing TV White Spaces. http://stakeholders.ofcom.org.uk/binaries/consultations/white-space-coexistence/statement/tvws-statement.pdf. Accessed 18 Apr 2018
2. ECC: Report 205 licensed shared access (2014)
3. FCC: 16-55 the second report and order and order on reconsideration finalizes rules for innovative citizens broadband radio service in the 3.5 GHz band (2016)
4. IEEE: Standard 802.22b-2015 wireless regional area networks, pp. 1–299 (2015)
5. Tuukkanen, T., Yrjölä, S., Matinmikko, M., Ahokangas, P., Mustonen, M.: Armed forces' views on Shared Spectrum Access. In: 2017 International Conference on Military Communications and Information Systems (ICMCIS), Oulu, pp. 1–8 (2017)
6. ETSI: Technical Specification 103 379. Information elements and protocols for the interface between LSA controller (LC) and LSA repository (LR) for operation of licensed shared access (LSA) in the 2300–2400 band. V1.1.1. (2017). http://www.etsi.org/deliver/etsi_ts/103300_103399/103379/01.01.01_60/ts_103379v010101p.pdf. Accessed 18 Apr 2018
7. ETSI: Technical Report 103 588. Feasibility study on temporary spectrum access for local high-quality wireless networks. V1.1.1. (2018). http://www.etsi.org/deliver/etsi_tr/103500_103599/103588/01.01.01_60/tr_103588v010101p.pdf. Accessed 18 Apr 2018
8. Yrjölä, S., Kokkinen, H.: Licensed Shared Access evolution enables early access to 5G spectrum and novel use cases. EAI Endorsed Trans. Wirel. Spectr. **17**(12), e1 (2017)
9. WINNF Spectrum Sharing Committee: SAS Functional Architecture (2016). http://groups.winnforum.org/d/do/8512. Accessed 18 Apr 2018
10. Petersen, G.: Licensed Shared Access pilot in the Netherlands. CEPT Frequency Management Working Group Meeting Document, Prague (2016). https://cept.org/Documents/wg-fm/33535/5-3_pmse-lsa-in-the-band-2300-2400-mhz-nl. Accessed 18 Apr 2018

A Low-Latency Wireless Network
for Cloud-Based Robot Control

Seyed Ali Hassani$^{(\boxtimes)}$ ⓘ and Sofie Pollin ⓘ

Department of Electrical Engineering, KU Leuven, Heverlee 3001, Belgium
{seyedali.hassani,sofie.pollin}@esat.kuleuven.be
https://www.esat.kuleuven.be/telemic/research/NetworkedSystems

Abstract. We demonstrate a reliable network for robot remote control
in which a cross-layer PHY-MAC architecture is exploited to establish
a low-latency and time-critical data transmission. In our demo, three
reverse pendulum robots share the spectrum to communicate their sensory data to a processing unit which can instantly generate and transmit
appropriate commands to maintain the robots' balance.

To this end, we upgrade CLAWS (Cross-Layer Adaptable Wireless
System) with a two-layer MAC platform which accelerates and facilities
interrupt handling. To grant the network operational reliability, we elaborately coupled the FPGA-based IEEE 802.15.4 PHY in the CLAWS
architecture with a set of hardware blocks that play the role of the
low-level MAC. CLAWS also offers a run-time programmable module
in which we deploy the high-level functionalities of the MAC protocol.
Jointly with the implemented bi-layer MAC structure, we demonstrate
how the CLAWS' flexibility allows either standard compliant or ad-hoc
network prototyping to establish a reliable cloud-based robot remote
control.

Keywords: Software-defined radio · Cross-layer architecture
Cloud-based processing

1 Introduction

Software-defined radio (SDR) enables reconfigurability in wireless communication systems, and as such it has played a key role in technology development
in the last decade. In addition to programmability, the latest communication
technologies (e.g., 5G, wireless edge computing) have to provide a high level
of performance to satisfy new and emerging applications such as cloud-based
processing.

Today's challenge on SDR is to bring together both flexibility and high-
performance functionality in one platform. To overcome this challenge, the platform has to provide a wide variety of capabilities in the hardware-reliant network
layers. The PHY and MAC, for instance, differ in their data-flow and control-flow
operations: PHY works with simple pipeline stages to deal with heavy data-flow

I. Moerman et al. (Eds.): CROWNCOM 2018, LNICST 261, pp. 46–51, 2019.
https://doi.org/10.1007/978-3-030-05490-8_5

and is dominated by processing latency, whereas the MAC functionality needs complex control and complicated branch instructions to perform event handling and control functions [1].

1.1 The Programmable CLAWS Architecture for Reliable Communication

Recently, large FPGA-based SDRs have been introduced to fill the gap between latency requirements and reconfigurability. CLAWS [3] is one of the presented platforms which offers an IEEE 802.15.4 compliant transceiver including the physical and MAC layers respectively implemented by LabVIEW FPGA and C. The PHY is split into several functional adjustable blocks enabling granular modification and on-the-fly changes without recompiling of the FPGA code [5]. The MAC is also fully deployed in a Xilinx MicroBlaze softcore [4] to allow run-time reprogramming and facilitate MAC development.

The demo presented in [5] demonstrates the CLAWS PHY and network layers performance in a standard compliance network. The main objective of our demo is to illustrate how one can combine the CLAWS' pieces to prototype a high-reliable wireless system for time-critical messaging.

A crucial prerequisite for Ultra-Reliable Low Latency Communication (URLLC) is to deliver a packet within a certain time. One can define the reliability as the probability that the latency does not exceed a predescribed deadline [2]. Such a deadline might be dictated by the application itself or determined by the standard, e.g., the fixed time interval that within the receiver has to acknowledge a data receipt. A running MAC on CPU, may not fulfill this obligation as it can not handle multiple and successive interrupts properly.

In the case of the cloud-based wireless network, it can be shown that occurrence of consecutive interrupts, such as generating multiple succeeding Immediate Acknowledge (Imm-Ack) packets in the central node, affects the CPU performance negatively as it has to reinitiate the interrupted task each time. In full-duplex or multi-channel MAC protocols, the capability of handling events becomes even more essential. For instance, in a multi-channel vehicular network, the MAC CPU is more likely to be suspended by a high-priority packet at the control channel while it has to react to the service channels concurrently.

To mitigate this problem, we combine the CLAWS' CPU with a scalable set of low-level modules which enables agile interrupt handling while does not degrade the CLAWS flexibility. Then we employ the enhanced platform to establish a cloud-based system that controls three balancing robots. The resulting timing enhancement is presented.

2 Two-Level MAC Structure for Improving Interrupt Handling Capability

The CLAWS platform utilizes a MicroBlaze soft processor to run the MAC protocol. In addition to run-time reprogramability of this CPU, it significantly helps implementation of multi-stage procedures and sequential algorithms. In fact, some basic tasks in the MAC layer do not need deep flexibility and hence, can be implemented in hardware more efficiently.

Figure 1 depicts our proposed two-layer MAC structure in the CLAWS framework. This model benefits from a set of hardware level blocks which are interfaced carefully with the high-level flexible MAC running in the MicroBlaze. Operating close to the PHY layer, the low-level MAC can deliver a set of basic and interrupt-based tasks of the MAC layer and accelerate interrupt handling as well as facilitate the development of complicated networking protocols and retransmission algorithms.

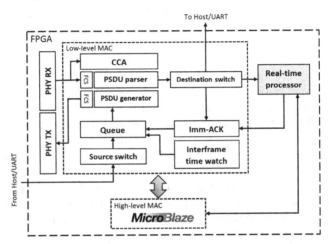

Fig. 1. High/Low level MAC in the CLAWS architecture.

2.1   High-Level MAC

The CLAWS cross-layer architecture enables to deploy the high-level MAC on MicroBlaze. In the enhanced platform, this CPU can initiate packet transmission process, run retransmission algorithm, drive the backoff timer to estimate the backoff time, trigger Clear Channel Assessment (CCA) module, configure the payload sources and destination switches (e.g., UART, host PC), etc.

2.2   Low-Level MAC

The hardware realized low-level MAC in the upgraded CLAWS reduces the workload of the CPU as it can perform somewhat non-sequential straightforward jobs of the MAC protocol and react to interrupts instantly. For instance, the CPU can configure the destination switch in the low-level MAC to pass a packet to the host, the UART interface, the MicroBlaze itself or any other hardware-implemented processor. This mechanism also allows spontaneous Imm-ACK packet transmission.

As shown in Fig. 1, these blocks are elaborately coupled with the related sections in PHY on one side and interfaced with the high-level MAC one the other side. The following functionalities can be accomplished by the presented low-level MAC; generating the PHY Service Data Unit (PSDU) and Imm-ACK packet, parsing the PSDU, controlling the packet queue, and measuring the interframe spacing times. This set of components is implemented by LabVIEW FPGA, running at 150 MHz and needs slight flexibility which is guaranteed by the CPU.

3   Demo Set-Up Overview

We show a star-topology network in which four SDRs run the upgraded CLAWS architecture. Each SDR has an NI USRP RIO [6] which is equipped with a Xilinx Kintex 7 FPGA. This SDR can transmit from 400 MHz to 4.4 GHz and provides a 120 MHz IQ sample rate at IF stage. We use the integrated PCIe interface to monitor the FPGA's internal signals and the results.

Figure 2 (Left) illustrates the structure of the test set-up. Each of the three SDRs is interfaced with a reverse pendulum robot which requires updating its balance status every 7 ms. The robots send their sensory data through the UART interface to the SDRs. The SDRs then transmit this information to the fourth node which plays the role of cloud processor and can produce appropriate commands to drive the robot's DC motors in such a way that they maintain balance.

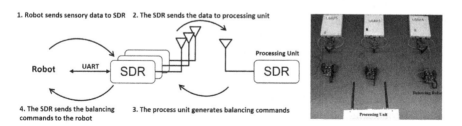

Fig. 2. (Left): The structure of the cloud-based wireless network. (Right): The test set-up including four SDRs and three balancing robots.

The payload carries 4 bytes of sensory data and jointly with the MAC's header and footer it forms a 12-Byte PSDU. In order to share the spectrum fairly, the nodes obey the CSMA/CA MAC scheme to transmit their sensory data. The processor in our set-up can either attach the balancing commands to the Imm-ACK in the low-level MAC or generate a new packet in the CPU. Due to the CCA procedure and the backoff mechanism in CSMA/CA scheme, the latter is accompanied by a non-deterministic latency. The processing unit can also acquire a control command, e.g., moving forward and backward, through an Ethernet connection and broadcast it to all robots. A video demonstrating this set-up is available in [7].

4   Experimental Results

To compare the performance of the presented two-layer MAC and the fully CPU-deployed MAC, we ran both structures at 150 MHz and interrupted them to produce 12-Byte Imm-ACK. Depending on its working state, the single-layer MAC needs 10 µs to generate and place the Imm-ACK packet in the queue. However, this time may exceed up to 16 µs depending on CPU's working status. Whereas, the bi-layer MAC behaves deterministically as it generates and inserts the packet, including the balancing command, into the queue within 0.41 µs.

In order to compare our ad-hoc command transmission scheme with a standard complaint MAC, we measured the time that the CPU needs to acquire the sensory data from the PHY's FIFO, generate and place the Imm-ACK, trigger the CCA module and apply the CMSA's exponential backoff time to transmit the commands. Depending on the network traffic load, this interval may vary from 156 µs to several milliseconds in a non-deterministic fashion.

5   Conclusion

In this paper, we illustrated how the flexibility of CLAWS architecture helps to prototype a standard compliant or an ad-hoc network which effectively satisfies the obligations of low-latency and time-critical messaging.

Using the CLAWS architecture, it is shown that the developed two-layer MAC model enables robust communication while it preserves the CLAWS' run-time configuration capability. Due to its efficient implementation, this low-level MAC can take up the time-sensitive workload of the MAC layer and enable reliable ad-hoc network prototyping.

Besides, our low-level MAC fits in <%2 of the Kintex7 FPGA while the MicroBlaze occupies %8 of the total logic resources. Therefore, a combination of multiple low-level MACs on top of one CPU module can form a practical and efficient solution for multi-channel and full-duplex MAC protocols as it delivers adequate processing power and multiple interrupt handling ability.

Acknowledgement. This work was partially funded by the European Union's Horizon 2020 under grant agreement no. 732174 (ORCA project).

References

1. Wu, H., et al.: The tick programmable low-latency SDR system. In: MobiCom, Snowbird, Utah, USA, October 2017
2. Popovski, P., et al.: Ultra-reliable low-latency communication (URLLC): principles and building blocks. CoRR, abs/1708.07862 (2017)
3. Van den Bergh, B., Vermeulen, T., Verhelst, M., Pollin, S.: CLAWS: cross-layer adaptable wireless system enabling full cross-layer experimentation on real-time software-defined 802.15. 4. EURASIP J. Wirel. Commun. Netw. **2014**(1), 187 (2014)
4. MicroBlaze soft processor. http://www.xilinx.com/tools/microblaze.htm.. Accessed 04 Apr 2018

5. Vermeulen, T., Van den Bergh, B., Pollin, S.: Demo: a software defined radio platform for rapid cross-layer prototyping, pp. 1–4 (2015)
6. Ni usrp-2942r - national instruments. http://sine.ni.com/nips/cds/view/p/lang/nl/nid/212434
7. https://www.youtube.com/watch?v=hP7aXoF9FVU

Licensed Shared Access and Dynamic
Spectrum Access

Comparison of Incumbent User Privacy Preserving Technologies in Database Driven Dynamic Spectrum Access Systems

He Li[(✉)], Yaling Yang, Yanzhi Dou, Chang Lu, Doug Zabransky,
and Jung-Min (Jerry) Park

Virgina Tech, Blacksburg, VA, USA
{heli,yyang8,yzdou,chang17,dmz5e,jungmin}@vt.edu

Abstract. Database driven dynamic spectrum sharing is one of the most promising dynamic spectrum access (DSA) solution to address the spectrum scarcity issue. In such a database driven DSA system, the centralized spectrum management infrastructure, called spectrum access system (SAS), makes its spectrum allocation decisions to secondary users (SUs) according to sensitive operational data of incumbent users (IUs). Since both SAS and SUs are not necessarily fully trusted, privacy protection against untrusted SAS and SUs become critical for IUs that have high operational privacy requirements. To address this problem, many IU privacy preserving solutions emerge recently. However, there is a lack of understanding and comparison of capability in protecting IU operational privacy under these existing approaches. In this paper, thus, we fill in the void by providing a comparative study that investigates existing solutions and explores several existing metrics to evaluate the strength of privacy protection. Moreover, we propose two general metrics to evaluate privacy preserving level and evaluate existing works with them.

Keywords: Dynamic spectrum access · Privacy preserving technology

1 Introduction

Using geolocation databases is one of the most practical approaches for enabling spectrum sharing. For example, to achieve dynamic spectrum access between Citizens Broadband Radio Service (CBRS) and government and non-government incumbents in 3.5 GHz band, a Spectrum Access System (SAS) is required to coordinate CBRS devices (CBSDs). Under SAS's coordination, CBSDs can satisfy the varying interference protection requirements of incumbent users (IUs), while maximizing the utilization of spectrum.

The operational privacy of IUs is crucial in this DSA paradigm, especially when IUs are federal government and military systems [9]. The Federal

© ICST Institute for Computer Sciences, Social Informatics and Telecommunications Engineering 2019
Published by Springer Nature Switzerland AG 2019. All Rights Reserved
I. Moerman et al. (Eds.): CROWNCOM 2018, LNICST 261, pp. 55–65, 2019.
https://doi.org/10.1007/978-3-030-05490-8_6

Communications Commission (FCC) and wireless innovation forum (WINNF) have regulatory requirements that the retention and disclosure of information related to IU operational privacy should be limited.

To satisfy these regulations of IU operational privacy, a few IU privacy preserving schemes have been proposed recently. These schemes can be divided into two categories. The first category, including [2–4,11,12], achieve their goals by obfuscating IUs' inputs to SAS. The second category achieves provable security through secure multi-party computation (MPC) protocols [7,8], where IU inputs are encrypted before being sent to SAS and SAS performs spectrum computation on ciphertext domain without seeing the plaintext of IU operational data.

In this paper, we present a comparative study on the two existing categories of proposals, and we explore different existing security metrics for evaluating these existing works. Furthermore, we propose two new and generic metrics, named *minimum adversarial estimation error* and *indistinguishable input*, to evaluate IU privacy preserving level that can be applied across different schemes.

Through simulation study, we show that data obfuscation-based solutions provide better protection against adversarial SUs, yet offer worse spectrum utilization. Secure MPC-based solutions provides better protection against untrusted SAS and offer worse protection against adversarial SUs.

The rest of the paper is organized as follows: Section 2 presents the general system model and attack model. Section 3 introduces existing works. Section 4 proposes our security metrics evaluating IU privacy protection strength. Section 5 presents the comparison on privacy preserving strength for existing works and Sect. 6 concludes the paper.

2   System Model

In this section, we introduce the general system model and attack model for an IU privacy preserving DSA system.

2.1   Model of Database Driven Dynamic Spectrum Access System

In this paper, we assume a general DSA service model, which consists of three entities: incumbent users (IUs, also known as "primary users" in some literature), Spectrum Access System (SAS), and secondary users (SUs). IUs update their operational status to SAS. SAS handles spectrum request from SUs by running a spectrum computation functionality $f(\cdot)$ that performs admission control for SUs. $f(\cdot)$ may also include channel assignment and/or power assignment operations. This system model summarizes the system models used in all existing privacy-protection works, including [2–4,7,8,11,12].

2.2   Attack Models

There exist several types of attackers focusing on breaking IU operational privacy in a database driven DSA system:

A1: (Intruders) the attacker is an intruder, which is not any entity in the DSA system. It can overhear, intercept, and synthesize any message exchanged across the network. Specifically it may directly extract IU operational status by looking at the messages sent from IUs to SAS. This threat model is also referred to as "Dolev-Yao model" [6]. Under this threat model, exchanging all messages under secure channels (e.g. using TLS) can provide confidentiality, which ensures IU privacy. Thus, existing works are not focusing on proposing countermeasures towards this type of attack.

A2: (Honest but curious SAS, or semi-honest SAS) the adversary is a faithful SAS. While it performs all spectrum computation faithfully, it is also interested in discovering the operational parameters of IUs from the information it receives from IUs. Under this attack model, IU privacy fails if IUs directly send their plain operational status to SAS. Works [3,4,7,8] consider this attack model.

A3: (Adversarial SU network) the adversary controls a group of compromised SUs, so that it can obtain their spectrum request results to infer IUs' operational parameters. This type of attack is also referred to as "database inference attack" [2], which is studied in [2–4,11].

A4: (Malicious colluding SAS) the adversary controls both a group of compromised SUs and a malicious SAS. The malicious SAS would deviate from the protocol to allure SUs to generate other observations to further infer IUs' operational status. In [7] such kind of attack is discussed.

3 Existing Works

In this section, we will introduce existing solutions for IU privacy protection.

3.1 Overview of Existing Works

Data Obfuscation Techniques: When we consider attacks that focus on inferring IU operational status, the straightforward countermeasure is to obfuscate the inputs from IUs to SAS by adding noise or distortion to the input data.

For example, in order to prevent adversaries from deriving an IU's location by the radius of its protection zone, [2,11] propose to replace k IUs' individual protection zones by a super-size protection contour that encloses these k individual protection zones. Thus, IU location privacy protection in terms of k-anonymity can be provided under these schemes.

Another approach is to directly add noise to the actual IU operational parameters before executing spectrum computation functionality $f(\cdot)$. In [3,4], such strategies are briefly discussed. In [12], a structured noise is added to the true location of IUs, so that differential location privacy is preserved for IUs.

It is also proposed in [3,4] to add fake IU entries to the database. As a result, both adversarial SAS and SUs will not be able to distinguish those false entries from the true IU entries.

Essentially, applying data obfuscation techniques achieves IU privacy protection at a cost of SU spectrum utility. In [2,4,11], simulation results show that data obfuscation techniques can achieve an advantageous trade-off in their simulation setup. However, it is not deeply studied on how to choose proper obfuscation techniques and how to set parameters for them. In [4], an optimization problem is setup to study this issue, but the authors also claimed it may not be practical to solve this optimization problem at runtime.

Secure Multi-party Computation Based Schemes: The basic idea of a secure multi-party computation (MPC) based solution for DSA system is for IUs to first encrypt their operational parameters by homomorphic cryptosystems before sending the encrypted parameters to SAS. SAS then executes spectrum computation functionality $f(\cdot)$ in ciphertext domain by leveraging the homomorphic property of the cryptosystems. The confidentiality properties of the underlying cryptosystems ensure that a semi-honest SAS is not able to extract any information from those encrypted messages.

In [8], such an MPC-based solution is proposed, where SAS is assumed to manage SU interference in "protection zone model", which ensures the aggregated interference generated from SUs to IUs does not exceed certain threshold. In [7], another MPC-based solution is proposed, where SAS is assumed to manage SU interference in "exclusion zone model", which ensures any spectrum request from an SU located in an exclusion zone will be declined.

3.2 Privacy Metrics in Existing Works

A few metrics have been used in existing DSA privacy-preserving works. In this section, we introduce these metrics and discuss whether they are appropriate for comparative studies of multiple privacy-preserving schemes.

Average Expected Location Estimation Error [2,4,11]: Assume an attacker can obtain a probability density function $A(loc'|\mathcal{O})$ as the guess of an IU location given some observation $\mathcal{O}$. Assuming n_I IUs exist in a target region, the actual IU locations are used to partition the region into n_I subregions using the Voronoi diagram approach. These subregions are denoted as $\mathcal{L}_i$. The *average expected location estimation error* metric is defined as:

$$Pri := \frac{1}{n_I} \sum_{i=1}^{n_I} \sum_{loc \in L_i} d(loc_i, loc) \frac{A(loc|\mathcal{O})}{\sum_{loc' \in \mathcal{L}_i} A(loc'|\mathcal{O})}, \tag{1}$$

where loc_i is the true location of the ith IU, $d(\cdot,\cdot)$ is the distance between two locations. This metric is proposed in [4] and is widely applicable. [2] and [11] use a special case of the metric that assumes $n_I = 1$.

Privacy Time [3]: Privacy time is a widely applicable metric that measures the degradation of location privacy level over time. It is the expected time that it takes for IU location estimation error to fall lower than a certain threshold.

Size of Search Space [4]: This is the size of search space of possible IU param-eters. After collecting some observations, an adversarial SAS or SU can exclude some locations as possible IU locations, which means the search space of true IU locations is reduced. This metric is essentially equivalent with a special case of the "expected location estimation error" metric where $A(loc'|\mathcal{O})$ is set to be a uniform distribution in the search space area.

ϵ-Differential Privacy [12]: When an attacker obtain observation $\mathcal{O}$ and attempts to distinguish the true location of an IU between l_0 and l_1 within a circle with radius r, ϵ-differential privacy requires the likelihood ratio is lower than $e^{\epsilon r}$, where ϵ is the parameter of differential privacy and r can be any radius value smaller than the radius of service area.

The formal definition is given as follows[1]:

$$\frac{P(\mathcal{O}|l_1)}{P(\mathcal{O}|l_0)} \le e^{\epsilon r} \qquad \forall r > 0 \; \forall l_1, l_0 : d(l_1, l_0) \le r. \tag{2}$$

This metric, however, cannot be applied in DSA systems where the inter-ference management policy of SAS protects IUs from harmful interference. For example, when $\mathcal{O}$ is a positive response for an SU query at location l_0 and l_0 is extremely close to an IU at the same time, it is easy to see that the denomina-tor $P(\mathcal{O}|l_0)$ in Eq. (2) must be 0, which makes differential privacy unachievable. Since most of the existing privacy-preserving works [2–4,7,8,11] except [12] are designed for systems where harmful interference to IUs is strictly prohibited, ϵ-differential is not a suitable metric for comparative study of DSA privacy schemes.

Provable Security with the Cryptographic Setting [7,8]: By defining prov-able security with the cryptographic setting for a privacy preserving DSA system, we attempt to abstract the attack model and formulate any attacker under this model as an adversarial algorithm $\mathcal{A}$. When the provable security is achieved, we expect that any probabilistic polynomial time (PPT) adversarial algorithm $\mathcal{A}$ cannot achieve its goal at a non-negligible probability. Note that we call these security features "provable" because usually we attempt to prove that it is at least harder for an adversary to achieve its goal, compared to breaking a secure cryptosystem or other underlying hard problems.

In [7,8], provable security feature on IU operational privacy protection is proposed and proved. However, security definitions in [7,8] are also tailored definitions towards a specific interference management policy ("protection zone" and "exclusion zone" respectively). We hereby propose a general definition of "indistinguishable input" in Sect. 4 to ensure wider applicability.

---

[1] There are three equivalent definitions proposed in [1], and in this paper we show the third one.

4   Proposed Security Metric

In this section, we propose two additional metrics to evaluate the level of IU operational privacy. These two metrics are named *minimum adversarial estimation error* and *indistinguishable input*.

4.1   Minimum Adversarial Estimation Error

Suppose M IUs are operating with parameter sets $P_1^*, \cdots, P_M^* \in \mathcal{P}$, where $\mathcal{P}$ is the set of parameters with all possible values. An adversary $\mathcal{A}$ can obtain a posterior distribution of IUs' true parameters through its observations $\mathcal{O}$, which are obtained from compromised SAS or SUs. We denote $p_{\mathcal{A}}(\mathcal{P})$ as the posterior probability and

$$p_{\mathcal{A}}(\mathcal{P}) := \Pr\left[\text{IUs' operational parameter set} = \mathcal{P} | \mathcal{A} \text{ observes } \mathcal{O}\right], \qquad (3)$$

where $\mathcal{P} := \{P_j\}_{j=1}^M$.

We assume that the adversary would sample a parameter set based on the posterior distribution $p_{\mathcal{A}}(\mathcal{P})$ as its guess of the IUs' true operational parameter sets. The privacy preserving level (PPL), thus, can be defined as the expectation of the minimum estimation error, which is the minimum distance between any true IU parameters and any adversarial guess. That is,

$$PPL := E\left[\min_{i \in [M]} \min_{j \in [M]} d(P_i, P_j^*)\right]. \qquad (4)$$

The above privacy preserving metric definition extends the "expected location estimation error" concept to privacy protection of any IU operational parameter. In addition, compared to the "average expected location estimation error" discussed in Sect. 3.2, this metric evaluates the minimum estimation error among multiple IUs.

Since different privacy preserving techniques have different format of observations and will result in different posterior distribution of IU parameters from the adversary's point of view, it is not efficient or possible to derive a closed-form math expression of the PPL. Thus, we choose to use numerical method to obtain PPL value. Specifically, note that given the specification of a privacy-preserving system, it is straightforward to generate a large set of possible adversary observations $\mathcal{O}$ for any given IU parameter set P^*. We can therefore employ Markov Chain Monte Carlo (MCMC) [10] method to generate samples of posterior distribution of IU parameters, and use them to obtain an approximate PPL.

4.2   Indistinguishable Input

We introduce the new metric called *indistinguishable input* to extend the concept of provable IU operational security, so that it can be applied on evaluating more privacy preserving DSA solutions under different attack models. Indistinguishable input requires that an adversary is not able to extract much information about an IU's operation parameters (e.g. location, transmit power, etc.) from this IU's input to SAS. In other words, indistinguishable input says that when SAS receives a message from an IU, the likelihoods that the message is generated under two different IU operational parameter settings are *almost* the same.

To formally define this metric, we setup the following guessing game:

- Initialization phase: setup the DSA system faithfully.
- Challenge phase: an adversary (e.g. a compromised SAS) chooses two arbitrary different IU operational parameters P_0 and P_1 on its will. IU picks a random bit $b \leftarrow_\$ \{0,1\}$ and sends the corresponding IU input $\mathcal{I}_b$ to the adversary.
- Finalization phase: the adversary attempts to find out the secret bit b and return its guess b^*. We say the adversary wins the game if $b^* = b$.

Indistinguishable input means that any adversary cannot win the above game with an effectively higher probability than randomly guessing. Formally, if for any polynomial time algorithm $\mathcal{A}$ through which the adversary wins the above game at a probability $\epsilon_\mathcal{A}(\lambda)$ (λ is the security parameter of underlying cryptosystem), a design that has indistinguishable input property must ensure $\max_\mathcal{A} |\epsilon_\mathcal{A}(\lambda) - \frac{1}{2}|$ is negligible. Here, "negligible" means that for any integer c, there exists some λ^* such that $\forall \lambda \geq \lambda^*$,

$$\max_\mathcal{A} \left| \epsilon_\mathcal{A}(\lambda) - \frac{1}{2} \right| < \frac{1}{\lambda^c}. \tag{5}$$

5 Comparisons on Privacy Preserving Strength

In this section, we compare the security strength for existing works [2–4,7,8,11]. We analyze the indistinguishable input property for all these works, and evaluate the average expected error, minimum adversarial estimation error and privacy time for all of them under attack model **A2** and **A3**.

As we have discussed in Sect. 3.2, "search space size" metric is essentially equivalent to a special case of "expected location estimation error" metric, and ϵ-Differential privacy is not a suitable metric since it is not applicable to most of the existing works. Therefore, we are not using these two metrics for evaluation.

Note that as we have discussed in Sect. 2.2, the security threat in attack model **A1** can be thwarted by using secure channel, and the security threats in attack model **A4** has not been deeply studied in existing works. Therefore, we are not evaluating existing works under these two attack models.

5.1 Comparison Based on Indistinguishable Input Property

Under attack model **A2**, indistinguishable input property is only achieved for secure MPC protocol based schemes [7,8]. This is because the obfuscated IU operational status still leaks non-negligible information. In the challenge phase of guessing game, a semi-honest SAS can generate two IU parameter sets that lead to different obfuscated results and directly distinguish them.

Under attack mode **A3**, when adversarial SUs are taken into consideration, indistinguishable input property is not expected to be achieved for all existing schemes. Under this attack model, what an adversary can obtain includes the final spectrum allocation results. Meanwhile under any DSA service model, the spectrum allocation result changes if the IU operational status changes. Hence, by synthesizing the spectrum allocation results, an adversary is able to distinguish IU operational statuses under different scenarios.

5.2   Comparison Using Adversarial Estimation Error and Privacy Time

The comparative study in this subsection is based on simulation. In the simulation setting, IUs are deployed in a 20 Km by 20 km rectangular region and there is one channel centered at frequency 3600 MHz. The IUs are military radars with 50 m height and -80 dBm interference threshold; SUs are assumed to be outdoor CBSD devices and their antenna heights are 6 m and transmission powers are 24 dBm. ECC-33 model [5] is used to formulate the path loss. The adversary collects two SU observations per minute.

We firstly compare the privacy preserving strength under attack model **A3**, i.e. attacker is an adversarial SUs network. Figure 1 compares the privacy preserving strength of MPC-based schemes [7,8], obfuscation-based schemes designed for k-anonymity [2,11], and obfuscation-based schemes that add false IU entries [3,4]. MPC-based schemes behave the worst in this case since essentially in the perspective of an adversarial SU network, the secure MPC protocols in [7,8] do not affect the spectrum computation result and hence introduce no additional confusion for the adversary to infer IU's operational parameters.

We then compare the privacy preserving strength under attack model **A2**, i.e. attacker is a semi-honest SAS. Table 1 shows the privacy preserving strength against semi-honest SAS between different approaches. For MPC-based schemes in [7,8], we assume that an adversary cannot break a cryptographic system and can only obtain inferred IU locations by randomly guessing.

In the table, we see that MPC-based schemes provide strong IU privacy protection against semi-honest SAS. Obfuscation schemes designed for k-anonymity do not grant strong privacy protection under attack model **A2**, compared to the same simulation setting under attack model **A3**. This is because when a semi-honest SAS has the full knowledge on k-anonymity algorithm and the equivalent protection zone information, it can estimate the true IU locations with much smaller error. For obfuscation-based schemes that add false IU items, it can be observed that the privacy preserving strength increases with more false IUs. Yet, intuitively we also expect the spectrum utility will decrease in this case, which will be analyzed in the next subsection.

5.3   Comparison Based on Spectrum Utilization

In this subsection we compare the spectrum utilization for different privacy-preserving approaches. Table 2 shows the privacy preserving strength measured

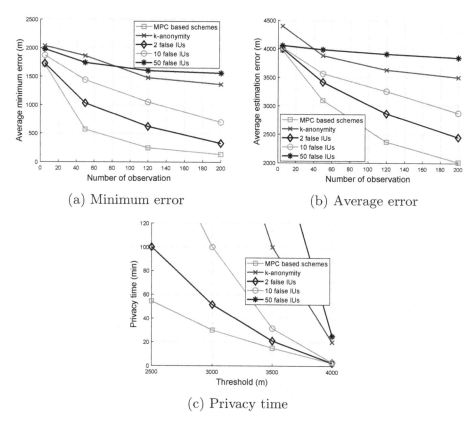

(a) Minimum error   (b) Average error

(c) Privacy time

Fig. 1. Privacy preserving strength evaluation under attack model **A3**.

Table 1. Privacy preserving strength under attack model **A2**.

	Minimum estimation error (m)	Average estimation error (m)
MPC-based schemes	1743.02	4006.33
k-anonymity	509.52	2394.24
Obfuscation (2 false IUs)	0	599.83
Obfuscation (10 false IUs)	71.07	2618.74
Obfuscation (50 false IUs)	701.96	3453.90

in minimum estimation error and spectrum utilization between different privacy preserving solutions. We observe that MPC-based schemes provide highest spectrum utilization and they also grant strong privacy protection against semi-honest SAS. For obfuscation-based schemes, we observe a trade-off between privacy protection and spectrum utilization under both **A2** and **A3** attack models. We also observe that schemes designed for k-anonymity sacrifice most spectrum utilization to achieve strong privacy protection under attack model **A3**.

Table 2. Spectrum utilization and privacy protection.

	Spectrum utilization (%)	Minimum estimation error (m)	
		Attack model **A2**	Attack model **A3**, 120 queries
MPC-based schemes	95.56	1743.02	249.14
k-anonymity	51.68	509.52	1478.35
Obfuscation (2 false IUs)	93.89	0	622.07
Obfuscation (10 false IUs)	87.92	71.07	1054.89
Obfuscation (50 false IUs)	62.67	701.96	1602.70

6   Conclusion and Discussions

In this paper, we present a comparative study on existing solutions that preserves incumbent user's operational privacy. We additionally propose minimum adversarial estimation error metric to evaluate privacy preserving strength, and we propose the indistinguishable input property to generalize the concept of provable security. Our study shows the effectiveness of MPC-based solutions against attacks from semi-honest SAS, and the trade-off between spectrum utilization and privacy preserving strength for obfuscation-based solutions. We also discover that obfuscation-based scheme provide stronger privacy protection against malicious SUs compared to MPC-based schemes. Combining both MPC-based and obfuscation-based schemes so that both adversarial SAS and SUs can be handled can be an interesting and promising future direction for IU operational privacy protection.

Acknowledgements. This work was partially sponsored by NSF through grants 1547366, 1265886, 1547241, 1563832, and 1642928.

References

1. Andrés, M.E., Bordenabe, N.E., Chatzikokolakis, K., Palamidessi, C.: Geo-indistinguishability: differential privacy for location-based systems. In: CCS 2013, pp. 901–914. ACM, New York (2013)
2. Bahrak, B., Bhattarai, S., Ullah, A., Park, J.M., Reed, J., Gurney, D.: Protecting the primary users' operational privacy in spectrum sharing. In: 2014 IEEE International Symposium on Dynamic Spectrum Access Networks (DYSPAN), pp. 236–247. IEEE (2014)
3. Clark, M., Psounis, K.: Can the privacy of primary networks in shared spectrum be protected? In: 35th Annual IEEE International Conference on Computer Communications, IEEE INFOCOM 2016, pp. 1–9. IEEE (2016)
4. Clark, M.A., Psounis, K.: Trading utility for privacy in shared spectrum access systems. IEEE/ACM Trans. Network. (TON) **26**(1), 259–273 (2018)
5. Electronic Communication Committee, et al.: Within the European conference of postal and telecommunications administration (CEPT), "the analysis of the coexistence of FWA cells in the 3.4–3.8 GHz band". Technical report, ECC Report 33 (2003)

6. Dolev, D., Yao, A.: On the security of public key protocols. IEEE Trans. Inf. Theory **29**(2), 198–208 (1983)
7. Dou, Y., et al.: Preserving incumbent users' privacy in exclusion-zone-based spectrum access systems. In: 2017 IEEE 37th International Conference on Distributed Computing Systems (ICDCS), pp. 2486–2493. IEEE (2017)
8. Dou, Y., et al.: P^2-SAS: preserving users' privacy in centralized dynamic spectrum access systems, pp. 321–330. ACM (2016)
9. The Office of the Federal Register (OFR): The Government Publishing Office: Title 47: Telecommunication, part 96-citizens broadband radio service. http://www.ecfr.gov/cgi-bin/text-idx?node=pt47.5.96&rgn=div5
10. Robert, C.P.: Monte Carlo Methods. Wiley Online Library, Hoboken (2004)
11. Zhang, L., Fang, C., Li, Y., Zhu, H., Dong, M.: Optimal strategies for defending location inference attack in database-driven CRNs. In: 2015 IEEE International Conference on Communications (ICC), pp. 7640–7645 (2015)
12. Zhang, Z., Zhang, H., He, S., Cheng, P.: Achieving bilateral utility maximization and location privacy preservation in database-driven cognitive radio networks. In: 2015 IEEE 12th International Conference on Mobile Ad Hoc and Sensor Systems (MASS), pp. 181–189. IEEE (2015)

Spectrum Leasing for Micro-operators Using Blockchain Networks

Junho Kim, Han Cha, and Seong-Lyun Kim[(✉)]

School of Electrical and Electronic Engineering, Yonsei University, Seoul, Korea
{jhkim, chan, slkim}@ramo.yonsei.ac.kr

Abstract. This paper introduces a spectrum sharing system for Micro Operators (MOs) using the blockchain network. In order to satisfy different network requirements for each service, the license for spectrum access should be dynamically allocated to the required spectrum bandwidth. We propose a spectrum lease contract for MOs to share spectrum with the Mobile Network Operator (MNO) is performed through the blockchain networks. Main reasons for applying the blockchain network to the spectrum sharing system are as follow. First, the blockchain networks share database with all participants. Second, networks have mutual trust among all participants. Third, it needs no central authority. Fourth, automated contract execution and transaction interactions are possible. The blockchain usage in the MO-based spectrum sharing system and the detailed process of spectrum lease contract are proposed. Then, the economic effects of spectrum sharing system for MOs is analyzed. The MO can be profitable by getting involved in the blockchain to take reward for a Proof of Work (PoW) and providing wireless service to its users.

Keywords: Spectrum sharing · Micro-operator · Blockchain
Dynamic Spectrum Access · Optimization · Network economics

1 Introduction

As the age of 5G approaches, increasing demand for Enhanced Mobile Broadband (eMBB), Ultra-reliable and Low-latency Communications (uRLLC), and Massive Machine Type Communications (mMTC) require more radio resources [1]. To satisfy those demands, securing available spectrum is one of the most important issues. The bands that are mainly studied in academic and industrial sectors are divided into mmWave and sub 6 GHz band. However, there are some engineering issues such as directivity and sensitivity to blockage to use mmWave in practical communication systems [2]. To compensate limitations and disadvantages of mmWave, it is important to utilize the existing spectrum band. Unfortunately, the lack of available spectrum is widely known [3].

Spectrum sharing concept is one of promising wireless technologies to make full use of the spectrum bandwidth that is allocated to license holders [4]. The key role of spectrum sharing is to look for balance among different services with their various Quality-of-Service (QoS) and system temporal dynamics so that the spectrum is efficiently utilized [5]. As an attempt to construct an efficient spectrum sharing system in a

I. Moerman et al. (Eds.): CROWNCOM 2018, LNICST 261, pp. 66–77, 2019.
https://doi.org/10.1007/978-3-030-05490-8_7

real environment, there have been researches on how to use idle spectrum bands such as TVWS [6]. Based on a decade of profound spectrum sharing research, a couple of practical spectrum licensing-based sharing models have been emerged. Citizens Broadband Radio Service (CBRS) [7] and Licensed Shared Access (LSA) [8] are such examples. Efforts to more efficiently use a limited spectrum have led to Micro Operator (MO) research beyond CBRS and LSA [9].

The concept of MO is local service delivery in wireless networks to build indoor small cell communication infrastructure and to provide context related vertical contents [10]. Cell densification and network slicing realize the service of MO. It is inefficient that assigning exclusive rights to MOs whose service region and time are specific. Therefore, it is persuasive to receive a certain spectrum of authority distribution from existing Mobile Network Operator (MNO). Spectrum can be efficiently used through dynamic spectrum allocation to support the services such as automated medical services, smart factories and VR/ARs in tight space.

With the emergence of Bitcoin proposed by an anonymous engineer named Satoshi, the blockchain technology, which is a distributed ledger system, attracted considerable attention. The blockchain is a system where all clients equally own the distributed ledger and update the new information. Information of transactions between users are stored permanently in the chain form of blocks. The blocks are copied and shared among clients across the networks. Reliability of data is guaranteed by a mechanism of consensus of blockchains [11]. Unlike the conventional method based on centralized authority [12], the blockchain guarantees stability from malicious attacks even in the trustless environment. Since there is no central administrator, single point of failure and attack is technically immune [13].

Blockchains are being discussed in various distributed systems and multiple access network scenarios, e.g., smart grid systems [14], vehicular networks [15], mobile edge computing [16], Internet-of-Things (IoT) [17] and spectrum sharing system such as CBRS [19]. In particular, MO based spectrum sharing systems that require short term transactions on spectral license holders like MNOs, can utilized the advantages of blockchains. Sensing values stored in a block serving as a distributed database has potential for Dynamic Spectrum Access (DSA), Peer-to-Peer (P2P) transaction.

In this paper, the spectrum sharing system where MOs Ware granted DSA rights by using the blockchain network is proposed. A reasonable reward system that can maintain the blockchain network ecosystem is also designed. Then, the detailed process of wireless services from MOs to the end is described.

2 Blockchain Technology

The blockchain comes from the birth of a cryptocurrency called Bitcoin in 2008, proposed by Satoshi, an anonymous individual or a group [11]. The fundamental idea of blockchain is that blocks serving as databases are continually created and updated in a chain [13]. Each node in the blockchain network has the same verified transactions, information, and contracts etc. The public ledgers, which are distributed databases shared across all participants, are tamper-proof, cryptographically secured, and permanent records of all the transactions that ever took place among the participants. The

information about every transaction completed is shared and available to all participants, which imply that there is no need for a central certification authority anymore.

The reason that the blockchain can be kept constant is that the information in the
blocks is not counterfeit. There are various consensus algorithms to guarantee this trust.
A Proof of Work (PoW) is described as the most popular algorithm being used by
currencies such as Bitcoin and Ethereum [20]. Blockchains use PoW to elect a leader
who will decide the contents of the next block. In PoW procedure, nodes who want to
be elected as a leader have to solve a simple mathematical quiz. The mathematical quiz
is finding out what a number *nonce* is. Since the hash function is cryptographically
secure, trying all possible combinations of *nonce* is the only way. The node who firstly
solve the aforementioned problem has the right of updating the blockchain update [21].
These solvers are called a *minor*. Whenever a new block is generated, that winner node
gets rewarded with transaction fees and system rewards. The other nodes verify validity
of the block by checking whether the nonce is the right answer.

Then, our motivation of applying the blockchain technology to the MO-based
spectrum sharing system is as follows: First, MOs and MNOs should make sure that the
spectrum sharing system is running securely and reliably. This is possible because all
nodes participating in the block chain have a shared database called ledgers. In addition, the interference from incumbent users sensed by an MO, which has duty protecting MNO service, stored in the block and shared with MNOs. If MNO leases the
spectrum bandwidth considering interference level, spectrum utilization is maximized.

In situations where spectrum bands are traded, a complete trust relationship
between stakeholders is needed. In the blockchain network, the record of transactions
only can be modified when all *nonce* of blocks are known. But, it is technically
impossible knowing all numbers n simultaneously. This property prevents transaction
records from forgery.

3   MO-Based Spectrum Sharing System

Considering the wireless network, there are a number of MOs that provide the various
local services. One MNO provides the primary access. The MNO already has authorized spectrum band allocated from the government. MOs lease the spectrum from
MNO because they do not have exclusive spectrum usage rights. From the perspective
of spectrum license holders like MNO, the license holders can share their spectrum to
generate additional revenue.

3.1   Blockchain Usage in Spectrum Sharing System

The MO provides local services via spectrum sharing through the blockchain network
as shown in Fig. 1. The blockchain network is based on a distributed P2P network
among user nodes, and mining nodes [19]. In the blockchain network, user nodes are
composed of MO and MNO. Dedicated miners not associated with any spectrum
leasing are defined as mining nodes. When the spectrum license lease is approved as a
smart contract in the blockchain, the actual deployed MOs can provide each local
service to the users.

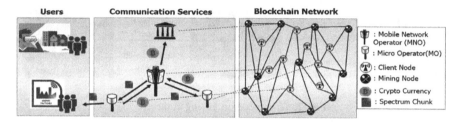

Fig. 1. Spectrum sharing system based on blockchain network

For the spectrum lease transaction to take place through the blockchain, the client nodes transact with cryptocurrency which we call as *Sharecoins*. It can be exchanged with cashes. It is assumed that base currency for spectrum leasing transactions is *Sharecoin*. It is not only used as bids for leasing spectrum but also serves as a reward for efforts to update the blockchain.

The reward received by the winning node for the block generation should be set appropriately. The rewards for mining are defined as follows: The winner node who the fastest accomplishes PoW gets reward as *Sharecoins*. The reward is given for block generation and transaction validation fee on the block. The other nodes that fail to conduct fastest PoW cannot receive any reward. Reward can be obtained in proportion to the mining capacity of the node versus the total mining capacity in the long-term perspective. The spectrum lease transaction in the blockchain network is conducted by several network components as follows:

- Mobile Network Operator (MNO): A spectrum license holder from the authorized organization. It participates as a client node in the blockchain network. It performs spectrum leasing transaction in the blockchain network. *Sharecoin* is given for the reward of spectrum leasing.
- Micro Operator (MO): Provide wireless communication service to users with spectrum bandwidth leased from MNO. MO is also a client node that performs the actual spectrum license transaction with its *Sharecoin* in the blockchain network. The MO participates in mining to maintain blockchain. As reward of mining, MO gets *Sharecoin*.

3.2 System Model

The wireless communication service market consists of MNO, MO and users of MO. We assume there is plenty of miners that guarantees security our blockchain. This means the blockchain network is maintained even if MO does not perform PoW at all. From now on, we refer wireless communication service as service. In Fig. 2, the MNO determines the unit price for the shared spectrum. The MO jointly determines the service price and involvement to maintaining blockchain to maximize its net profit. Each user of MO maximizes its payoff by determining how much it leases the spectrum from MO. The profit maximization is solved by applying the concept of backward induction as shown in Fig. 2 [22].

Fig. 2. The spectrum leasing contract

Let p_M is the unit price of the shared spectrum bandwidth for service. Note that the unit price for leased spectrum p_s and the spectrum bandwidth for MO W is determined by MNO. The parameters p_m and p_s is bounded in $[0,1]$. Each user demands the quantity of spectrum denoted by Q. As a result, MO's profit is $(p_M - p_s)Q$.

Because MO manages its spectrum sharing system with blockchain, MO processes PoW of its blockchain. Let p_w is rewards for the PoW. MO's reward p_w is directly proportional to the computing resource allocation for PoW denoted by m. Computing resource allocation for PoW, m is a value between 0 and 1. If m is one, MO allocates all its computing resources to PoW. Otherwise, MO allocate computing resource to service. We denote γ as redundant computing resource for providing service. Accordingly, if m exceeds γ, the quality of service deteriorates.

MO jointly chooses the optimal unit price of spectrum bandwidth p_M and the computing resource allocation for PoW m to maximize its profit. Then the maximum profit of MO is as follows:

$$\max_{0 \le p_M \le 1, 0 \le m \le 1} \pi^{MO}(p_M, m) = max(p_M - p_s)Q(p_M, m) + mp_w. \tag{1}$$

The *service* type of users is varies depending on MO's local service. The service type represents different willingness to pay of each user which is denoted as v. Assume that the parameter v is uniformly distributed in $[0,1]$ [23]. The utility of user with willingness to pay v is defined as $u(v, b, m)$ when spectrum bandwidth is b and the computing resource for PoW of MO is m. If m is lower than γ, the utility of user is retained. But m is greater than γ, the utility of the user is reduced. Then $u(v, b, m)$ is:

$$u(v,b,m) = \begin{cases} v\ln(1+b), & \text{if } 0 \le m < \gamma, \\ v\ln\left(1 + \left(\frac{1-m}{1-\gamma}\right)b\right), & \text{if } \gamma \le m \le 1. \end{cases} \tag{2}$$

The MO imposes users a linear payment p_M per unit spectrum bandwidth. Then, net utility of the user with service type v is the difference of its utility and payment, i.e.,

$$u(v,b,m) = \begin{cases} v\ln(1+b) - p_M b, & \text{if } 0 \le m < \gamma, \\ v\ln\left(1 + \left(\frac{1-m}{1-\gamma}\right)b\right) - p_M b, & \text{if } \gamma \le m \le 1. \end{cases} \tag{3}$$

4 Numerical Analysis

In this section, the utility of users and the profit of MO are analyzed from an economic perspective in the proposed spectrum sharing system

4.1 Users of MO' Demand

The optimal amount of spectrum bandwidth that maximizes the net utility of user is

$$
b^*(v, p_M, m) =
\begin{cases}
\frac{v}{p_M} - \frac{1-\gamma}{1-m}, & \text{if } \left(\frac{1-\gamma}{1-m}\right)p_M \leq v \text{ and } m > \gamma, \\
\frac{v}{p_M} - 1, & \text{if } p_M \leq v \text{ and } m \leq \gamma, \\
0, & \text{otherwise.}
\end{cases}
\tag{4}
$$

For a user who has willingness to pay v, the maximum of the Eq. (2) is:

$$
u(v, b^*(v, p_M), p_M, m) =
\begin{cases}
v \ln\left(\frac{1-m}{1-\gamma}\frac{v}{p_M}\right) - v + \frac{1-\gamma}{1-m}p_M, & \text{if } \frac{1-\gamma}{1-m}p_M \leq v \text{ and } m < \gamma, \\
v \ln\left(\frac{v}{p_M}\right) - v + p_M, & \text{if } p_M \leq v \text{ and } m \leq \gamma, \\
0, & \text{otherwise.}
\end{cases}
\tag{5}
$$

which is nonnegative in every case. The total sum of net utility of users is:

$$
U_M =
\begin{cases}
p_M\left(1 - \frac{p_M}{4}\right) - \frac{1}{2}\ln(p_M) - \frac{3}{4}, & \text{if } m \leq \gamma, \\
\frac{1-\gamma}{1-m}p_M\left(1 - \frac{1-m}{1-\gamma}\frac{p_M}{4}\right) - \frac{1}{2}\ln\left(\frac{1-m}{1-\gamma}p_M\right) - \frac{3}{4}, & \text{if } m > \gamma
\end{cases}
\tag{6}
$$

Equation (6) is derived from integral of (5) in $[p_M, 1]$ when m is greater than γ, and $[\frac{1-\gamma}{1-m}p_M, 1]$ when m is lower or equal to γ with respect to willingness to pay v.

4.2 MO's Pricing and Mining

MO determines price p_M and the computing resource for PoW m to achieve the maximum profit. Consider m is divided by two cases: the one is less or equal than redundant computing resource for providing service γ, the other is greater than γ.

- Case $m \leq \gamma$: Since MO's involvement in the blockchain does not affect services, MO's profit is the maximum when m is equal to γ. Thus, problem (1) is replaced by the follow problem:

$$
\max_{0 \leq p_M \leq 1} \pi^{MO}(p_M) = \max(p_M - p_s)Q(p_M) + \gamma p_w.
\tag{7}
$$

Since the bandwidth that can be provided by MNO is W, the overall optimization problem is as follows:

$$\max_{0 \leq p_M \leq 1} \pi^{MO}(p_M) = max(p_M - p_s)Q(p_M) + \gamma p_w,$$

$$subject\ to\ \ Q(p_M) \leq W. \tag{8}$$

Given demand of users as (4), the total demand of shared spectrum in the MO network is derived as follows

$$Q(p_M) = \int_{p_M}^1 \left(\frac{v}{p_M} - 1\right) dv = \frac{1}{2p_M} - 1 + \frac{p_M}{2}, \tag{9}$$

where Q_M is decreasing function in $p_M \in [0, 1]$.

Note that the user only uses the service when the price of service is less or equal than willingness to pay of user. The optimal solution of the above profit maximization problem is described in the following proposition.

Proposition 1. The optimal service price p_M is

$$p_M(p_s) = \frac{1}{3}\left(1 + \frac{p_s}{2}\right)\left(1 + 2\cos\left(\frac{\phi + 4\pi}{3}\right)\right),$$

where $\phi = \tan^{-1}\left(\frac{\sqrt{p_s\left(\frac{2}{27}\left(1 + \frac{p_s}{2}\right)^3 - \frac{p_s}{4}\right)}}{\frac{2}{27}\left(1 + \frac{p_s}{2}\right)^3 - \frac{p_s}{2}}\right)$ and p_s is normalized in $(p_M^3, 1]$.

Proof. See Appendix A.   ∎

- Case $m > \gamma$: Since MO's involvement in the blockchain affect its users utility introduced as (2). The problem of MO's profit maximization should be considered jointly with m and p_M:

$$\max_{0 \leq p_M \leq 1, \gamma \leq m \leq 1} \pi^{MO}(p_M, m) = max\ p_M Q(p_M, m) + m p_w \tag{10}$$

$$subject\ to\ \ Q(p_M, m) \leq W.$$

Given the demand of user of (4), the total shared spectrum demand in the MO network is calculated as

$$Q(p_M, m) = \int_{\frac{1-\gamma}{1-m}p_M}^1 \left(\frac{v}{p_M} - \frac{1-\gamma}{1-m}\right) dv = \frac{1}{2p_M} - \frac{1-\gamma}{1-m} + \left(\frac{1-\gamma}{1-m}\right)^2 \frac{p_M}{2}. \tag{11}$$

Under certain conditions for p_w, the optimal solution of (10) is derived in the following Proposition 2.

Proposition 2. When the reward for PoW p_w is following condition $p_w > M_h$, the optimal solution p_M^* of (10) is p_w where M_h is $\frac{1}{p_M^2(1-\gamma)}$.

Proof. See Appendix B.   ∎

The variation of total profit of MO is greater than zero when the reward of PoW p_w is greater than M_h. According to Proposition 2, the MO abandon to providing services and allocate all computing power to PoW when p_w is greater than M_h.

Proposition 3 introduces the optimal point of objective function (10).

Proposition 3. When p_w is less than M_l, the optimal solution (p_M^*, m^*) of the objective function (10) is:

$$(p_M^*, m^*) = \left(\frac{1}{3}\left(1 + \frac{p_s}{2}\right)\left(1 + 2\cos\left(\frac{\phi + 4\pi}{3}\right)\right), \gamma\right),$$

where ϕ is $\tan^{-1}\left(\frac{\sqrt{p_s\left(\frac{2}{27}\left(1 + \frac{p_s}{2}\right)^3 - \frac{p_s}{4}\right)}}{\frac{2}{27}\left(1 + \frac{p_s}{2}\right)^3 - \frac{p_s}{2}}\right)$ and M_l is $(1 - \gamma)(p_M - p_s)(1 - p_M)$.

Proof. See Appendix C. ∎

The variation of total profit of MO is less than zero when the reward of PoW p_w is less than M_l. From the Proposition 3, the MO would keep providing services and allocate only redundant computing power to PoW when p_w is lower than M_l.

We analyze the effects of rewards for the PoW p_w on the utility of users and MO's profit, which is divided into three cases:

- $p_w < M_l$: This case implies the rewards of the PoW are very low so that MO allocates only redundant computing power to PoW.
- $p_w > M_h$: The rewards of the PoW are considered as high price. Therefore, MO allocates its all computing power to performing PoW.
- $M_l \leq p_w \leq M_h$: MO allocates more resources than the redundant computing power to get the rewords of PoW by reducing the revenue from providing service.

Figure 3 shows the total net utility of users of MO U_M according to the rewards of PoW p_w. When p_w is lower than M_l, MO can fully focus on providing services. As p_w increase, the computing resource for PoW m is allocated by taking the portion of

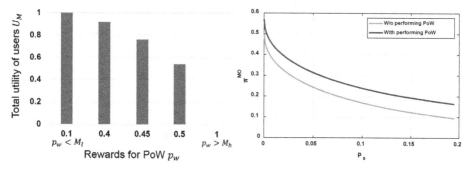

Fig. 3. The total net utility of users of MO U_M when $p_s = 0.15$ and $\gamma = 0.7$.

Fig. 4. MO's equilibrium profits π^{MO} depending on the unit price of leased spectrum p_s when $p_w = 0.1 < M_l$ and $\gamma = 0.7$.

computing resource for service. As a result, U_M decrease. If p_w is greater than M_h, MO only processes the PoW and the service is halted.

Figure 4 shows MO can make additional profit without affecting the total net utility through involving in the blockchain.

By setting the appropriate rewards of PoW p_w, the total users of MO utility and MO's profit can be maximized. When MOs have limited computing power, p_w is needed to be under M_l to preserve the utility of users. Otherwise, MO has no incentive for service whose profit is less than that of processing the PoW. It may disrupt the motivation of the spectrum sharing system using the blockchain networks.

5 Conclusion

In this paper, the spectrum sharing system based on blockchain network is introduced. The motivations of applying the blockchain network to the spectrum sharing system are as follow. First, the blockchain networks share database with all participants. Second, networks have mutual trust among all participants. Third, there is no need for central authority. Fourth, automated contract execution and transactions are possible.

The role of blockchain network in the Micro Operator (MO) spectrum sharing system is described. The system is designed where users of the MO receive wireless communication service via the spectrum leased from the Mobile Network Operator (MNO). The roles and functions are introduced by matching the subjects constituting the actual wireless communication network to the blockchain network.

The utility of users and the profit of MO are analyzed in economic perspective. The MO can achieve its profit not only from providing wireless communication service to users, but also from processing PoW which is essential procedure for maintaining the blockchain. By setting the appropriate PoW rewards, the total utility of users and MO's profit can be maximized. Note that too high PoW rewards can disrupt the motivation of the MO to provide wireless communication services. In worst case, MO halt providing wireless communication service to users.

Acknowledgement. This work was supported by Institute for Information & communications Technology Promotion (IITP) grant funded by the Korea government (MSIT) (No. 2018-0-00923, Scalable Spectrum Sensing for Beyond 5G Communication).

Appendix

A. Proof of Proposition 1

To find the equilibrium price $p_M^*(p_s)$, it is verified that the objective function of (7) should be a concave function of $p_M(p_s)$. Differentiate (7) is as follow:

$$\frac{\partial^2 \pi^{MO}}{p_M(p_s)^2} = 1 - \frac{p_s}{p_M^3} < 0, \text{ if } p_M^3 < p_s.$$ (12)

Concavity of (7) for $p_M(p_s)$ is guaranteed in $p_s \in (p_M^3, 1]$. The equilibrium price can be obtained by solving the first order derivative of (7) as follows:

$$\frac{\partial \pi^{MO}}{\partial p_M(p_s)} = p_M(p_s) - 1 - \frac{p_s}{2}\left(1 - \frac{1}{p_M(p_s)^2}\right) = 0$$ (13)

$$2p_M(p_s)^3 - (2 + p_s)p_M(p_s)^2 + p_s = 0$$

Finally, three candidate solutions to maximize MO's profit as follows:

$$p_M(p_s) = \frac{1}{3}\left(1 + \frac{p_s}{2}\right)\left(1 + 2\cos\left(\frac{\phi + 2n\pi}{3}\right)\right), \text{ where } n \in \{1, 2, 3\}.$$ (14)

There is a unique optimal solution when $n = 3$ because $p_M(p_s)$ is either 1 or negative when $n = 1$ or $n = 2$. ∎

B. Proof of Proposition 2

The first order partial derivative of the objective function of (10) respect to m is

$$\frac{\partial \pi^{MO}}{\partial m} = p_w + (p_M - p_s)\left(\frac{p_M(1 - \gamma)^2}{(1 - m)^3} - \frac{1 - \gamma}{(1 - m)^2}\right)$$ (15)

If the Eq. (15) is greater than 0 for all m, the objective function has the maximum value when m is maximum, that is, when $m = 1$.

If $p_w > \frac{1}{p_M^2(1-\gamma)}$, the Eq. (15) has following relationship:

$$\frac{\partial \pi^{MO}}{\partial m} > \frac{1 - (p_M - p_s)}{p_M^2(1 - \gamma)} + (p_M - p_s)\left(\frac{1}{p_M^2(1 - \gamma)} - \frac{1 - \gamma}{(1 - m)^2}\right) \cdots (*)$$ (16)

Note that the function $\frac{1-\gamma}{(1-m)^2}$ is an increasing function for m. Substitute m with the value $1 - p_M(1 - \gamma)$ which is maximum value of m then the Eq. (16) is

$$(*) > \frac{1 - (p_M - p_s)}{p_M^2(1 - \gamma)} + (p_M - p_s)\left(\frac{1}{p_M^2(1 - \gamma)} - \frac{1 - \gamma}{(p_M(1 - \gamma))^2}\right)$$

$$= \frac{1 - (p_M - p_s)}{p_M^2(1 - \gamma)} > 0$$ (17)

Finally, $\frac{\partial \pi^{MO}}{\partial m} > 0$ for all m when $p_w > \frac{1}{p_M^2(1-\gamma)}$. ∎

C. Proof of Proposition 3

The first order partial derivative of (10) respect to m is (18).

$$
\begin{aligned}
\frac{\partial \pi^{MO}}{\partial m} &= p_w + (p_M - p_s)\frac{1-\gamma}{(1-m)^2}\left(\frac{1-\gamma}{1-m}p_M - 1\right)\\
&< (p_M - p_s)\frac{1-\gamma}{(1-m)^2}\left((1-m)^2 + \left(1 - \frac{1}{1-m}\right)\frac{1-\gamma}{1-m}p_M - 1\right) \cdots (**)
\end{aligned}
\tag{18}
$$

The Eq. (18) is negative when $m \geq \gamma$ and $0 < m < 1$.

Finally, $\frac{\partial \pi^{MO}}{\partial m} < 0$ for all m when $p_w < (1-\gamma)(p_M - p_s)(1 - p_M)$. ∎

References

1. Andrews, J.G., et al.: What will 5G be? IEEE J. Sel. Areas Commun. **32**(6), 1065–1082 (2014). https://doi.org/10.1109/JSAC.2014.2328098. ISSN 0733-8716
2. Park, J., Kim, S.L., Zander, J.: Tractable resource management with uplink decoupled millimeter-wave overlay in ultra-dense cellular networks. IEEE Trans. Wireless Commun. **15**(6), 4362–4379 (2016)
3. Valenta, V., Maršálek, R., Baudoin, G., Villegas, M., Suarez, M., Robert, F.: Survey on spectrum utilization in Europe: measurements, analyses and observations. In: Proceedings of the 5th International Conference on Cognitive Radio Oriented Wireless Network and Communication (CROWNCOM), pp. 1–5 (2010)
4. Jorswieck, E.A., Badia, L., Fahldieck, T., Karipidis, E., Luo, J.: Spectrum sharing improves the network efficiency for cellular operators. IEEE Commun. Mag. **52**(3), 129–136 (2014)
5. Peha, J.M.: Approaches to spectrum sharing. IEEE Commun. Mag. **43**(2), 10–12 (2005)
6. Ofcom: TV White Spaces Pilots. http://stakeholders.ofcom.org.uk/spectrum/tv-white-spaces/white-spaces-pilot/
7. WINNF Spectrum Sharing Committee. http://www.wirelessinnovation.org/spectrumsharing-committee
8. ECC: Licensed Shared Access (LSA). ECC report 205 (2014)
9. Ahokangas, P., et al.: Future micro operators business models in 5G. In: Proceedings International Conference on Restructuring of the Global Economy (ROGE) (2016)
10. Matinmikko, M., Latva-aho, M., Ahokangas, P., Yrjölä, S., Koivumäki, T.: Micro operators to boost local service delivery in 5G. Wirel. Pers. Commun. J. **95**, 69–82 (2017)
11. Nakamoto, S.: Bitcoin: A Peer-to-Peer Electronic Cash System (2008)
12. O'Hara, K.: Smart contracts - dumb idea. IEEE Internet Comput. **21**(2), 97–101 (2017)
13. Greenspan, G.: Avoiding the pointless blockchain project, November 2015

14. Kang, J., Yu, R., Huang, X., Maharjan, S.: Enabling localized peer-to-peer electricity trading among plug-in hybrid electric vehicles using consortium blockchains. IEEE Trans. Ind. Inform. **13**(6), 3154–3164 (2017)

15. Yang, Z., Zheng, K., Yang, K., Leung, V.C.: A blockchain-based reputation system for data credibility assessment in vehicular networks. In: Proceedings of IEEE International Symposium on Personal, Indoor and Mobile Radio Communication (PIMRC), pp. 1–5 (2017)

16. Xiong, Z., Feng, S., Niyato, D., Wang., Han., Z.: Edge Computing Resource Management and Pricing for Mobile Blockchain. arXiv:1710.01567 (2017)

17. Christidis, K., Devetsiokiotis, M.: Blockchains and smart contracts for the Internet of Things. IEEE Access **4**, 2292–2303 (2016)

18. Kotobi, K., Bilen, S.G.: Blockchain-enabled spectrum access in cognitive radio networks. In: 2017 Wireless Telecommunications Symposium (WTS), pp. 1–6 (2017)

19. Yrjölä, S.: Analysis of blockchain use cases in the citizens broadband radio service spectrum sharing concept. In: Marques, P., Radwan, A., Mumtaz, S., Noguet, D., Rodriguez, J., Gundlach, M. (eds.) CrownCom 2017. LNICST, vol. 228, pp. 128–139. Springer, Cham (2018). https://doi.org/10.1007/978-3-319-76207-4_11

20. Ethereum, White Paper (2016). https://github.com/ethereum/wiki/wiki/White-Paper

21. Yli-Huumo, J., Ko, D., Choi, S., Parka, S., Smolander, K.: Where is current research on blockchain technology? — a systematic review (2016)

22. Jung, S.Y., Yu, S.M., Kim, S.L.: Utility-optimal partial spectrum leasing for future wireless services. In: 2013 IEEE 77th Vehicular Technology Conference (VTC Spring), pp. 1–5 (2010)

23. Walrand, J.: Economic models of communication networks. In: Liu, Z., Xia, C.H. (eds.) Performance Modeling and Engineering, pp. 57–87. Springer, New York (2008). https://doi.org/10.1007/978-0-387-79361-0_3

SZ-SAS: A Framework for Preserving Incumbent User Privacy in SAS-Based DSA Systems

Douglas Zabransky[⊠], He Li, Chang Lu, and Yaling Yang

Virginia Polytechnic Institute and State University, Blacksburg, VA 24060, USA
{dmz5e,heli,changl7,yyang8}@vt.edu

Abstract. Dynamic Spectrum Access (DSA) is a promising solution to alleviate spectrum crowding. However, geolocation database-driven spectrum access system (SAS) presents privacy risks, as sensitive Incumbent User (IU) operation parameters are required to be stored by SAS in order to perform spectrum assignments properly. These sensitive operation parameters may potentially be compromised if SAS is the target of a cyber attack or SU inference attack. In this paper, we propose a novel privacy-preserving SAS-based DSA framework, Suspicion Zone SAS (SZ-SAS). This is the first framework which protects against both the scenario of inference attacks in an area with sparsely distributed IUs and the scenario of untrusted or compromised SAS. Evaluation results show SZ-SAS is capable of utilizing compatible obfuscation schemes to prevent the SU inference attack, while operating using only homomorphically encrypted IU operation parameters.

Keywords: Dynamic Spectrum Access · Inference attack
Location privacy

1 Introduction

Dynamic Spectrum Allocation (DSA) allows Secondary Users (SUs) to transmit opportunistically on underutilized spectrum while avoiding the creation of interference which would impact the operation of the legacy users, known as Incumbent Users (IUs).

Because the IUs in bands of interest are comprised of federal government and military systems, the operational security (OPSEC) of these users is of paramount importance. The authors of [4] identify several operational attributes of these systems which should remain confidential, including geolocation, transmit protection contours, and times of operation. However, current DSA designs include exclusion zone (E-Zone) based spectrum access systems (SAS), in which SAS is a database containing plaintext information allowing the determination of regions (E-Zones) in which SUs are not permitted to operate because they will

I. Moerman et al. (Eds.): CROWNCOM 2018, LNICST 261, pp. 78–88, 2019.
https://doi.org/10.1007/978-3-030-05490-8_8

create harmful interference to IUs. The authors of [3] first addressed this security risk by proposing a SAS framework which utilizes homomorphic encryption in order to prevent SAS from directly accessing IU operation parameters.

However, the framework proposed in [3] is susceptible to inference attacks, as it has no method of determining queries which could indicate the execution of an inference attack and no method of obfuscating responses to these queries. The SU inference attack, first defined in [2], allows adversarial SUs to correlate the results of seemingly innocuous queries in order to infer the geolocation or transmit protection contour information of an IU by simply observing which areas are available for transmission and which areas fall within the boundaries of an E-Zone. The most effective proposed countermeasure against this attack is the introduction of obfuscation [2,6]. However, the proposed obfuscation strategies require SAS to have intimate knowledge of IU operation parameters, rendering them incompatible with the secure SAS designs proposed in [3]. Additionally, many of these obfuscation techniques are not particularly effective in the case of sparse IUs, as they either rely upon grouping nearby IUs or result in obfuscated E-Zones which maintain the same geolocation center as their unobfuscated counterparts. We address this gap in the literature with our contributions described in the remainder of this paper.

Our contributions can be summarized as follows:

- We propose a novel database-driven DSA framework, Suspicion Zone SAS (SZ-SAS), the first such framework which allows for obfuscation to be applied on a per-user or per-group basis based upon the query history of an individual user and the first such framework which protects against both the scenario of inference attacks in an area with sparsely distributed IUs and the scenario of untrusted SAS.
- We introduce a modified inference attack, showing a lower bound of privacy provided by non-obfuscated SAS responses than previously suspected.
- We provide and analyze multiple obfuscation techniques which are compatible with the proposed DSA framework.

The rest of this paper is structured as follows: Section 2 introduces SZ-SAS and the cryptographic background upon which it is built, Sect. 3 discusses the problem of inference attacks and techniques which could be employed in SZ-SAS to prevent such attacks, and Sect. 4 concludes the paper.

2   SZ-SAS Background and System Model

From a high-level view, SZ-SAS leverages homomorphic proxy re-encryption to encrypt operation parameters from IUs such that SAS has no direct knowledge of these parameters. Utilizing the homomorphic nature of the chosen cryptosystem, SZ-SAS uses a novel method for maintaining and utilizing an encrypted count of potentially suspicious queries made by each SU. Then, it restricts SUs which have exceeded a given IU's specified threshold of suspicious queries from querying the IU's actual E-Zone. Instead, it calculates their query results from obfuscated E-Zones, which hide the true geolocation of the IU in question.

In this section, we first discuss the cryptographic basis of our framework. We then introduce the details of SZ-SAS framework and define its operations.

2.1   Cryptographic Preliminaries

SZ-SAS utilizes the AFGH cryptosystem [1], which is a single-hop, unidirectional, homomorphic proxy re-encryption scheme based upon bilinear maps. In this section, we discuss the basis of this cryptosystem and the cryptographic assumptions upon which it was designed.

The AFGH Homomorphic Proxy Re-encryption Scheme. The AFGH cryptosystem was chosen based upon several criteria, primary of which are functionality and overhead. SZ-SAS requires a cryptosystem in which SAS can perform operations securely on encrypted parameters. Because SZ-SAS will potentially be processing thousands of queries per minute and thus will need to reduce its computation and communication overhead, the relatively light-weight partially homomorphic AFGH scheme was chosen.

AFGH as proposed in [1] is homomorphic with respect to multiplication. However, our scheme requires an accumulator and so we must modify AFGH to become homomorphic with respect to addition. In order to accomplish this, we simply exponentiate the generator, Z of G_T, by our plaintext prior to encryption as Z^{PT}. This will allow us to perform addition, but the discrete log problem (DLP) will need to be solved in order to recover the actual plaintext. Thus, we have built our system to operate without requiring the plaintext to be recovered from Z^{PT} in order to avoid the computations required to solve the DLP. We are also able to perform multiplication of a ciphertext by a plaintext value using exponentiation. We define the encrypted addition operation and the plaintext multiplication created by our modification as $\oplus$ and $\otimes$ for the remainder of this paper and describe the construction and important features of the additive AFGH cryptosystem below:

- **System Parameters:** $e : G \times G \rightarrow G_T$ is a Type 1 bilinear map, g is a random generator of G, and $Z = e(g, g)$ is a random generator of G_T.
- **Key Generation:** Set a group secret key $SK_a \leftarrow_{\$} Z_p^*$ and public key $PK_a = g^{SK_a}$ for all IUs.
- **Re-encryption Key Generation:** To re-encrypt a level 2 ciphertext which was originally encrypted with IUs' public key into a level 1 ciphertext which can be decrypted by SU b's secret key, a re-encryption key must be generated. This key is generated with SU b's public key, PK_b, and IUs' private key, SK_a, as $RK_{a \rightarrow b} = PK_b^{1/SK_a}$. This is equivalent to g^{SK_b/SK_a}.

2.2   System Model, Operations, and Correctness

The structure of SZ-SAS is depicted in Fig. 1 and is comprised of a 4-party SAS structure consisting of key manager, IUs, SAS, and SUs.

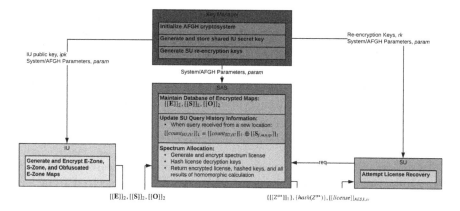

Fig. 1. SZ-SAS system framework overview

Key Manager Operations. The key manager generates re-encryption keys for each SU during the SU's initial registration with SAS. The key manager should either be controlled by a government entity or trusted-third party as re-encryption key generation requires knowledge of the shared IU secret key.

IU Operations. Each IU is responsible for the generation of its E-Zone, Suspicion Zone (S-Zone), and obfuscated E-Zone maps. Each of these maps is represented by an $M \times N$ matrix and contains information for the entire area covered by SAS. A series of E-Zone maps, each represented by a matrix $\mathbf{E}$, are generated via a chosen path loss model and a set of discretized SU maximum transmit power levels, (TP). Any grid location for which the path loss value exceeds the interference threshold of the IU is considered part of the E-Zone. If channel f at grid location (m, n) and transmit power level (tp) is considered to be E-Zone by the IU, then the value of the E-Zone map $\mathbf{E}_{f,m,n,tp}$ is a random non-zero element picked from Z_p. Otherwise, $\mathbf{E}_{f,m,n,tp}$ is set to 0.

Because the area around the protection contour provides the most information to a SU performing an inference attack, the IU defines the cells adjacent to the protection contour as S-Zone cells and generates a series of maps, represented by matrix $\mathbf{S}$, corresponding to the contour of each E-Zone map. If channel f at grid location m, n and and transmit power level (TP) is considered to be S-Zone by the IU, then the value of the S-Zone map $\mathbf{S}_{f,m,n,tp}$ is set to 1. Otherwise, $\mathbf{S}_{f,m,n,tp}$ is set to 0.

Obfuscated E-Zone maps essentially are distorted and enlarged E-Zones and are generated using an obfuscation scheme as described in Sect. 3.3. These maps, represented by matrix $\mathbf{O}$, follow the same value assignment rules as E-Zone maps. The IU also determines a suspicious request threshold, represented by τ, which is the number of queries an SU is allowed to make from S-Zone areas.

Each IU prepares these three categories of maps, encrypts each map value with the IU public key, and commits the resulting encrypted maps and the unencrypted threshold value to SAS. The encryption of these maps is essential as SAS can potentially be compromised and these maps may be used to derive sensitive parameters, such as the geolocation and operation times of the IU.

SAS Operations. SAS is responsible for performing three main operations, maintaining the database of all encrypted maps, $[\![\mathbf{E}]\!]$, $[\![\mathbf{S}]\!]$, $[\![\mathbf{O}]\!]$, updating the encrypted number of suspicious queries made by each SU for each IU, represented by $[\![count_{SU,IU}]\!]$, and performing spectrum assignment computations in response to SU requests.

SAS updates $[\![count_{SU,IU}]\!]$ whenever a query is initially received from an SU which is querying from a new location. When a query is received from location (m, n) for channel f at transmit power level tp, SAS first determines if this is the querying SU's first query from this location. If it is, SAS updates $[\![count_{SU,IU}]\!] = [\![count_{SU,IU}]\!] \oplus [\![\mathbf{S}_{f,m,n,tp}]\!]$. Otherwise, SAS does not update $[\![count_{SU,IU}]\!]$. This allows SAS to maintain an encrypted count of queries originating from grid locations which have been designated as potentially suspicious due to the potential information revealed in a SAS response to an SU performing an inference attack from this location.

The spectrum assignment computation is the primary functionality of SAS. SAS must generate a spectrum license consisting of the SU's access information (expiration time, transmit power level, location, etc.) and a digital signature over this access information. This license will be transmitted to the SU in two possible situations. In the first situation, the SU has not exceeded the threshold of suspicious requests (i.e. $count_{SU,IU} < \tau$) and is not located in the E-Zone of any IU. In the second situation, the threshold has been exceeded and, thus, the SU must not be in the obfuscated E-Zone.

Because SAS does not have direct knowledge of $[\![\mathbf{E}]\!]$, $[\![\mathbf{S}]\!]$, $[\![\mathbf{O}]\!]$, it cannot directly determine whether the SU is located within an IU's E-Zone or obfuscated E-Zone. Therefore, the assignment is performed via a special process which leverages the properties of AFGH. First, SAS updates $[\![count_{SU,IU}]\!] = [\![count_{SU,IU}]\!] \oplus [\![\mathbf{S}_{f,m,n,tp}]\!]$ as described previously. Next, SAS generates the spectrum license, which must be encrypted in a manner such that it may only be decrypted if it is a valid spectrum request, as described previously. In order to accomplish this, SAS utilizes a cascade encryption scheme and a specialized homomorphic calculation as described in the following paragraph.

First, SAS generates a separate symmetric encryption key for each IU by selecting a random element α in G_T, and uses this element to exponentiate the generator, Z, resulting in Z^α. Then, SAS hashes Z^α with a cryptographic hash function and the resulting hash digest is split into two bit strings, k and iv. The hash function used in this step will be referred to as the primary hash function for the remainder of this paper. Each IU's k and iv bit strings are then used as the secret key and initialization vector for a block cipher operating in a stream-like mode, such as CTR mode AES, and the license is sequentially encrypted by each k and iv pair via cascade encryption, resulting in $[\![license]\!]_{AES,k,iv}$. Each IU's Z^α and a series of threshold values from 0 to τ, denoted as ϵ_i for $i \in$

$[0, \tau]$, are then encrypted to level 1 ciphertexts, $[\![Z_{IU}^{\alpha}]\!]$ and $[\![\epsilon_{i,IU}]\!]$, with the querying SU's AFGH public key. Next, $[\![\mathbf{E}_{f,m,n,tp}]\!]$, $[\![\mathbf{S}_{f,m,n,tp}]\!]$, and $[\![\mathbf{O}_{f,m,n,tp}]\!]$ are re-encrypted from level 2 ciphertexts to level 1 ciphertexts with the SU's re-encryption keys. SAS then performs the following homomorphic calculation for each IU and corresponding Z_{IU}^{α}:

$$\forall i \in [0, \tau] : [\![Z_{i,IU}^{\alpha*}]\!] \leftarrow [([\![count_{SU,IU}]\!] \oplus [\![\epsilon_i]\!]^{-1}) \otimes R] \oplus [\![\mathbf{E}_{f,m,n,tp}]\!] \oplus [\![Z_{IU}^{\alpha}]\!] \quad (1)$$

in which R is a random, large, negative nonce. The first portion of this calculation, $([\![count_{SU,IU}]\!] \oplus [\![\epsilon_i]\!]^{-1}) \otimes R$, ensures that if the current value of $[\![count_{SU,IU}]\!]$ is greater than τ, the resulting decrypted $Z_{i,IU}^{\alpha*}$ will be equal to Z_{IU}^{α} distorted by a multiple of the random nonce, R. Additionally, if the query originated from a cell inside of the E-Zone, $[\![\mathbf{E}_{f,m,n,tp}]\!] \oplus [\![Z_{IU}^{\alpha}]\!]$ will distort the result by the random value in G_T to which $\mathbf{E}_{f,m,n,tp}$ was initialized. If the current value of $[\![count_{SU,IU}]\!]$ is less than τ and the query originated from a cell outside of the E-Zone, there will be one resulting $Z^{\alpha*}$ which is equal to Z_{IU}^{α}. SAS also produces one $[\![Z_{i,IU}^{\alpha*}]\!]$ for each IU based upon the obfuscated E-Zone map by simply calculating $[\![Z_{i,IU}^{\alpha*}]\!] \leftarrow [\![\mathbf{O}_{f,m,n,tp}]\!] \oplus [\![Z_{IU}^{\alpha}]\!]$. When decrypted, this $Z_{i,IU}^{\alpha*}$ will equal Z_{IU}^{α} if and only if the SU is located outside of the IU's obfuscated E-Zone and will allow the SU to recover a license if it is outside of the obfuscated E-Zone. Thus, $[\![Z_{i,IU}^{\alpha*}]\!]$ equals Z_{IU}^{α} when the request is from either of the valid SU request situations.

SAS then hashes each Z_{IU}^{α} with a different cryptographic hash function than was used as the primary hash function, which we shall refer to as the secondary hash function, and returns this list of hash digests, $[\![license]\!]_{AES,k,iv}$, and all resulting $[\![Z_{i,IU}^{\alpha*}]\!]$ rearranged in a randomized order, to the querying SU.

SU Operations. Each SU must initially register with SAS with the registration process specified by the FCC and may then query SAS by providing its current location, requested channel, and requested maximum transmit power. SAS will then respond to this query with a list of hash digests, $[\![license]\!]_{AES,k,iv}$, and a number of $[\![Z^{\alpha*}]\!]$ values. The SU then decrypts each $[\![Z^{\alpha*}]\!]$ using its private key and executes the secondary hash function on the resulting decrypted $Z^{\alpha*}$. If the result of this hash exists in the list of hash digests, the SU recognizes this digest corresponds to an IU's Z^{α}, recovers k and iv using the primary hash function, and removes it from the list. The SU then uses these k and iv values to remove one layer of encryption from $[\![license]\!]_{AES,k,iv}$. Once the $Z^{\alpha*}$ for each digest in the list has been found and the corresponding k and iv pair used to encrypt $[\![license]\!]_{AES,k,iv}$ has be recovered, the SU can successfully fully decrypt the license. If the SU hashes each $Z^{\alpha*}$ but is unable to find all digests in the list, its spectrum request was invalid and thus it is unable to recover the license.

Correctness of SZ-SAS. The correctness property requires that when an SU is located in an E-Zone of any IU, its spectrum request cannot be approved, and thus an SU cannot receive a valid spectrum license. Additionally, when an SU which has exceeded the query threshold of any IU and is located within the obfuscated E-Zone for this IU, its spectrum request cannot be approved. The SZ-SAS functionality can be donated as a function f:

$$\texttt{license}^* := f(\llbracket \mathbf{E}_{f,m,n,tp} \rrbracket, \llbracket \mathbf{O}_{f,m,n,tp} \rrbracket, \tau, \llbracket count_{SU,IU} \rrbracket, \texttt{req}), \qquad (2)$$

where $\texttt{req}$ is the information received from an SU during a spectrum request.

Definition 1. *SZ-SAS is correct if it satisfies the following condition: For any input ($\llbracket \mathbf{E}_{f,m,n,tp} \rrbracket, \llbracket \mathbf{O}_{f,m,n,tp} \rrbracket, \tau, \llbracket count_{SU,IU} \rrbracket, \texttt{req}$) to SZ-SAS, if the requested location (m, n) is within an IU's E-Zone, or $\llbracket count_{SU,IU} \rrbracket > \tau$ and (m, n) is within an IU's obfuscated E-Zone, $\texttt{license}^*$ is invalid. Conversely, if the requested location (m, n) is outside of all IU's E-Zone, and $\llbracket count_{SU,IU} \rrbracket < \tau$ for all IUs or (m, n) is outside of all IU's obfuscated E-Zone, $\texttt{license}^*$ is valid.*

Theorem 1. *The probability with which SZ-SAS is NOT correct is negligible.*

Proof. The correctness follows directly from the specification of the SZ-SAS protocols. $\llbracket count_{SU,IU} \rrbracket$ can be updated using the homomorphic addition specified in Sect. 3.1. Let (m, n) be the location of $\texttt{req}$. If (m, n) is located within an IU's E-Zone, then $\mathbf{E}_{f,m,n,tp} \leftarrow^\$ Z_p \backslash \{0\}$ for this IU. Thus, in the situation in which a query originates from the E-Zone of an IU, $Z_{IU}^{\alpha*} = Z_{IU}^\alpha + Z_p \backslash \{0\} \neq Z_{IU}^\alpha$. In the second situation, if $\llbracket count_{SU,IU} \rrbracket > \tau$, then $Z_{IU}^{\alpha*} = Z_{IU}^\alpha + R \neq Z_{IU}^\alpha$ where R is some random value in G_T. Additionally, if the query is also located in the obfuscated E-Zone of an IU, then $\mathbf{O}_{f,m,n,tp} \leftarrow^\$ Z_p \backslash \{0\}$ for this IU. As a result, the $Z_{IU}^{\alpha*} = Z_{IU}^\alpha + Z_p \backslash \{0\} \neq Z_{IU}^\alpha$ for the $Z_{IU}^{\alpha*}$ associated with the obfuscated E-Zone map. As a result, for all i, $Z_{IU,i}^{\alpha*} \neq Z_{IU}^\alpha$, and as such, the key and IV for this IU will not be recoverable, and the license will not be successfully decrypted by the SU. Conversely, if (m, n) is located outside of an IU's E-Zone, then $\mathbf{E}_{f,m,n,tp} = 0$ for this IU and additionally if $\llbracket count_{SU,IU} \rrbracket < \tau$, then $Z_{IU}^\alpha = Z_{IU}^\alpha + \mathbf{E}_{f,m,n,tp} = Z_{IU}^\alpha$. Also, if (m, n) is outside of an IU's obfuscated E-Zone map, then $\mathbf{O}_{f,m,n,tp} = 0$ for this IU. As a result, the $Z_{IU}^\alpha = Z_{IU}^\alpha$ for the $Z_{IU}^{\alpha*}$ associated with the obfuscated E-Zone map and the SU can recover the license. ∎

3 Preserving Location Privacy of Incumbent Users Against Inference Attacks

In this section, we describe the inference attack and analyze the compatibility and efficacy of potential obfuscation schemes.

3.1 Threat Model

We assume that there exists a singular honest-but-curious mobile SU with the ability to query SAS throughout the entirety of the region covered by SAS, this

SU shall henceforth be referred to as the adversary. The adversary's goal is to determine the grid location of a stationary IU using only information gained from the responses received from SAS. We assume the attacker has knowledge of $T(P_L, I_{th})$, the propagation model used by the IUs to calculate P_L, and I_{th}. We also assume the adversary has side knowledge indicating the existence of at least one IU operating on a channel of interest served by SAS.

3.2 Location Inference Algorithms

The Bayesian inference algorithm presented in [2] is robust and allows SUs to approximate the location of multiple IUs simultaneously. Thus, we will employ this algorithm to test the efficacy of our obfuscation techniques. However, we also propose a separate algorithm with the focus of locating a singular IU lacking the ability to inject false positive responses, as is the case of IUs in [3]. This algorithm emphasizes the importance of implementing protections against inference attacks and is introduced below.

First-Detected IU Inference Algorithm. We first define a Bernoulli random variable, $R_{xy}^{(k)}$, which represents the event of an IU existing in grid location $g(x, y)$ on channel k. Based upon the properties of the Bernoulli distribution, $P(R_{xy}^{(k)} = 1) = p_{xy}^{(k)}$ and $P(R_{xy}^{(k)} = 0) = 1 - p_{xy}^{(k)}$. Because the adversary has knowledge that there exists at least one IU on a channel of interest in the area covered by SAS, the IU is equally likely to be located in any of the grid locations covered by SAS. Thus, we initialize $p_{xy} = \frac{1}{MN} \ \forall \ g(x, y)$ on the given channel.

The adversary then queries the database from a chosen location and updates the value p_{xy} for all affected $g(x, y)$ based upon the response received from SAS. The adversary's inference regarding IU location for each possible combination of query responses is as follows:

- **Valid License for both TP_1 and TP_2:** This first case implies that there are no IUs operating in any cells with path loss values less than P_{L2} relative to the query location. The adversary first sets $p_{xy} = 0$ for all $P_{L_{xy}} < P_{L2}$, then adjusts p_{xy} for each remaining non-zero p_{xy} to reflect the current number of possible IU locations. As all non-zero locations are equally likely to contain the IU, $p_{xy} = \frac{1}{(MN) - n_{p0}}$, where n_{p0} is the total count of $g(x, y)$ with $p_{xy} = 0$.
- **Invalid License for TP_2, Valid License for TP_1:** In this case, the adversary's queries for TP_2 and TP_1 imply that there is an IU operating in some cell with $P_{L1} < P_{L_{xy}} < P_{L2}$ with respect to the queried location. The adversary uses this information to update the affected values of p_{xy} by first setting $p_{xy} = 0$ for all $P_{L_{xy}} > P_{L2}$ or $P_{L_{xy}} < P_{L1}$. The adversary then adjusts all remaining non-zero p_{xy} using the same logic as in the first scenario.
- **Invalid License for both TP_2 and TP_1:** This final case indicates the existence of an IU operating in a cell with $P_{L_{xy}} < P_{L1} < P_{L2}$. The adversary sets $p_{xy} = 0$ for all $P_{L_{xy}} > P_{L1}$ and uses the same logic as in the first scenario to update all remaining non-zero p_{xy}.

The two inference attack algorithms can be compared by determining the number of queries required to locate the IU with some degree of certainty, which can be quantified either as the value of p_{xy} for the IU's actual location or as the calculated incorrectness (IC) as defined in [5], representing the distance between the actual and inferred location of the IU (Table 1).

Table 1. Queries required to geolocate IU using the two inference attack algorithms based upon two threshold metrics averaged over 1000 trials.

	IC < 0.01	p(x, y) > 0.90
Standard algorithm	142.12022	161.18045
Modified algorithm	115.75138	111.24599

3.3   Obfuscation Schemes

Previous works regarding obfuscation have focused entirely on techniques which could be applied directly by SAS. Because SZ-SAS encrypts IU parameters and SAS responses, obfuscation schemes cannot be applied by SAS and thus must be applied by the IUs. We propose a novel obfuscation scheme below.

Envelopment by Offset False IUs (OFIU). This obfuscation scheme covers the entirety of the true E-Zone map with exclusion zones generated by artificially generated IUs. In order to simulate each IU, we first select a random x and y location offset, and add this offset to the IU's true location to create a new location for the artificially generated IU. We then select a random negative noise value for each, and add this to the actual IU's maximum transmit power level. We adjust these parameters until the true IU's exclusion zone is completely enveloped by the newly generated IU exclusion zones. This results in a new exclusion map which is not centered around the IU's true location.

3.4   Experimental Results

We conducted a series of experiments testing each of the proposed obfuscation schemes. We consider an area covered by SAS to be a 50×50 grid with grid side lengths of $250\,\mathrm{m}$, a total area of $156.25\,\mathrm{km}^2$. In this situation, the total communication overhead for each SU request is only $3\,\mathrm{kB}$ and $231\,\mathrm{kB}$ for SAS responses when the region contains 100 IUs.

Figure 2a shows that as the zone is enlarged by OFIU, the lower bound of incorrectness increases, implying that an adversary should not be successful in locating the IU. Additionally, the adversary is able to accurately locate the IU when obfuscation is not applied as in 2b, but is unable to locate this same IU when obfuscation is applied in 2c.

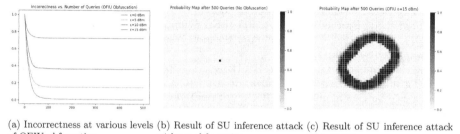

(a) Incorrectness at various levels of OFIU obfuscation   (b) Result of SU inference attack without obfuscation   (c) Result of SU inference attack with OFIU

Fig. 2. Results of SU inference attack on IUs with and without OFIU obfuscation

4 Conclusion

A novel framework which protects sensitive IU parameters from both untrusted SUs and untrusted SAS was successfully developed. We demonstrate the effectiveness of an inference attack, and show the necessity of obfuscation in the prevention of such an attack. Our experimental analysis demonstrates the ability of our framework to utilize compatible obfuscation schemes to prevent such an inference attack. In future works, this framework can be utilized as a building block when designing SAS-based DSA systems. Other obfuscation methods may also be developed and analyzed. Additionally, as light-weight fully homomorphic cryptosystems are developed, AFGH may be replaced by one such cryptosystem in our framework, which would allow researchers more flexibility when designing novel obfuscation schemes.

References

1. Ateniese, G., Fu, K., Green, M., Hohenberger, S.: Improved proxy re-encryption schemes with applications to secure distributed storage. ACM Trans. Inf. Syst. Secur. **9**(1), 1–30 (2006). https://doi.org/10.1145/1127345.1127346
2. Bahrak, B., Bhattarai, S., Ullah, A., Park, J.M.J., Reed, J., Gurney, D.: Protecting the primary users' operational privacy in spectrum sharing. In: 2014 IEEE International Symposium on Dynamic Spectrum Access Networks (DYSPAN), pp. 236–247, April 2014. https://doi.org/10.1109/DySPAN.2014.6817800
3. Dou, Y., et al.: Preserving incumbent users' privacy in server-driven dynamic spectrum access systems. In: 2016 IEEE 36th International Conference on Distributed Computing Systems (ICDCS), pp. 729–730, June 2016. https://doi.org/10.1109/ICDCS.2016.40
4. Park, J.M., Reed, J.H., Beex, A.A., Clancy, T.C., Kumar, V., Bahrak, B.: Security and enforcement in spectrum sharing. Proc. IEEE **102**(3), 270–281 (2014). https://doi.org/10.1109/JPROC.2014.2301972

5. Shokri, R., Theodorakopoulos, G., Le Boudec, J.Y., Hubaux, J.P.: Quantifying location privacy. In: Proceedings of the 2011 IEEE Symposium on Security and Privacy, SP 2011, pp. 247–262. IEEE Computer Society, Washington, DC (2011). https://doi.org/10.1109/SP.2011.18
6. Zhang, L., Fang, C., Li, Y., Zhu, H., Dong, M.: Optimal strategies for defending location inference attack in database-driven CRNs. In: 2015 IEEE International Conference on Communications (ICC), pp. 7640–7645, June 2015. https://doi.org/10.1109/ICC.2015.7249548

Secrecy Outage Probability of Cognitive Small-Cell Network with Unreliable Backhaul Connections

Jinghua Zhang$^{(\boxtimes)}$, Chinmoy Kundu, and Emi Garcia-Palacios

Queen's University Belfast, Belfast BT9 5AH, UK
{jzhang22,c.kundu}@qub.ac.uk, e.garcia@ee.qub.ac.uk

Abstract. In this paper, we investigate the secrecy performance of underlay cognitive small-cell radio network with unreliable backhaul connections. The secondary cognitive small-cell transmitters are connected to macro base station by wireless backhaul links. The small-cell network is sharing the same spectrum with the primary network ensuring that a desired outage probability constraint in the primary network is always satisfied. We propose an optimal transmitter selection (OTS) scheme for small-cell network to transfer information to the destination. The closed-form expression of secrecy outage probability are derived. Our result shows that increasing the primary transmitter's transmit power and the number of small-cell transmitter can improve the system performance. The backhaul reliability of secondary and the desired outage probability of the primary also have significant impact on the system.

Keywords: Unreliable backhaul · Cognitive radio network
Small-cell network · Physical layer security · Secrecy outage probability

1 Introduction

Due to the explosion of data-intensive applications and wireless systems such as the Internet of Things (IoT) and smart cities, the deployment of wireless infrastructure is expected to get more dense and heterogeneous in the near future [1]. To reach such high data rate, the backhaul links connecting the macro-cell and many small-cells in the heterogeneous networks (HetNets) are also expected to become dense. In the conventional wired backhaul network, high reliability wired links and high data rate can be expected, however, the deploying and sustaining the large-scale wired links require excessive capital investment for all the connections [2,3]. This leads wireless backhaul as alternative solution since it has been proven cost-effective and flexible in practical systems. However, wireless

---

This work was supported in part by the Royal Society-SERB Newton International Fellowship under Grant NF151345.

I. Moerman et al. (Eds.): CROWNCOM 2018, LNICST 261, pp. 89–98, 2019.
https://doi.org/10.1007/978-3-030-05490-8_9

backhaul is unlikely reliable as wired backhaul due to non-line-of-sight (n-LOS) propagation and fading of wireless channels [4].

The aforementioned rapid development in wireless devices and services is also pushing the demand for spectrum while most of licensed spectrum bands are occupied [5]. In recent years, the investigation on cognitive radio (CR) techniques [6] has attracted many experts' attention. CR optimises the current spectrum usage, which allows unlicensed secondary users to share the same spectrum with the licensed primary users in an opportunistic manner. The authors in [7] analysed the impact of the primary network on the secondary network. In [8], the authors optimizing the time and power allocation in the secondary network. To improve the CR or noncognitive network performance, user selection is always among the secondary users and relays in the literature [9–12].

For a complete study, we also consider the challenges of security in the wireless communication network. Due to the broadcasting nature of wireless channels, the confidential information in wireless network is vulnerable to eavesdropping and security attacks. In reality, CR networks are easily susceptible to eavesdropping. The conventional way from upper layer security is deploying data encryption for secure communication, on the other hand, physical layer security (PLS) obtains the advantage from the randomness of the wireless channels for information security extensively. PLS has become increasingly popular to deal with wiretapping and possible loss of confidentiality. Some research has investigated the secrecy performance using PLS [9,13–16].

Nevertheless, all the aforementioned work did not take into account the impact of unreliable backhaul on PLS of CR network. Some literatures in CR network only consider the interference on the primary network. In some literature on backhaul CR networks [4,17–19], authors investigated the secrecy performance but not consider the system with secondary user selection schemes. The impact of guaranteeing outage as a quality-of-service (QoS) in the primary networks was not considered either in aforementioned paper. Our research address these key issues in CR network with backhaul. We investigate the secrecy performance of CR network with unreliable backhaul connections. Based on those considerations, our contribution of this paper is summarised as follows:

1. We take into account the backhaul unreliability in secrecy performance. We develop the close-form expression of the secrecy outage probability.
2. We consider interference both in primary and secondary receiver.
3. We consider primary QoS constraint metric as outage probability, which is different from other works in CR.
4. Our model investigates a small-cell transmitter selection schemes, namely, optimal transmitter selection (OTS) which prioritizes the maximum channel gain S–D, and also assesses the influences of varying the number of small-cell transmitter.

The rest of the paper is organised as follows. In Sect. 2, the system channel models are described. Section 3 demonstrates the secrecy outage probability of propose system. Numerical results from monte-carlo simulations are showcased in Sect. 4. Finally, the paper is concluded in Sect. 5.

2 System and channel models

As illustrated in Fig. 1, the system is consisting of a primary network with one primary transmitter, T, one primary receiver, R and a secondary network consisting of K small-cells transmitters, $\{S_1, ..., S_k, ..., S_K\}$ which are connected to a macro-base station, BS, by unreliable backhaul links, one secondary destination, D, and one eavesdropper, E. All nodes are equipped with single antenna. We assume all nodes are sufficiently separated from each other so that $T-R$, $T-D$, $T-E$, $S-R$, $S-D$ and $S-E$ experience independent and identically distributed Rayleigh fading. The channel between nodes are denoted by h_X where X = $\{$ TR, TD, TE, SR, SD, SE $\}$ channel power gains are exponential distributed with parameters λ_x for x = $\{$ tr, td, te, sr, sd, se $\}$, respectively. The noise at R , E and D is modelled as the additive white Gaussian noise (AWGN) with zero mean and variances N_0. One best transmitter will be selected among K small-cell transmitters, to transfer information to D. While the message is sent from the BS to small-cell transmitters, the backhaul link might have certain probability of failure. Backhaul reliability is modelled as Bernoulli process with success probability, $\mathbb{P}(\mathbb{I}_k = 1) = \Lambda$, and failure probability is $\mathbb{P}(\mathbb{I}_k = 0) = 1 - \Lambda$ for each $k = 1, \cdots, K$. We investigate the secrecy outage probability (SOP) of the secondary network.

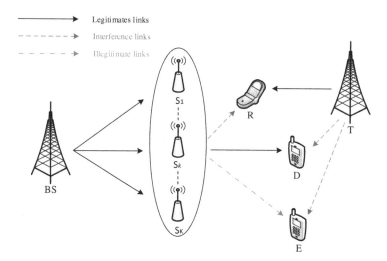

Fig. 1. Underlay cognitive radio network with unreliable backhaul connections.

2.1 Interference at Primary and Secondary Power Constraint

The primary network is interfered from the selected secondary transmitter, S_k, for $k = \{1, ..., K\}$ via interference channels $h_{S_k R}$ during the secondary network transmission. The signal-to-interference-plus-noise-ratio (SINR) at R is given as

$$\Gamma_R = \frac{P_T |h_{TR}|^2}{P_S |h_{S_k R}|^2 + N_0}, \tag{1}$$

where P_S is the maximum allowed transmit power of small-cell transmitter which satisfies the primary network QoS constraint, h_{TR} is the channel coefficient of the $T - R$ link, and $h_{S_k R}$ is the channel coefficient of the $S - R$ link. To protect the primary network, the secondary network transmitters must adapt their transmit power. Moreover, the secondary network transmit power must be limitedly the QoS of the primary network which characterized by its desired outage probability. The primary network outage probability should be below a desired level, Φ. The desired outage probability constraint is defined as follows

$$\mathbb{P}\left[\Gamma_R < \Gamma_0\right] \leq \Phi, \tag{2}$$

where $\Gamma_0 = 2^\beta - 1$, β is the target rate of the primary network, and $0 < \Phi < 1$. From (1) and (2), output power of secondary transmitter can be derived from the desired outage probability at the primary network

$$P_S = \begin{cases} P_T \lambda_{sr} \xi, & \text{if } \xi > 0 \\ 0, & \text{otherwise.} \end{cases} \tag{3}$$

where

$$\xi = \frac{1}{\lambda_{tr} \Gamma_0} \left[\frac{\exp\left(\frac{-\lambda_{tr} \Gamma_0}{\Gamma_T}\right)}{1 - \Phi} - 1 \right]. \tag{4}$$

Here, we used CDF of $\Gamma_R(x)$ to find P_S in close-form. The CDF of $\Gamma_R(x)$ can be derived from the definition of CDF as

$$F_R(x) = 1 - \frac{\frac{\lambda_{sr} \Gamma_T}{\lambda_{tr} \Gamma_S}}{x + \frac{\lambda_{sr} \Gamma_T}{\lambda_{tr} \Gamma_S}} \exp\left(\frac{-\lambda_{tr} x}{\Gamma_T}\right), \tag{5}$$

where $\Gamma_T = \frac{P_T}{N_0}$ and $\Gamma_S = \frac{P_S}{N_0}$.

2.2　Proposed Source Selection and Interference at the Secondary

To mitigate the eavesdropping, OTS scheme is proposed where a source is selected to forward the message such that it maximize $S_k - D$ link power gain as

$$k^* = \arg \max_{1 \leq k \leq K} P_S |h_{S_k D}|^2. \tag{6}$$

Due to the unreliability of the backhaul, the selected link may not be active. To consider backhaul reliability into the performance analysis, we model backhaul reliability using Bernoulli random variable $\mathbb{I}$. The SINR at D can be given as

$$\Gamma_{SD} = \mathbb{I} \tilde{\Gamma}_{SD}, \tag{7}$$

where

$$\tilde{\Gamma}_{SD} = \frac{P_S \max[|h_{S_k D}|^2]}{P_T |h_{TD}|^2 + N_0}. \tag{8}$$

SINR at E can be similarly expressed as

$$\Gamma_{SE} = \frac{P_S |h_{S_k E}|^2}{P_T |h_{TE}|^2 + N_0}. \tag{9}$$

Conditioned on the source has already been selected, E always experience its intercepted signal power as independent exponentially distributed, hence, while finding the distribution of Γ_{SE} no backhaul reliability parameter comes into play in (9). However, that is not true for Γ_{SD} in (7). The distribution of Γ_{SD} will be the mixture distribution of $\mathbb{I}$ and $\tilde{\Gamma}_{SD}$. Now the distribution of Γ_{SD} can be obtained from the mixture distribution due to backhaul reliability as

$$f_{SD}(x) = (1 - \Lambda)\delta(x) + \Lambda \tilde{f}_{SD}, \tag{10}$$

where $f_{SD}(x)$, $\tilde{f}_{SD}(x)$ are the PDFs of Γ_{SD} and $\tilde{\Gamma}_{SD}$, respectively and $\delta(x)$ is delta function. CDF of $f_{SD}(x)$ can be obtained just by integrating it and finding the CDF of $\tilde{\Gamma}_{SD}$.

The CDF of $\tilde{\Gamma}_{SD}$ can be evaluate from the definition of CDF with the help of the CDF of $\max |h_{S_k D}|^2$ and the PDF of $|h_{TD}|^2$ as

$$\tilde{F}_{SD}(x) = \mathbb{P}\left[\frac{P_S \max |h_{S_k D}|^2}{P_T |h_{TD}|^2 + N_0} < x\right]$$

$$= \mathbb{P}\left[P_S \max_{k=1,\dots,K} |h_{S_k D}|^2 < (P_T |h_{TD}|^2 + N_0)x\right]$$

$$= 1 - \sum_{k=1}^{K} \binom{K}{k} \frac{(-1)^{k+1} \frac{\lambda_{td} \Gamma_S}{k \lambda_{sd} \Gamma_T}}{x + \frac{\lambda_{td} \Gamma_S}{k \lambda_{sd} \Gamma_T}} \exp\left(\frac{-k \lambda_{sd} x}{\Gamma_S}\right). \tag{11}$$

The CDF of Γ_{SD} then can be evaluate with the help of (10) as

$$F_{SD}(x) = 1 - \Lambda \sum_{k=1}^{K} \binom{K}{k} \frac{(-1)^{k+1} \frac{\lambda_{td} \Gamma_S}{k \lambda_{sd} \Gamma_T}}{x + \frac{\lambda_{td} \Gamma_S}{k \lambda_{sd} \Gamma_T}} \exp\left(\frac{-k \lambda_{sd} x}{\Gamma_S}\right). \tag{12}$$

The CDF of $\Gamma_{S_k E}$ can be obtained from the definition of CDF similar to $\tilde{F}_{SD}$ as

$$F_{SE}(x) = 1 - \frac{\frac{\lambda_{te} \Gamma_S}{\lambda_{se} \Gamma_T}}{x + \frac{\lambda_{te} \Gamma_S}{\lambda_{se} \Gamma_T}} \exp\left(\frac{-\lambda_{se} x}{\Gamma_S}\right), \tag{13}$$

and the PDF of Γ_{SE} can be expressed after differentiating (13) as

$$f_{SE}(x) = \frac{\frac{\lambda_{te}}{\Gamma_T} \exp\left(\frac{-\lambda_{se} x}{\Gamma_S}\right)}{x + \frac{\lambda_{te} \Gamma_S}{\lambda_{se} \Gamma_T}} + \frac{\frac{\lambda_{te} \Gamma_S}{\lambda_{se} \Gamma_T} \exp\left(\frac{-\lambda_{se} x}{\Gamma_S}\right)}{\left(x + \frac{\lambda_{te} \Gamma_S}{\lambda_{se} \Gamma_T}\right)^2}. \tag{14}$$

3   Secrecy Outage Probability

In this section, we investigate the SOP of the secondary network where the eavesdropper's CSI is assumed unavailable in the proposed network. So, the transmitters encode and transfer the information with the certain target rate of ρ. We denoted the instantaneous secrecy capacity by C_S in bits/s/HZ, and the secrecy gain is guaranteed when C_S is greater than R_{th}. Otherwise, information-theoretic security is compromised [20]. Towards deriving those performances, the secrecy capacity is required to be defined first. The secrecy capacity can be expressed for as [21,22]

$$C_S = [\log_2(1 + \Gamma_{SD}) - \log_2(1 + \Gamma_E)]^+, \tag{15}$$

where $\log_2(1 + \Gamma_{SD})$ is the instantaneous capacity at D, $\log_2(1 + \Gamma_E)$ is the instantaneous capacity of the wiretap channel at E, $\Gamma_E = \Gamma_{SE}$ and $[x]^+ = \max(x, 0)$. The SOP is defined as the probability that the secrecy rate is lower than a certain threshold, R_{th}, can be expressed as

$$
\begin{aligned}
\mathcal{P}_{out}(R_{th}) &= Pr(C_S < R_{th}) \\
&= \mathbb{P}\left[\Gamma_{SD} < R_{th}(1 + \Gamma_E) - 1\right] \\
&= \int_0^\infty F_{SD}(\rho(x + 1) - 1) f_{SE}(x) dx,
\end{aligned}
\tag{16}
$$

where $\rho = 2^{R_{th}} - 1$, R_{th} is the target rate of the secondary network. Substituting (11) and (14) into (16), outage secrecy probability can be evaluated as

$$\mathcal{P}_{out}(R_{th}) = 1 - A \cdot I_1 - B \cdot I_2, \tag{17}$$

where I_1 and I_2 can be expressed respectively as

$$I_1 = \int_0^\infty \frac{1}{(x + a)(x + b)} \exp\left(-cx\right) dx, \tag{18}$$

$$I_2 = \int_0^\infty \frac{1}{(x + a)(x + b)^2} \exp\left(-cx\right) dx, \tag{19}$$

with $a = \frac{\lambda_{td}\Gamma_S + k\rho\lambda_{sd}\Gamma_T - k\lambda_{sd}\Gamma_T}{k\rho\lambda_{sd}\Gamma_T}$, $b = \frac{\lambda_{te}\Gamma_S}{\lambda_{se}\Gamma_T}$ and $c = \frac{k\rho\lambda_{sd} + \lambda_{se}}{\Gamma_S}$

$$A = \sum_{k=1}^K \binom{K}{k} \Lambda(-1)^{k+1} \frac{\lambda_{te}\lambda_{td}\Gamma_S}{k\rho\lambda_{sd}\Gamma_T^2} \exp\left(\frac{-k\lambda_{sd}(\rho - 1)}{\Gamma_S}\right), \tag{20}$$

$$B = \sum_{k=1}^K \binom{K}{k} \Lambda(-1)^{k+1} \frac{\lambda_{te}\lambda_{td}\Gamma_S^2}{k\rho\lambda_{se}\lambda_{sd}\Gamma_T^2} \exp\left(\frac{-k\lambda_{sd}(\rho - 1)}{\Gamma_S}\right). \tag{21}$$

We can utilize the partial fraction to transform multiplication into summation and solve (18) and (19) using

$$\frac{1}{(x + a)(x + b)} = -\frac{1}{(a - b)(x + a)} + \frac{1}{(a - b)(x + b)}, \tag{22}$$

$$\frac{1}{(x+a)(x+b)^2} = \frac{1}{(a-b)^2(x+a)} - \frac{1}{(a-b)^2(x+b)} + \frac{1}{(a-b)(x+b)^2}. \quad (23)$$

For the final solution, we have used the integral solution of the form [23], eq.(3.352.4) and [23], eq.(3.353.3) to get

$$I_1 = \frac{1}{a-b} \exp{(ac)} \operatorname{Ei}{(-ac)} - \frac{1}{a-b} \exp{(bc)} \operatorname{Ei}{(-bc)}, \quad (24)$$

$$I_2 = -\frac{1}{(a-b)^2} \exp{(ac)} \operatorname{Ei}{(-ac)} + \frac{1}{(a-b)^2} \exp{(bc)} \operatorname{Ei}{(-bc)}$$
$$+ \frac{1}{a-b}\left(c\exp{(bc)} \operatorname{Ei}{(-bc)} + \frac{1}{b}\right). \quad (25)$$

4 Numerical Results and Discussions

In this section, Monte Carlo simulations are provide to validate the theoretical analyses. Without loss of generality, we assume all nodes are affected by the same noise power N_0, and the following parameters are set: $\beta = 0.5$ bits/s/Hz, $R_{th} = 0.5$ bits/s/Hz, $\lambda_{tr} = 3, \lambda_{td} = -6, \lambda_{sd} = 3, \lambda_{sr} = -3, \lambda_{te} = 6, \lambda_{se} = -3$ dB.

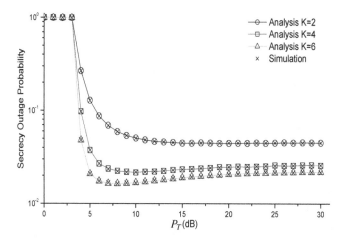

Fig. 2. SOP versus P_T(dB) for different numbers of secondary users.

Figure 2 shows the SOP versus P_T for different number of small-cell transmitters, K = 2, K = 4, and K = 6. The network parameters are set as $\Phi = 0.1$ and $\Lambda = 0.99$. It shows that the analysis match with simulation. It can be observed that the number of small-cell transmitters strongly affects the SOP. As the number of smell-cell transmitter increase, SOP improves. However, the increase of transmitter i.e. K = 2 to K = 4 has more improvement compared to

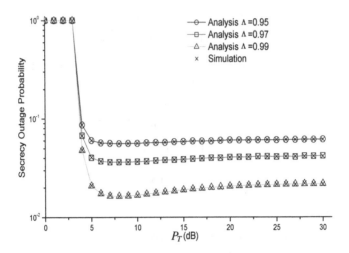

Fig. 3. SOP versus P_T(dB) for different values of Λ .

k = 4 to K = 6. As we increase P_T SOP decreases first and converges to its floor after certain values.

Figure 3 plots the SOP versus P_T for different value of backhaul reliability, $\Lambda = 0.95$, $\Lambda = 0.97$ and $\Lambda = 0.99$ with K = 6, $\Phi = 0.1$. We observed that the SOP reduces when the Λ increases. This is intuitive that as the reliability of the backhaul link improve of secrecy also improves.

In Fig. 4, the SOP is investigated versus P_T with three different value of primary QoS constraint, $\Phi = 0.01$, $\Phi = 0.05$ and $\Phi = 0.1$ with K = 6, $\Lambda = 0.99$. We observed that increasing Φ result in a reduction in the SOP. This is because

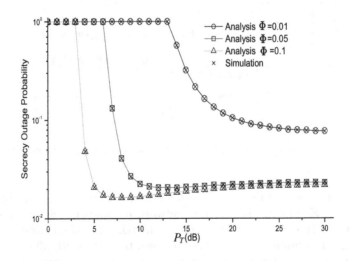

Fig. 4. SOP versus P_T(dB) for different values of Φ.

the secondary network are allowed to have higher transmit power by relaxing the QoS requirement of the primary network.

5   Conclusion

In this paper, we have taken into account the backhaul connection reliability of studying the SOP of underlay cognitive radio network. A proposed selection scheme enhance the system's secrecy performance. The small-cell transmitter power met the desired outage probability. The results have proved that increasing the primary transmitter's power and the number of small-cell transmitter enhance the system's secrecy performance. In addition, our results shows that the backhaul reliability and the desired outage probability of the primary network are important parameter relative to the scaling of the secrecy performance. Increasing backhaul reliability will result in base station having higher success rate to connect with small-cell transmitters, and relaxing the QoS requirement of the primary network will allow small-cell transmitter to have higher transmit power, which will improve over all secrecy of the system.

Acknowledgment. This work was supported in part by the Royal Society-SERB Newton International Fellowship under Grant NF151345.

References

1. Andrews, J.G., Buzzi, S., Choi, W., et al.: What will 5G be? IEEE Trans. Signal Process. **32**(6), 1065–1082 (2014)
2. Tipmongkolsilp, O., Zaghloul, S., Jukan, A.: The evolution of cellular backhaul technologies: current issues and future trends. IEEE Commun. Surv. Tutor. **13**(1), 97–113 (2011)
3. Ge, X.H., Cheng, H., Guizani, M., et al.: 5G wireless backhaul networks: challenges and research advances. IEEE Netw. **28**(6), 6–11 (2014)
4. Kim, K.J., Yeoh, P.L., Orlik, P.V., et al.: Secrecy performance of finite-sized cooperative single carrier systems with unreliable backhaul connections. IEEE Trans. Signal Process. **64**(17), 4403–4416 (2016)
5. Kolodzy, P.: Avoidance, interference: spectrum policy task force. Federal Communications Commission, Washington, DC, Report ET Docket, vol. 40, no. 4, pp. 147–158 (2002)
6. Mitola, J., Maguire, G.Q.: Cognitive radio: making software radios more personal. IEEE Pers. Commun. **6**(4), 13–18 (1999)
7. Zhang, J.H., Nguyen, N.P., Zhang, J.Q., et al.: Impact of primary networks on the performance of energy harvesting cognitive radio networks. IET Commun. **10**(18), 2559–2566 (2016)
8. Lee, S., Zhang, R.: Cognitive wireless powered network: spectrum sharing models and throughput maximization. IEEE Trans. Cogn. Commun. Netw. **1**(3), 335–346 (2015)
9. Nguyen, N.P., Duong, T.Q., Ngo, H.Q., et al.: Secure 5G wireless communications: a joint relay selection and wireless power transfer approach. IEEE Access **4**, 3349–3359 (2016)

10. Bao, V.N.Q., Duong, T.Q., Da Costa, D.B., et al.: Cognitive amplify-and-forward relaying with best relay selection in non-identical Rayleigh fading. IEEE Commun. Lett. **17**(3), 475–478 (2013)
11. Kundu, C., Ngatched, T.M.N., Dobre, O.A.: Relay selection to improve secrecy in cooperative threshold decode-and-forward relaying. In: Proceedings of IEEE GLOBECOM 2016, Washington, DC, USA, 4–8 (2016)
12. Zhang, J., Kundu, C., Nguyen, N.P., et al.: Cognitive wireless powered communication networks with secondary user selection and primary QoS constraint. IET Commun. **12**, 1873–1879 (2018)
13. Huang, Y.Z., Wang, J.L., Zhong, C.J., et al.: Secure transmission in cooperative relaying networks with multiple antennas. IEEE Trans. Wirel. Commun. **15**(10), 6843–6856 (2016)
14. Yin, C., Nguyen, H.T., Kundu, C., et al.: Secure energy harvesting relay networks with unreliable backhaul connections. IEEE Access **6**, 12074–12084 (2018)
15. Vu, T., Nguyen, M.N., Kundu, C., et al.: Secure cognitive radio networks with source selection and unreliable backhaul connections. IET Commun. **12**, 1771–1777 (2017)
16. Kundu, C., Jindal, A., Bose, R.: Secrecy outage of dual-hop amplify-and-forward relay system with diversity combining at the eavesdropper. Wireless Pers. Commun. **97**, 539–563 (2017)
17. Khan, T.A., Orlik, P., Kim, K.J., et al.: Performance analysis of cooperative wireless networks with unreliable backhaul links. IEEE Commun. Lett. **19**(8), 1386–1389 (2015)
18. Nguyen, H.T., Duong, T.Q., Hwang, W.J.: Multiuser relay networks over unreliable backhaul links under spectrum sharing environment. IEEE Commun. Lett. **21**(10), 2314–2317 (2017)
19. Nguyen, H.T., Zhang, J.Q., Yang, N., et al.: Secure cooperative single carrier systems under unreliable backhaul and dense networks impact. IEEE Access **5**, 18310–18324 (2017)
20. Wang, L.F., Elkashlan, M., Huang, J., et al.: Secure transmission with antenna selection in MIMO Nakagami-m fading channels. IEEE Trans. Wireless Commun. **13**(11), 6054–6067 (2014)
21. Wang, L.F., Kim, K.J., Duong, T.Q., et al.: Security enhancement of cooperative single carrier systems. IEEE Trans. Inf. Forensics Secur. **10**(1), 90–103 (2015)
22. Yang, N., Yeoh, P.L., Elkashlan, M., et al.: Transmit antenna selection for security enhancement in MIMO wiretap channels. IEEE Trans. Commun. **61**(1), 144–154 (2013)
23. Jeffrey, A., Zwillinger, D.: Table of Integrals, Series and Products, 7th edn. Academic Press, Cambridge (2007)

Polarization-Space Based Interference Alignment for Cognitive Heterogeneous Cellular Network

Xiaofang Gao[1(✉)], Caili Guo[2], and Shuo Chen[1]

[1] Beijing Laboratory of Advanced Information Networks, Beijing University of Posts and Telecommunications, Beijing, China
nitup@bupt.edu.cn
[2] Beijing Key Laboratory of Network System Architecture and Convergence, Beijing University of Posts and Telecommunications, Beijing, China

Abstract. In underlay cognitive heterogeneous cellular network (CHCN), small cells can transmit their signals as long as the interference to macro cell is below a threshold. Consider a two-layer CHCN with polarized MIMO small cells, a novel polarization-space based interference alignment scheme is proposed. The cross-tier interference between macro cell and small cells is addressed by two given algorithms with different purposes. Orthogonal projection based polarization-space interference alignment (OP-PSIA) for ensuring the minimum effect to macro cell and interference constrained polarization-space interference alignment (IC-PSIA) for maximizing the performances of small cells if permitted. The co-tier interference between small cells are reduced by a minimum total mean squared error (MMSE) algorithm. Then we give specific solutions for two algorithms both including orthogonal projection processing and analytically iterative calculations. Simulation results show the improvement of two algorithms in BER performance of small cells while ensuring the protection of macro cell and keeping maximum overall sum rate.

Keywords: Polarization · Interference alignment
Orthogonal projection · Cognitive heterogeneous cellular network

1 Introduction

Cognitive heterogeneous cellular network (CHCN) is regarded as a promising solution to solve the urgent spectrum shortage problem [1] in wireless communication system. However, small cells in CHCN fully reuse the spectrum of macro cell in underlay mode and cause complex interference situation. Interference alignment (IA) has been paid much attention to solve the problem effectively with the development of multi-input multi-output (MIMO) technology

This work was supported by the National Natural Science Foundation of China under Grant No. 61571062 and No. 61271177, and the Fundamental Research Funds for the Central Universities2014ZD03-01

I. Moerman et al. (Eds.): CROWNCOM 2018, LNICST 261, pp. 99–108, 2019.
https://doi.org/10.1007/978-3-030-05490-8_10

[2]. Recently, co-located orthogonally dual-polarized antenna (ODPA) has been widely used in practice [3] because of its less antenna correlation and smaller physical size. Polarization, as an intrinsic characteristic of electromagnetic wave, doubles the system's degrees of freedom (DoFs). So with the advantages of ODPAs and the large diversity gains of MIMO array, polarized MIMO antennas are designed to solve more complex interference. Based on polarized MIMO small cells, we consider an effective IA scheme.

The multiple interference is usually handled hierarchically in CHCN. First, it is necessary to restrict the interference to macro cell when small cells access to the authorized spectrum. And the interference from macro cell to small cells should be eliminated too. To reduce those cross-tier interference, limiting the transmissions of small cells to the null spaces of channels from their transmitters to the macro cell in spatial domain [4,5] or using the orthogonal polarization states for two layers in polarization domain [6]. [7] proposes a polarization based cross-tier IA scheme to minimize the interference from macro cell to small cell under the interference constraint. Second, small cells also cause severe co-tier interference with the increase of their number. [8] considers it as a standard IA problem with proper antenna configuration to satisfy the feasible conditions. And authors in [9] propose a spectrum sharing scheme based on joint polarization adaption and MIMO beamforming for polarized MIMO system. However, IA scheme for CHCN with polarized MIMO small cells has not been tackled in the literature which brings better performances as expected.

So in this paper, we propose a novel polarization-space based IA scheme for underlay CHCN with polarized MIMO small cells. The main contributions are:

- The cross-tier interference suppression takes into account two different purposes and the corresponding algorithms are given. One is the orthogonal projection based polarization-space IA (OP-PSIA) algorithm which suppresses the cross-tier interference completely and aims to guarantee the minimum degradation for macro cell. The other is interference constrained polarization-space IA (IC-PSIA) algorithm which minimizes the interference from macro cell to small cells while reduces the interference from small cells to macro cell within the tolerable constraint. It aims to improve the performances of small cells if permitted.
- The co-tier interference between small cells is dealt with a standard minimum total mean squared error (MMSE) algorithm instead of other practical IA algorithms such as minimizing the leakage interference [8] and maximizing the SINR [8,9]. Because MMSE algorithm is analytically proved to have IA-like behavior [10] and it achieves better performances, especially bit-error rate (BER) performance [11]. With the development of high reliability services, such as vehicle-to-vehicle (V2V), real-time gaming, live streaming services, better BER performance requirement is put forward for the physical layer.
- Unlike existing work, we construct system model based on the polarization-space characteristics of signals. The specific and novel solutions for two algorithms are given including orthogonal projection processing and analytically iterative calculations.

2 System Model

Considering a two layer downlink scenario, one macro cell serving as primary network coexists with K small cells as secondary networks sharing the same spectrum. The disjoint subcarrier allocation is adopted to avoid the intra-user interference. From Fig. 1, small cell base stations (SBSs) and their user equipment (SUEs) are configured with N_t transmitting and N_r receiving ODPAs respectively. $\mathbf{H}_{kl}$ represents the channel state information (CSI) from the k-th small cell base station to l-th small cell subscriber. $\mathbf{H}_{pk}$ and $\mathbf{H}_{kp}$ are the inter-tier CSI of interfering links. A polarized MIMO channel model with Rayleigh fading and depolarization effect is adopted containing polarized and spatial information [12] as $\mathbf{H} = \mathbf{H}^s \odot \mathbf{H}^p$ where the Hadamard product $\odot$ separates the spatial fading channel $\mathbf{H}^s$ and the polarized channel $\mathbf{H}^p$ with depolarization effect.

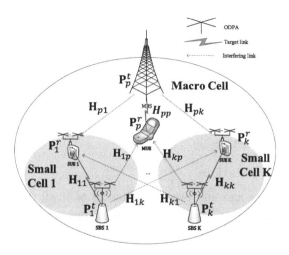

Fig. 1. Coexistence scenario of macro cell and small cells.

Besides, the intra-tier CSI is obtained by traditional channel estimation methods of orthogonal frequency division multiplexing (OFDM) system while the learning of inter-tier CSI is an open issue. A possible solution is SBS has the ability of cognising the sounding reference signal (SRS) from near macro cell user and the CSI from macro cell base station to small cell users is measured by the cognition of macro cell base station's pilot signal [5].

In small cells, the transmitting polarization-space matrices $\overrightarrow{\mathbf{P}_k^t}$, $k = 1, 2, \ldots, K$ also contain both spatial and polarization information as $\overrightarrow{\mathbf{P}_k^t} = \mathbf{W}_k \odot \mathbf{P}_k^t = [w_1^k w_2^k \ldots w_{N_t}^k]^H \odot [\mathbf{P}_{k,1}^t \mathbf{P}_{k,2}^t \ldots \mathbf{P}_{k,N_t}^t]^H$ where $\odot$ separates the beamforming vector $\mathbf{W}_k$ with spatial coefficients w_i^k and the polarization matrix $\mathbf{P}_k^t$ with state vector $\mathbf{P}_{k,i}^t$ of each ODPA. In an orthogonal coordinate system, polarization state is denoted as Jones vector $\mathbf{P}_{k,i}^t = \begin{pmatrix} cos\gamma_{k,i} \\ sin\gamma_{k,i} \ e^{j\phi_{k,i}} \end{pmatrix}$ where

$\gamma_{k,i} \in [0, \pi/2]$ is the amplitude ratio of two orthogonal branches of i-th ODPA in k-th small cell and $\phi_{k,i} \in [0, 2\pi]$ is the phase difference between them. The structure of receiving matrices $\overrightarrow{\mathbf{P}_k^r}$, $(k = 1, 2, \ldots, K)$ are similar. As for macro cell, the configurations of macro base station (MBS) and user equipment (MUE) depend on their own design. Denote their transmitting and receiving polarization states as $\mathbf{P}_p^t$ and $\mathbf{P}_p^r$. So macro cell received signal $\mathbf{r}_p$ and k-th small cell received signal $\mathbf{r}_k$ are as follows

$$\mathbf{r}_p = (\mathbf{P}_p^r)^H (\mathbf{H}_{pp}\mathbf{P}_p^t\sqrt{G_p}\mathbf{s}_p + \underbrace{\sum_{k=1}^{K} \mathbf{H}_{kp}\overrightarrow{\mathbf{P}_k^t}\sqrt{G_k}\mathbf{s}_k}_{cross-tier\ interference} + \mathbf{n}_p) \tag{1}$$

$$\mathbf{r}_k = (\overrightarrow{\mathbf{P}_k^r})^H (\mathbf{H}_{kk}\overrightarrow{\mathbf{P}_k^t}\sqrt{G_k}\mathbf{s}_k + \underbrace{\mathbf{H}_{pk}\mathbf{P}_p^t\sqrt{G_p}\mathbf{s}_p}_{cross-tier\ interference} + \underbrace{\sum_{l \neq k, l=1}^{K} \mathbf{H}_{lk}\overrightarrow{\mathbf{P}_l^t}\sqrt{G_l}\mathbf{s}_l}_{co-tier\ interference} + \mathbf{n}_k) \tag{2}$$

where $(\cdot)^H$ is conjugate transpose. $\mathbf{s}_p$ and $\mathbf{s}_k$ $(k = 1, 2, \ldots, K)$ are bit sequences of macro cell and k-th small cell with powers G_p and G_k, respectively. $\mathbf{n}_p$ and $\mathbf{n}_k$ are additive white Gaussian noises (AWGNs) with covariances σ_p^2, σ_k^2.

3   Proposed Scheme

3.1   Problem Formulation

To reduce interference and improve performances of small cells, define a set of polarization-space based transmitting and receiving matrices $\{(\overrightarrow{\mathbf{P}_k^t}, \overrightarrow{\mathbf{P}_k^r}), k = 1, 2, \ldots, K\}$ to minimize the total mean square error (MSE). It is constructed as $MSE_k = E\{\|\widetilde{\mathbf{s}}_k - \mathbf{r}_k\|_F^2\} = E\{tr[(\widetilde{\mathbf{s}}_k - \mathbf{r}_k)(\widetilde{\mathbf{s}}_k - \mathbf{r}_k)^H]\}$ for k-th small cell where $\widetilde{\mathbf{s}}_k = \sqrt{G_k}\mathbf{s}_k$ is the target signal and $tr(\cdot)$ is the trace. As for macro cell, the total interference power I_{total} from small cells is $I_{total} = \sum_{k=1}^{K} E\{\|(\mathbf{P}_p^r)^H \mathbf{H}_{kp}\overrightarrow{\mathbf{P}_k^t}\sqrt{G_k}\mathbf{s}_k\|_F^2\}$. So the optimization problem is

$$(\mathcal{P}_1) \quad \min_{\{(\overrightarrow{\mathbf{P}_k^r}, \overrightarrow{\mathbf{P}_k^t}), k=1,2,\ldots,K\}} \sum_k^K MSE_k \tag{3}$$
$$s.t.\ I_{total} \leq I_{th}$$

where I_{th} is the tolerable interference power of macro cell. Notice that $\mathcal{P}_1$ is a quadratic constraint quadratic programming (QCQP) problem with respective to $2K$ variable vectors and it's very difficult to find an analytically optimal solution. So we simplify it by processing interference at the transmitter and receiver. Two algorithms are given: orthogonal projection based polarization-space IA (OP-PSIA) algorithm which aims to guarantee the minimum degradation for macro cell and interference constrained polarization-space IA (IC-PSIA) algorithm which aims to maximize the performances of small cells if permitted.

3.2   Orthogonal Projection Based Polarization-Space IA Algorithm

The essence of simplifying $\mathcal{P}_1$ is to eliminate the interference terms of objective function. Firstly, reduce the cross-tier interference from macro cell to small cells by introducing the orthogonal projection filter [13] at the receiver. Assuming $\mathbf{H}_{pk}$ and $\mathbf{P}_p^t$ is known, the orthogonal projection filter operator $\mathbf{E}_{\mathbf{H}_{pk}\mathbf{P}_p^t}^{\perp}$ is

$$\mathbf{E}_{\mathbf{H}_{pk}\mathbf{P}_p^t}^{\perp} = \mathbf{I} - \mathbf{H}_{pk}\mathbf{P}_p^t[(\mathbf{H}_{pk}\mathbf{P}_p^t)^H\mathbf{H}_{pk}\mathbf{P}_p^t]^{-1}(\mathbf{H}_{pk}\mathbf{P}_p^t)^H \tag{4}$$

Since the operator has the property $\mathbf{E}_{\mathbf{H}_{pk}\mathbf{P}_p^t}^{\perp}\mathbf{H}_{pk}\mathbf{P}_p^t = 0$, the filter eliminates the interference from macro cell completely. Define equivalent channel $\widehat{\mathbf{H}}_{ij} = \mathbf{E}_{\mathbf{H}_{pk}\mathbf{P}_p^t}^{\perp}\mathbf{H}_{ij}$ and the received signal becomes $\widehat{\mathbf{r}}_k = (\overrightarrow{\mathbf{P}_k^r})^H(\sum_{l=1}^{K}\widehat{\mathbf{H}}_{lk}\overrightarrow{\mathbf{P}_l^t}\sqrt{G_l}\mathbf{s}_l + \mathbf{n}_k)$.

Secondly, to eliminate the interference from small cells to macro cell, we construct an orthogonal projection based precoding at the transmitter in the same way. Assuming $\mathbf{H}_{kp}$ and $\mathbf{P}_p^r$ of macro cell is known, the precoding is

$$\mathbf{E}_{\mathbf{H}_{kp}^H\mathbf{P}_p^r}^{\perp} = \mathbf{I} - \mathbf{H}_{kp}^H\mathbf{P}_p^r[(\mathbf{H}_{kp}^H\mathbf{P}_p^r)^H\mathbf{H}_{kp}^H\mathbf{P}_p^r]^{-1}(\mathbf{H}_{kp}^H\mathbf{P}_p^r)^H \tag{5}$$

And $(\mathbf{P}_p^r)^H\mathbf{H}_{kp}\mathbf{E}_{\mathbf{H}_{kp}^H\mathbf{P}_p^r}^{\perp} = 0$ based on the property. So far, the cross-tier interference is cancelled. Defining the further equivalent channel $\widehat{\mathbf{H}}_{OP,ij} = \widehat{\mathbf{H}}_{ij}\mathbf{E}_{\mathbf{H}_{kp}^H\mathbf{P}_p^r}^{\perp}$, the k-th small cell signal is $\widehat{\mathbf{r}}_{OP,k} = (\overrightarrow{\mathbf{P}_k^r})^H(\sum_{l=1}^{K}\widehat{\mathbf{H}}_{OP,lk}\overrightarrow{\mathbf{P}_l^t}\sqrt{G_l}\mathbf{s}_l + \mathbf{n}_k)$.

Thirdly, $\mathcal{P}_1$ is reduced to a standard MMSE IA problem after twice orthogonal projection processing. To solve the problem easily, the individual maximum transmitting power constraint $G_{max,k}$ is introduced and we have

$$(\mathcal{P}_2) \quad \min_{\{(\overrightarrow{\mathbf{P}_k^r},\overrightarrow{\mathbf{P}_k^t}),k=1,2,\dots,K\}} \sum_{k}^{K}\widehat{MSE}_{OP,k} = \sum_{k}^{K}E\{\|\widehat{\mathbf{s}}_k - \widehat{\mathbf{r}}_{OP,k}\|_F^2\} \tag{6}$$

$$s.t. E\{\|\overrightarrow{\mathbf{P}_l^t}\sqrt{G_l}\mathbf{s}_l\|_F^2\} \preceq G_{max,k}$$

$\mathcal{P}_2$ is solved by Lagrange multiplier method [14] with $\lambda_{\mathcal{P}_2,k}$ and get

$$\overrightarrow{\mathbf{P}_k^t} = [\sum_{l=1}^{K}(\widehat{\mathbf{H}}_{OP,kl})^H\overrightarrow{\mathbf{P}_l^r}(\overrightarrow{\mathbf{P}_l^r})^H\widehat{\mathbf{H}}_{OP,kl} + \lambda_{\mathcal{P}_2,k}\mathbf{I}]^{-1}(\widehat{\mathbf{H}}_{OP,kk})^H\overrightarrow{\mathbf{P}_k^r} \tag{7}$$

$$\overrightarrow{\mathbf{P}_k^r} = [\sum_{l=1}^{K}\widehat{\mathbf{H}}_{OP,lk}\overrightarrow{\mathbf{P}_l^t}(\widehat{\mathbf{H}}_{OP,lk}\overrightarrow{\mathbf{P}_l^t})^H + \sigma_k^2\mathbf{I}]^{-1}\widehat{\mathbf{H}}_{OP,kk}\overrightarrow{\mathbf{P}_k^t} \tag{8}$$

$$E\{\|\overrightarrow{\mathbf{P}_l^t}\sqrt{G_l}\mathbf{s}_l\|_F^2\} = G_{max,k} \tag{9}$$

where $k = 1, 2, \dots, K$. $\lambda_{\mathcal{P}_2,k}$ is solved by (9) in the same way as PC-PSIA, and omitted here. Then iteratively computes $\overrightarrow{\mathbf{P}_k^r}$ and $\overrightarrow{\mathbf{P}_k^t}$ until the final convergent result is obtained. It's clear that MMSE objective function is lower bounded which implies it converges. Besides, this general iterative algorithm allows for a distribution implementation in each small cell. The details are shown in Algorithm 1.

Algorithm 1. Orthogonal Projection based Polarization-Space IA Algorithm

Require: $\mathbf{P}_p^t$, $\mathbf{P}_p^r$, $\mathbf{H}_{ij}$, $\mathbf{H}_{ip}$, $\mathbf{H}_{pi}$, I_{th} and σ_k^2 for $i,j \in \{1,2,\ldots,K\}$.

Ensure: $\overrightarrow{\mathbf{P}}_k^t$, $\overrightarrow{\mathbf{P}}_k^r$, $\mathbf{E}_{\mathbf{H}_{kp}^H\mathbf{P}_p^r}^{\perp}$, $\mathbf{E}_{\mathbf{H}_{pk}\mathbf{P}_p^t}^{\perp}$, $k = 1,2,\ldots K$.

1: Construct $\mathbf{E}_{\mathbf{H}_{pk}\mathbf{P}_p^t}^{\perp}$ based on (4) and $\widehat{\mathbf{H}}_{ij} = \mathbf{E}_{\mathbf{H}_{pk}\mathbf{P}_p^t}^{\perp}\mathbf{H}_{ij}$, for $i,j \in \{1,2,\ldots,K\}$;

2: Construct $\mathbf{E}_{\mathbf{H}_{kp}^H\mathbf{P}_p^r}^{\perp}$ by (5) and $\widehat{\mathbf{H}}_{OP,ij} = \widehat{\mathbf{H}}_{ij}\mathbf{E}_{\mathbf{H}_{kp}^H\mathbf{P}_p^r}^{\perp}$, for $i,j \in \{1,2,\ldots,K\}$;

3: Initialize $\overrightarrow{\mathbf{P}}_k^t$, $k = 1,2\ldots,K$;

4: Calculate $\overrightarrow{\mathbf{P}}_k^r$, $k = 1,2,\ldots,K$ based on (8);

5: Solve $\lambda_{\mathcal{P}_2,k}$, $k = 1,2,\ldots K$ according to (9) and (7);

6: Update $\overrightarrow{\mathbf{P}}_k^t$, $k = 1,2\ldots,K$ according to (7) with solved $\lambda_{\mathcal{P}_2,k}$, $k = 1,2,\ldots K$;

7: Repeat step 4, 5 and 6 until converge or a certain number of iteration.

3.3 Interference Constrained Polarization-Space IA Algorithm

Obviously, we could further improve the performance of small cells with the cost of the limited interference to macro cell. Firstly, simplify $\mathcal{P}_1$ using filter $\mathbf{E}_{\mathbf{H}_{pk}\mathbf{P}_p^t}^{\perp}$ to eliminate the interference from macro cell to small cells. $\mathcal{P}_1$ becomes

$$(\mathcal{P}_3) \quad \min_{\{(\overrightarrow{\mathbf{P}}_k^r,\overrightarrow{\mathbf{P}}_k^t),k=1,2,\ldots,K\}} \sum_k^K \widehat{MSE}_{IC,k} = \sum_k^K E\{\|\widetilde{\mathbf{s}}_k - \widehat{\mathbf{r}}_k\|_F^2\} \tag{10}$$

$$s.t. \ I_{total} \leq I_{th}$$

Secondly, the interference constraint and the interference between small cells are addressed jointly based on $\mathcal{P}_3$. It is easy to have the receiving matrix

$$\overrightarrow{\mathbf{P}}_k^r = [\sum_{l=1}^K \widehat{\mathbf{H}}_{lk}\overrightarrow{\mathbf{P}}_l^t(\widehat{\mathbf{H}}_{lk}\overrightarrow{\mathbf{P}}_l^t)^H + \sigma_k^2\mathbf{I}]^{-1}\widehat{\mathbf{H}}_{kk}\overrightarrow{\mathbf{P}}_k^t \tag{11}$$

Unfortunately, the transmitting matrix is hard to solve. So an alternative and heuristic approach is provided by introducing a scalar factor $\beta \in \mathbb{C}$ which combats the effect of noise and scales the amplitude [15]. Rewrite $\mathcal{P}_3$ as

$$(\mathcal{P}_4) \quad \min_{\{(\overrightarrow{\mathbf{P}}_k^t,\beta_k),k=1,2,\ldots,K\}} \sum_k^K E\{\|\widetilde{\mathbf{s}}_k - \beta_k^{-1}\widehat{\mathbf{r}}_k\|_F^2\} \tag{12}$$

$$s.t. \ I_{total} \leq I_{th}$$

The construction of Lagrange dual objective function and the Karush-Kuhn-Tucker (KKT) conditions are omitted because of the space. We have

$$\overrightarrow{\mathbf{P}}_k^t = \beta_k\widetilde{\overrightarrow{\mathbf{P}}}_k^t \tag{13}$$

with

$$\widetilde{\overrightarrow{\mathbf{P}}}_k^t = [\sum_{l=1}^K (\widehat{\mathbf{H}}_{kl})^H\overrightarrow{\mathbf{P}}_l^r(\overrightarrow{\mathbf{P}}_l^r)^H\widehat{\mathbf{H}}_{kl} + \lambda_{\mathcal{P}_4,k}\beta_k^2(\mathbf{H}_{kp})^H\mathbf{P}_p^r(\mathbf{P}_p^r)^H\mathbf{H}_{kp}]^{-1}(\widehat{\mathbf{H}}_{kk})^H\overrightarrow{\mathbf{P}}_k^r \tag{14}$$

where $\lambda_{\mathcal{P}_4,k}$ is the Lagrange multiplier. Hypothesize all small cells contribute equally to the total interference power. Based on KKT conditions, we derive

$$\lambda_{\mathcal{P}_4,k}\beta_k^2 = \frac{K\sigma_k^2(\overrightarrow{\mathbf{P}_k^r})^H\overrightarrow{\mathbf{P}_k^r}G_k}{I_{th}} \tag{15}$$

The scale factor β_k aims to scale up the received target signal's power to maximize the sum rate of small cell. With the interference constraint I_{th} and the individual transmitting power constraint $G_{max,k}$, we have

$$(\mathcal{P}_5) \quad \max_{\{\beta_k,k=1,2,...,K\}} \sum_{k}^{K} Blog_2(1 + \frac{\|(\overrightarrow{\mathbf{P}_k^r})^H\widehat{\mathbf{H}}_{kk}\beta_k\overrightarrow{\mathbf{P}_k^t}\sqrt{G_k}\mathbf{s}_k\|_F^2}{\sum_{l\neq k}^{K}\|(\overrightarrow{\mathbf{P}_k^r})^H\widehat{\mathbf{H}}_{lk}\beta_l\widetilde{\mathbf{P}_l^t}\sqrt{G_l}\mathbf{s}_l\|_F^2 + (\overrightarrow{\mathbf{P}_k^r})^H\overrightarrow{\mathbf{P}_k^r}\sigma_k^2})$$

$$s.t. \quad I_{total} \leq I_{th}$$

$$E\{\|\overrightarrow{\mathbf{P}_l^t}\sqrt{G_l}\mathbf{s}_l\|_F^2\} \preceq G_{max,k} \tag{16}$$

where B is the identical bandwidth for each small cell. Since the objective function of (16) is easily verified to increase monotonically with β_k^2, so we have

$$\beta_k = \min(\sqrt{\frac{I_{th}}{Ktr((\mathbf{P}_p^r)^H\mathbf{H}_{kp}\widetilde{\mathbf{P}_k^t}G_k(\widetilde{\mathbf{P}_k^t})^H(\mathbf{H}_{kp})^H\mathbf{P}_p^r)}}, \sqrt{\frac{G_{max,k}}{(\widetilde{\mathbf{P}_k^t})^HG_k\widetilde{\mathbf{P}_k^t}}}) \tag{17}$$

Finally, iteratively compute $\overrightarrow{\mathbf{P}_k^r}$ and $\overrightarrow{\mathbf{P}_k^t}$ until the final convergent results are obtained. The considerations of convergence and distribution implementation are the same as that of OP-PSIA. The details are shown in Algorithm 2.

Algorithm 2. Interference Constrained Polarization-Space IA Algorithm

---

Require: $\mathbf{P}_p^t$, $\mathbf{P}_p^r$, $\mathbf{H}_{ij}$, $\mathbf{H}_{ip}$, $\mathbf{H}_{pi}$, I_{th} and σ_k^2 for $i,j \in \{1,2,\ldots,K\}$.

Ensure: $\overrightarrow{\mathbf{P}_k^t}, \overrightarrow{\mathbf{P}_k^r}, \mathbf{E}_{\mathbf{H}_{pk}\mathbf{P}_p^t}^{\perp}, k = 1,2,\ldots K.$

1: Construct $\mathbf{E}_{\mathbf{H}_{pk}\mathbf{P}_p^t}^{\perp}$ based on (4) and $\widehat{\mathbf{H}}_{ij} = \mathbf{E}_{\mathbf{H}_{pk}\mathbf{P}_p^t}^{\perp}\mathbf{H}_{ij}$, for $i,j \in \{1,2,\ldots,K\}$;

2: Initialize $\overrightarrow{\mathbf{P}_k^t}, k = 1,2\ldots,K$;

3: Calculate $\overrightarrow{\mathbf{P}_k^r}, k = 1,2,\ldots,K$ based on (11);

4: Solve $\lambda_{\mathcal{P}_4,k}\beta_k^2$ and $\beta_k, k = 1,2,\ldots K$ according to (15) and (17) respectively;

5: Update $\overrightarrow{\mathbf{P}_k^t}, k = 1,2\ldots,K$ by (13)(14) with solved $\lambda_{\mathcal{P}_4,k}\beta_k^2$ and $\beta_k, k = 1,2,\ldots K$;

6: Repeat step 3, 4 and 5 until converge or a certain number of iteration.

---

4   Simulation and Discussion

In this section, the performances of the proposed scheme are evaluated. Based on 3GPP specification for Long Term Evolution (LTE) [16] and cross-polarization

Table 1. Simulation parameters.

Parameter	Value	Parameter	Value
Macro cell transmit power	5 W	Small cell transmit power	1 W
XPD in macro cell	5 dB	XPD in small cell	7.5 dB
Number of small cells	3	Channel coding	Turbo-1/3
Data modulation	OFDM $\pi/4$-QPSK	Carrier frequency	2 GHz
Bandwidth	5 MHz	Number of subcarriers	512
Useful symbol time	6.4×10^{-6} s	Guard interval	1.25×10^{-6} s

discrimination (XPD) values of a typical Urban NLOS cell [17], the simulation parameters are shown in Table 1.

As is known, MIMO system with N_r receiving ODPAs and N_t transmitting ODPAs provides $2\min\{N_r, N_t\}$ DoFs. We consider two different scenarios. The first scenario sets $N_r = 2, N_t = 2$ meaning 4 DoFs for three small cells; The second scenario sets $N_r = 2, N_t = 1$ providing 2 DoFs. Three algorithms are compared with the proposed algorithms: (1) Iterative IA (IIA) [8]; (2) Max-SINR [8]; (3) Joint polarization adaption and beamforming (JPAB) [9].

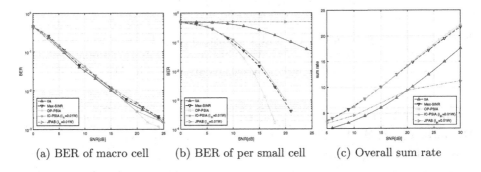

(a) BER of macro cell   (b) BER of per small cell   (c) Overall sum rate

Fig. 2. First scenario with $N_r = 2$, $N_t = 2$.

Comparing Figs. 2 and 3, three performances of each algorithm are significantly reduced with the decrease of DoFs. For example, the maximum overall sum rate in Fig. 2(c) is 1.2 times bigger than that in Fig. 3(c). This is because the less the DoFs, the less interference-free transmission dimensions are provided. Thus, the remaining interference and performance degradation are inevitable.

In the first scenario, OP-PSIA outperforms the other counterparts in BER performance of per small cell from Fig. 2(b) when macro cell's BER performances of all algorithms are almost equal in Fig. 2(a). The reason is OP-PSIA focuses on not only eliminating interference but also improving BER performance of small cell by MMSE optimization while IIA only cares about reducing interference and Max-SINR aims to maximize the receiving SINR. And performances of

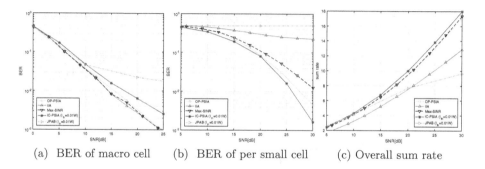

(a) BER of macro cell   (b) BER of per small cell   (c) Overall sum rate

Fig. 3. Second scenario with $N_r = 2$, $N_t = 1$.

JPAB are limited since only beamforming at transmitter is considered while the others jointly consider the beamforming at the transmitter and the interference suppression at the receiver. And it solves a sum rate optimization problem in a suboptimal way causing poor BER of small cells. As for IC-PSIA, the interference constraint term in (14) is considered as a little additional interference if DoFs is enough. From Fig. 2(c), the proposed algorithms and Max-SINR perform best because the goal of Max-SINR is to maximize the sum rate and the proposed algorithms using MMSE optimization perform as well as it.

In the second scenario from Fig. 3, the performance analyses of OP-PSIA, IIA and Max-SINR algorithms are the same as those in the first scenario. It is noted that the macro cell's BER performances of IC-PSIA and JPAB algorithms are degraded at high SNR from Fig. 3(a) because of the interference constraint. At high SNR, the decrease of noise makes the cross-tier interference from small cells a major effect for macro cell which degrades the BER performance. However, the per small cell's BER performance of IC-PSIA is greatly improved from Fig. 3(b). The reason is that the interference constraint condition enables IC-PSIA to further improve the BER performance of per small cell at the cost of the BER performance loss of macro cell. And another benefit is an improvement in the overall sum rate performance from Fig. 3(c).

5   Conclusion

We consider a cognitive heterogeneous cellular network (CHCN) with several polarized MIMO underlay small cells. And a novel polarization-space based interference alignment scheme is proposed to address the complex interference and improve the performances. Two algorithms, OP-PSIA and IC-PSIA, are given by orthogonal projection processing and MMSE optimization with analytically iterative solutions. OP-PSIA guarantees the protection of macro cell in any scenario while IC-PSIA, which maximizes the performance of small cells if permitted, is more suitable for the situation where DoFs are inadequate to the demand. The simulation results show the effectiveness of the proposed algorithms.

References

1. Tanab, M., Hamouda, W.: Resource allocation for underlay cognitive radio networks: a survey. IEEE Commun. Surv. Tuts. **19**(2), 1249–1276 (2017)
2. Peng, M., Wang, C., Li, J., Xiang, H., Lau, V.: Recent advances in underlay heterogeneous networks: interference control, resource allocation, and self-organization. IEEE Commun. Surv. Tuts. **17**(2), 700–729 (2015)
3. Guo, C., Liu, F., Chen, S., Feng, C., Zeng, Z.: Advances on exploiting polarization in wireless communications: channels, technologies, and applications. IEEE Commun. Surv. Tuts. **19**(1), 125–166 (2017)
4. Sharma, S.K., Chatzinotas, S., Ottersten, B.: Interference alignment for spectral coexistence of heterogeneous networks. EURASIP J. Wirel. Commun. Netw. **1**, 1–14 (2013)
5. Chen, Y., Wang, L., Sheen, W.: Joint user scheduling and interference alignment beamforming in heterogeneous wireless networks. In: IEEE PIMRC, pp. 1083–1087 (2014)
6. Lin, X., Guo, C., Zeng, Z., Li, D.: A novel interference avoidance scheme based on blind polarization signal processing for cognitive Femtocell network. In: Proceedings International Symposium Wireless Personal Multimedia Communications, pp. 40–44 (2012)
7. Gao, X., Guo, C., Chen, S.: Polarization-based cross-tier interference alignment in cognitive heterogeneous cellular network. In: International Symposium on Wireless Communication Systems (ISWCS), pp. 1–5 (2018)
8. Xu, T., Ma, L., Sternberg, G.: Practical interference alignment and cancellation for MIMO underlay cognitive radio networks with multiple secondary users. In: Proceedings IEEE GLOBECOM, pp. 1009–1014 (2013)
9. Li, D., Guo, C., Zeng, Z., Lin, X.: Dynamic spectrum sharing for TD-LTE and FD-LTE users based on joint polarization adaption and beamforming. In: IEEE 79th Vehicular Technology Conference (VTC Spring), Seoul, pp. 1–5 (2014)
10. Lu, E., Ma, T., Lu. I.T.: Interference alignment-like behaviors of MMSE designs for general multiuser MIMO systems. In: IEEE GLOBECOM, pp. 1–5 (2011)
11. Moreira, D.C., Silva, Y.C.B., Ardah, K., Freitas, W.C., F. R. P. Cavalcanti: Convergence analysis of iterative interference alignment algorithms. In: 2014 International Telecommunications Symposium (ITS), Sao Paulo, pp. 1–5 (2014)
12. Oestges, C., Clerckx, B.: MIMO Wireless Communications: From Real-World Progation to Space-Time Code Design. China Machine Press (2010)
13. Behrens, R.T., Scharf, L.L.: Signal processing applications of oblique projection operators. IEEE Trans. Sig. Process. **42**(6), 1413–1424 (1994)
14. Shen, H., Li, B., Tao, M., Luo. Y.: The new interference alignment scheme for the MIMO interference channel. In: Proceedings IEEE WCNC, pp. 1–6 (2010)
15. Joham, M., Utschick, W., Nossek, J.A.: Linear transmit processing in MIMO communications systems. IEEE Trans. Sig. Process. **53**(8), 2700–2712 (2005)
16. Evolved Universal Terrestrial Radio Access (E-UTRA): Further advancements for E-UTRA physical layer aspects, Third-Generation Partnership Project TR 36.814 (2010)
17. Guo, C., Wu, X., Feng, C., Zeng, Z.: Spectrum sensing for cognitive radios based on directional statistics of polarization vectors. IEEE J. Sel. Areas Commun. **31**(3), 379–393 (2013)

The Vision of 5G and the Need for Change in Mobile Spectrum Access

Peter Anker[1,2]([⊠])

[1] Technical University Delft, Delft, the Netherlands
peter.anker@telecomabc.com
[2] Ministry of Economic Affairs,
Bezuidenhoutseweg 73, 2594 AC The Hague, The Netherlands

Abstract. This paper discusses the need for change in the regulatory environment to cater for the next generation of mobile technology (5 G). It gives particular attention to provisioning of spectrum access for business specific services and applications and to possibilities to improve shared use of spectrum. It is proposed to broaden the market for mobile communication from a mobile operator specific market to a broadened market which is comprised of mobile operators, niche operators and service providers targeting specific business segments and private networks.

Keywords: 5G · Spectrum access · Sharing · LSA · Private networks
Unlicensed spectrum

1 Introduction

The vison of the next generation of mobile communications (5G) that differentiates it from the previous generations of mobile communications was first described by the International Telecommunications Union (ITU) when defining the overall vision and requirements for International Mobile Telecommunications for 2020 and beyond [1].

In the vision of the ITU, IMT-2020 is envisaged to expand and support diverse usage scenarios and applications that go beyond the usage scenarios of existing mobile communications. IMT-2020 is supposed to enable three different classes of usage scenarios:

1. Enhanced Mobile Broadband,
2. Massive Machine Type communications,
3. Ultra-reliable and low latency communications.

Enhanced Mobile Broadband expands the existing Mobile Broadband service offering. It addresses the human-centric use cases for access to multi-media content, services and data. Enhanced Mobile Broadband will improve the user experience in both wide area coverage as well as in hot spots, i.e. areas with high user density, a high traffic demand per user and low mobility compared to wide area coverage.

Massive Machine Type communications addresses the machine-centric use cases characterized by a very large number of connected devices typically transmitting a relatively low volume of non delay sensitive data. Devices are required to be low cost, and have a very long battery life. As such, it is an enabler of the Internet of Things.

© ICST Institute for Computer Sciences, Social Informatics and Telecommunications Engineering 2019
Published by Springer Nature Switzerland AG 2019. All Rights Reserved
I. Moerman et al. (Eds.): CROWNCOM 2018, LNICST 261, pp. 109–118, 2019.
https://doi.org/10.1007/978-3-030-05490-8_11

Ultra-reliable and low latency communications addresses use cases with stringent requirements for connectivity such as the throughput, latency and availability of the connection. Some examples include wireless control of industrial manufacturing or production processes, remote medical surgery, distribution automation in a smart grid and transportation safety.

This vision of 5G ties in with the trend in modern society with respect to (wireless) connectivity. Mobile connectivity is becoming a necessity for society with strong positive external effects on the economy. Connectivity is becoming a basic need for consumers who rely upon a diverse and affordable range of services. Connectivity is also becoming crucial for businesses for their services and internal business operations. Reliable connectivity is an enabler to strengthen their competitive position through costs savings, increased productivity and development of new applications.

5G is expected to drive industrial and societal transformations and economic growth by offering flexible and versatile mobile connectivity. It provides high-speed, reliable mobile broadband connectivity to enhance the capacity of wireless networks, to support new types of applications, to connect devices and objects in the Internet of Things and to cater for tailored services that fulfill the specific and stringent requirements needed by different industry sectors, also referred to as verticals [2, 3].

The question then is, how this vision of 5G can be realized and what the implications are on the regulatory provisions for spectrum access and spectrum sharing?

2   Providing 5G Services

The vision, as given in Sect. 1 above, gives an indication that 5G can be regarded as both an evolution of 4G, as well as a revolution. Many of the use cases build on the services provided by existing infrastructure. The existing mobile network already provides broadband services and IoT capabilities that will remain to be used. 5G will be introduced gradually to enhance the user experience and to provide ubiquitous connectivity for users and devices.

The capabilities that differentiates 5G from the previous generations is that it offers the possibility to tailor mobile data services to the particular characteristics of specific (business) users. Software Defined Networking and network virtualization provide possibilities to support a number of virtual networks over a single physical network. These so-called network slices will provide services to various business segments with performance characteristics such as bit rate, capacity, latency, availability and resilience, tailored for the needs of the specific business segment.

Business specific services may be offered by the existing mobile operators. However, not all business segments will need nationwide or wide area coverage. Many of the specific business needs will be needed in a limited area ranging from a somewhat larger area, such as a harbor, an airport or an industrial area to an even more limited area of a single factory. This area may even be limited to an indoor environment, e.g. in the case of industrial automation. As a consequence, it remains to be seen if the mobile operator will provide tailored solutions to these specific business segments in limited areas. It will depend on many factors if a mobile operators will serve a particular business segment. Factors that are of relevance are e.g. if there is a need for wide area coverage; how specific the requirements of the business customer are, as some business customers might have a requirement that is too specific or too difficult to meet for a mobile operator; and, how unique the solution is, as an operator is more inclined to offer a specific service if the same type of service can also be offered to other customers as well.

Another point is that the demand side will not have detailed knowledge of mobile connectivity. This will make it very hard for a customer to clearly specify their own requirements in terms of the performance characteristics of mobile connectivity.

This will provide opportunities for two new types of players. First of all, there is a role for a service provider or a Virtual Mobile Network Operators (VMNO) that targets one or more specific business segments. A VMNO that has specific and thorough knowledge of a specific business segment can serve as an intermediary between the mobile operator and the customer to translate the requirements of its customers to a targeted offer.

Secondly, this will provide opportunities for niche players to provide a business propositions for specific industries or factories, e.g. to the petrochemical industry in a harbor area or solutions for industrial automation in a factory or warehouse. There are already niche players active in the field of private mobile radio[1] and fixed wireless access that are in a good position to play a role. These kind of services have historically been delivered through distinct technologies. However, the technologies for these services are now converging. Both fixed wireless access and private mobile radio can make use of the same type of LTE and 5G technology as the mobile operators. Niche operators with a thorough understanding of a business segment can provide specific business services based on local infrastructure that is not easily delivered by mobile operators on their wide area network, e.g. a service that requires very low latency over a wireless connection for real-time control of an industrial process at an industrial plant. A recent study from Harbor Research indicated that the global private LTE network market will grow from $22.1 billion in 2017 to $118.5 billion in 2023 [4].

Other possibilities for niche players are to provide indoor solutions. A large portion of mobile communication needs are indoors and this will continue to be the case in the future. This market is hard to address for a mobile operator with his outdoor mobile network. This will provide opportunities for specific operators to provide indoor coverage with small cell infrastructure to complement the service offering of mobile operators [5].

The introduction of niche operators of local private outdoor and indoor networks can be arranged by providing licenses with a limited geographical area of operation. The ability to enter the market, although only on a local level, will make the market more contestable. Licenses for local usage will constrain the market power of the dominant (national) operators by the competitive fringe, which is important because the market for mobile communications tends towards consolidation. The national mobile operators cannot behave as being protected by high entry barriers, but must take the

---

[1] Private mobile radio means the use of radio communications for business purposes within a company, e.g. a taxi company to have contact between the drivers and the central dispatching unit.

activity of the competitive fringe into consideration. Hence there will be less need for government to regulate the behavior of the dominant national mobile operators [6].

3 Spectrum for 5G

The evolution of mobile communications cannot be decoupled from the availability of "new" spectrum. In Europe, the step from the first analogue systems to the second generation digital system (GSM) was made through the harmonized designation of the 900 MHz band, later followed by the 1800 MHz band. The third generation (UMTS) was developed in the 2100 MHz band.[2] The introduction of the 4th generation (LTE) started with the designation of the 2600 MHz band and later the 800 MHz bands. Nowadays, the different bands for mobile communication services are used for all generations of mobile technology with the introduction of UMTS and especially LTE in other bands to provide both coverage and capacity to the end user based on the requirements of the users and the actual spectrum holdings of the mobile operators.

To fulfill the requirements of 5G there is a need for additional spectrum. The Radio Spectrum Policy Group (RSPG), a high level group of Member States that advices the European Commission, has identified three bands for the introduction of 5G [3]:

1. The 3.6 GHz (3400–3800 MHz) band is seen as the primary band for the introduction of 5G services.
2. The 26 GHz (24.25–27.25 GHz) band is seen as the pioneering mm-wave band.
3. The 700 MHz band, together with existing bands for mobile communications.

These three bands have radically different characteristics and will be used differently. The 700 MHz band can be used to provide wide area and indoor coverage. The 3.6 GHz band can be used to provide high capacity and coverage, using both existing macro cells and small cells. The 26 GHz band is likely to be deployed in areas with very high demand, to provide ultra-high capacity for innovative new services, enabling new business models to benefit from 5G for example transport hubs, entertainment venues, industrial sites and retail sites. Because of its propagation characteristics, the 26 GHz band will not be used to create wide area coverage. In due course, the mobile operators could perform transition of lower frequency mobile spectrum (800, 900, 1800, 2100, 2600 MHz) to 5G, but some studies suggest that 4G LTE and its evolutions will continue to develop in parallel to 5G deployments [3].

The CEPT is studying the technical conditions and regulatory options for the use of the 3.6 and 26 GHz band in order to facilitate European harmonized introduction of 5G. The 3.4–3.8 GHz band is in Europe already harmonized for mobile and fixed communications networks (MFCN). The harmonized technical conditions are updated to incorporate the new 5G technology [7]. CEPT published harmonized technical conditions of the 26 GHz band (24.25 27.5 GHz) to enable its use in Europe and to promote the band for worldwide harmonization at the WRC-19 [8, 9].

---

[2] UMTS was first developed for 1920–1980 MHz paired with 2110–2170 MHz.

Frequency bands for the future development of International Mobile Telecommunications (IMT) are on the agenda for the World Radio Conference of 2019. The agenda item is especially targeted to the identification of frequency bands in the mm-wave range between 24 and 86 GHz. There are already a number of initiatives started in various countries and regions of the world to use mm-wave bands ahead of any decision made by the WRC-19. The main focus of these initiatives is in the 24.25–27.5 GHz (the 26 GHz band) and 27.5–29.5 GHz (the 28 GHz band). Whereby the United States, as well as Japan and Korea focus on the 28 GHz band, and Europe as well as other regions focus on the 26 GHz band.

In the European preparation of the WRC-19, the focus is on the 40.5–43.5 GHz band and the 66–71 GHz band, next to the pioneering 26 GHz band. The 66-71 GHz band is foreseen as a band for license exempt frequency use. License exempt frequency use is regarded as important breeding ground for innovation and will contribute towards a dynamic market environment [3].

4   Authorization of 5G Spectrum

Until now, mobile spectrum has been allocated usually on an exclusive, national basis. This approach has allowed mobile operators to avoid interference and deliver the expected Quality of Service experience for end users on a national level. However, it remains to be seen if the authorization of spectrum for 5G should be based totally on a national exclusive basis to realize the vision of 5G. As described above, the demand for business specific applications is to a large extend restricted to local areas without the need for wide area coverage. These applications may be provided by local networks. Realization of the vision of 5G may require local spectrum access by niche players and private networks to provide specific localized business applications and services next to national spectrum access for mobile operators.

4.1   Spectrum for Mobile Operators

Mobile operators will need additional spectrum to take advantage of the new possibilities 5G technology will offer. Their first applications will likely be enhanced mobile broadband services. Additional frequency bands for mobile operators is in Europe focused on the bands cited above in Sect. 3.

The 700 MHz band should be assigned to mobile operators and made available for wireless broadband use by 30 June 2020 at the latest in all EU Member states [10]. Moreover, the latest (stable) version of the new European Electronic Communications Code stipulates to assign sufficiently large blocks of spectrum in the 3,4–3,8 GHz band and at least 1 GHz of the 24.25 to 27.5 GHz frequency band, provided that there is clear evidence of market demand, before 31 December 2020 in order to facilitate roll-out of 5G.

Both the 700 MHz band and the 3.6 GHz band will be used to enhance wide area coverage and are therefore of vital importance for the mobile operators to facilitate 5G. European countries are now in a process of auctioning the 700 MHz band and the whole or a large part of the 3.6 GHz band. The 26 GHz will probably only be used in areas with a high demand and there is still some uncertainty around the technology as well as the market demand for this band. As a consequence, most countries in Europe are still in the process of defining the regulatory framework for the authorization of this band.

4.2   Spectrum for Niche Players and Private Networks

Business specific applications are already provided by PAMR operators and by solution providers to build a privately owned (PMR) network. The current offer is based on dedicated technology, such as TETRA, and is voice oriented, with restricted possibilities for data communications. There is a tendency to migrate to LTE and ultimately 5G to enable business specific broadband communications. However, this will require new and larger chunks of spectrum than available in the core bands for PMR and PAMR, mainly in the 400 MHz range.

Many of these networks will and can make use of existing unlicensed spectrum in the 5 GHz range. However, regulatory restrictions to allow unlicensed access, such as strict power limitations, will limit the possibilities to mainly indoor solutions. There might be a need for dedicated spectrum that can be used on an exclusive basis on the business premises (indoor and outdoor) to provide tailored solutions with the necessary quality of service.

Examples of private broadband networks can be found in e.g. France, where AGURRE (Association des Grands Utilisateurs de Réseaux Radio d'Exploitation) groups eleven key organizations, in the sectors of transport and energy, who need a broadband professional mobile network to fulfil the evolution of their operating and safety tasks.[3] A dedicated LTE network is built in the 2.6 GHz TDD band for airport operations. Other examples can be found in the Netherlands, where more than 100 licenses are issued in the 3.6 GHz band for local networks of which many are based on LTE. These licenses are used for a variety of (business) specific applications ranging from an automated container terminal in the Rotterdam harbor, to security and surveillance in cities and provisioning of wireless broadband services in underserved rural areas.

Since there is a need for mobile operators to introduce 5G in the 3.6 GHz band, the 3.6 GHz band will offer limited possibilities for local networks for niche players and privately owned solutions. The most likely opportunities are in the upper part of the band (especially 3700 to 3800 MHz) where licenses on a local basis could be made available in order to protect satellite earth stations that are active in the 3800–4200 MHz band. This possibility is chosen in e.g. Germany. In larger countries with limited satellite earth stations, there might also be possibilities in the 3800–4200 MHz itself. This possibility is under study in various countries, including the UK. [11].

Niche Spectrum for Niche Players

A more feasible possibility is to find "niche spectrum" for niche players to provide tailored local solutions. "Niche spectrum" in the sense that the spectrum is outside the

---

[3] Those organizations are the Aéroports de Paris Group, Air France, EDF, RATP, RTE, the Sanef Group, SNCF Mobilités, SNCF Réseau, Société du Grand Paris, SYTRAL and TIGF.

scope of the European harmonized bands for wide area coverage such as the existing bands for mobile operators. However, these niche bands should be part of the 3GPP standardization effort in order to take advantage of the economies-of-scale of the LTE and 5G ecosystem.

Various countries in Europe have already made spectrum available that is used to provide indoor solutions, based on spectrum in the 1800 MHz band (the Netherlands), 2.6 GHz TDD spectrum (e.g. in Belgium) or in the 3.6 GHz band (e.g. in Portugal and Ireland)

A "niche" band that could be used is the 2.3–2.4 GHz band. This band is harmonized for mobile communications, but in many countries not available for nationwide coverage due to incumbent use (mainly wireless cameras). Possibilities to make this band available will be explored in more detail in the next section.

Another possibility is the 1880–1900/1920 MHz band. The lower part of the band (1880–1900 MHz) is now harmonized in Europe for indoor cordless telecommunications (DECT). Possibilities to make the band available for other mobile technology (LTE and 5G) should be explored. The upper part of the band (1900–1920 MHz) could be made part of this study as a possible extension. This band is in most European countries not used. It used to be part of the 3G (UMTS) licenses, but the TDD component of UMTS was never used in Europe. The whole band of 1880–1920 is within the remit of 3 GPP standardization, and the band is used in China. Therefore, the handsets are already available.

A third possibility is the use of (parts of) the 26 GHz band. The band will only be used to provide ultra-high capacity in restricted areas. This will give possibilities to share the band between mobile operators and local networks.

4.3   Spectrum for Specific Verticals

5g is able to deliver a versatile and flexible mix of services that is tailored to the needs of a specific user group or a specific kind of usage. This includes the possibility to deliver public and societal services and applications that currently are provided through the use of dedicated spectrum allocations, such as public safety services (Public Protection and Disaster Relief) and services related to transport and traffic management (Intelligent Transport Systems). This may reduce the need for exclusive assignment of spectrum for those specific applications. Examples are the next generation of PPDR projects such as the Emergency Services Network (ESN) in the UK and FirstNet in the US.

However, there might still be instances where the vertical has very specific requirement and these will have to be assured to serve the public objectives. In that case, there still might be a need for dedicated spectrum. A good example can be found in the safety related aspects of ITS. Dedicated spectrum is set aside to assure the related safety service at all cost.

Governments should be very reluctant to set spectrum aside. Many verticals might state that the requirements are so unique that they need dedicated spectrum, while their needs could be served by a more generic network, as shown for PPDR above. Another example of today is the utility sector that claimed dedicated spectrum for smart meters. However, there are possibilities to provide smart meter readings as a service on an existing mobile or IoT network. This reduces the need for dedicated spectrum. However, there may be a need for the vertical sector to be involved in the standardization to assure that the needs of the vertical sector will be supported by the next generation of mobile technology as has been done by the PPDR and railway community. Both user groups provided their user requirements to the standardization activities of 3GPP.

5   The Need for Sharing

5G will provide new opportunities for spectrum sharing in both licensed and unlicensed spectrum. Spectrum sharing solutions can be used to make spectrum available on a local level for niche players. Sharing is thereby used to protect incumbent users and to allow different local 5G networks to coexist. Spectrum sharing will go beyond the traditional static sharing whereby spectrum is shared on a geographical basis. Spectrum sharing in 5G will be more dynamic. It will expand and enhance the spectrum sharing technologies already introduced in LTE.

A promising area of investigation is sharing between mobile operators and private local networks. These private networks are in most cases used in isolated spots (such as an industry plant or a warehouse) where there will be limited demand for wide area connectivity as provided by mobile operators. This gives possibilities to re-use part of the spectrum from the mobile operators for local networks. Coordination and time synchronization may be needed to prevent interference between the networks. Studies are needed to investigate the support of guaranteed QoS when sharing spectrum as well as QoS support when roaming from the local network to the wide area network.

Listen before talk mechanisms are used to share unlicensed spectrum, as e.g. introduced for MulteFire in the 5 GHz range. However the use of directional antennas and beamforming will pose a challenge. These narrow beams will be more difficult to detect. Although the chances of a collision are also reduced, the level of interference will be more excessive. Various mechanisms have been proposed to overcome this problem, ranging from beam coordination to centrally organized spectrum pooling arrangements [12, 13].

More dynamic forms of shared access that are already present in regulations are Licensed Shared Access (LSA) in Europe and Citizens Broadband Radio Service (CBRS) in the United States. CBRS is a three-tier sharing model for the 3550–3700 MHz band. This model allows secondary licensed access and tertiary unlicensed access to accommodate a variety of commercial uses on a shared basis with the primary incumbent federal and non-federal users of the band [14].

LSA is a sharing concept that is introduced in Europe to share spectrum between incumbents and (licensed) LSA-users. Licensed access would result in guarantees for spectrum access for both the incumbent and the licensed secondary user. It was introduced to provide spectrum access for mobile broadband in the 2.3–2.4 GHz range. New LSA work has started to address spectrum access for new entrants to provide locally deployed high-quality 5G networks [15].

The scope of LSA could be broadened to improve efficient shared use not only for the mobile operator, but also for incumbent users. To give an example, in a number of European countries, the incumbent users of the 2.3–2.4 GHz band are wireless cameras. These cameras are used on a temporarily basis in a limited geographical area to capture media events. In the Netherlands, a so-called booking system is used to reserve and acquire a license for this temporarily and local use. The booking system is used to optimize shared use of the band between the wireless cameras. Investigations are now ongoing if this optimized use will provide possibilities to introduce mobile communications in the band. There seem to be possibilities especially for local mobile networks targeted at specific business segments. Sharing between wireless cameras and local mobile networks is more promising than sharing between wireless cameras and mobile operators to provide enhanced mobile broadband. The reason being that the wireless cameras will normally not be used at company premises and industrial areas whereas wireless cameras are used to capture media events which are often also a hot spot area for mobile operators.

LSA based concepts can also be used to optimize the shared use of a band based on actual propagation conditions. Currently shared use is based on a worst case scenario for the propagation conditions. Hence there is ample room for improvement in shared use if the sharing can be based on more realistic and actual propagation conditions.

Recent measurements in the 3.6 GHz range have shown that the propagation conditions in this band are highly depending on the weather conditions. Worst case propagation conditions occur only for a very limited period of time per year and mainly in the evening till early morning hours [16]. Shared use of the 3.6 GHz band by mobile communications whilst protecting satellite earth stations could be greatly improved if the weather conditions are monitored and the geographical exclusion zone surrounding the satellite earth station is made smaller as long as the weather conditions allow to do so.

6   Conclusion

Realization of the vision of 5G to deliver reliable wireless connectivity tailored to the versatile needs of different business segments will require changes in the regulatory environment for mobile communications. It will require a departure from authorization purely based on auctioning nationwide licenses. Realization of the vision of 5G requires local spectrum access by niche players and private networks to provide specific localized business applications and services next to national spectrum access for mobile operators. Access to spectrum for 5G should be based on a combination of nationwide available exclusive licensed spectrum, exclusive local licensed spectrum and unlicensed spectrum access. This will put more emphasis on spectrum sharing. Technology can be used to make sharing more dynamic based on the actual demand and realistic propagation conditions to improve efficient use of shared spectrum.

References

1. ITU-R: Recommendation ITU-R M.2083 IMT Vision - Framework and overall objectives of the future development of IMT for 2020 and beyond. ITU, Geneva (2015)
2. GPPP: 5G empowering vertical industries. The 5G public private partnership, Brussels, April 2016
3. RSPG: RSPG18-005 Second Opinion on 5G networks: Strategic Spectrum Roadmap Towards 5G for Europe. RSPG, Brussels (2018)
4. Research, H.: Private LTE Networks Market Opportunity Paper (2017)
5. Matinmikko, M., et al.: Micro operators to boost local service delivery in 5G. Wireless Pers. Commun. **95**(1), 69–82 (2017)
6. Anker, P.: From spectrum management to spectrum governance. Telecommun. Policy **41**(5–6), 486–497 (2017)
7. CEPT Report 67: Report A from CEPT to the European Commission in response to the Mandate "to develop harmonised technical conditions for spectrum use in support of the introduction of next-generation (5G) terrestrial wireless systems in the Union" - Review of the harmonised technical conditions applicable to the 3.4–3.8 GHz ('3.6 GHz') frequency band, July 2018
8. ECC: ECC(16)110 Annex 17: CEPT roadmap for 5G 2016
9. ECC Decision : Harmonised technical conditions for Mobile/Fixed Communications Networks (MFCN) in the band 24.25–27.5 GHz, July 2018
10. Decision (EU) 2017/899 of the European Parliament and of the Council of 17 May 2017 on the use of the 470–790 MHz frequency band in the Union, Official Journal of the European Union L 138, pp. 131–137, 25 May 2017
11. Ofcom: Enabling 5G in the UK, discussion document, March 2018
12. Semaan, E., et al.: An outlook on the unlicensed operation aspects of NR. In: IEEE Wireless Communications and Networking Conference (WCNC) (2017)
13. Nekovee, M. Rudd, R.: 5G spectrum sharing, Crowncom (2017)
14. FCC 15–47: Order of reconsiderations and second report and order in the matter of Amendment of the Commission's rules with regard to commercial operations in the 3550–3650 MHz band, Federal Communications Commission, Washington (2015)
15. Matinmikko, M., et al.: On regulations for 5G: micro licensing for locally operated networks. Telecommun. Policy, **42**(8), 622–635 (2017)
16. Colussi, L.C., et al.: Multiyear trans-horizon radio propagation measurements at 3.5 GHz. IEEE Trans. Antennas Propag. **66**(2), 884–896 (2018)

Coexistence of LTE Networks Under LSA Paradigm in 2.6 GHz Band

Jaakko Ojaniemi[1,2]($\boxtimes$) (iD), Heikki Kokkinen[1], Arto Kivinen[1],
Georgios Agapiou[3], Stamatis Perdikouris[3], August Hoxha[3],
and Adrian Kliks[4] (iD)

[1] Fairspectrum, Otakaari 5, 02150 Espoo, Finland
{jaako.ojaniemi,heikki.kokkinen,arto.kivinen}@fairspectrum.com
[2] Aalto University School of Electrical Engineering, Espoo, Finland
[3] Hellenic Telecommunications Organization S.A. (OTE S.A.) OTE Group,
99 Kifissias Ave., 15124 Maroussi, Athens, Greece
gagapiou@ote.gr,{sperdikouris,ahoxha}@oteresearch.gr
[4] Poznan University of Technology, pl. M. Skłodowskiej-Curie 5,
60-965 Poznan, Poland
adrian.kliks@put.poznan.pl
https://www.fairspectrum.com
https://www.cosmote.gr

Abstract. This paper proposes a sharing scenario based on License Shared Access (LSA) framework with coexistence management between licensed Mobile Network Operator (MNO) and vertical MNOs. This allows the primary LSA license holder to lease the spectrum to the vertical operators when it is not used by the primary operator. We demonstrate the system in a real network consisting of two LTE-A base stations and core network, LSA Repository and LSA Controller. Furthermore, we implement the communication of the relevant network configuration parameters between the LSA Controllers in order to enable coexistence with interference-free conditions.

Keywords: Vertical spectrum sharing · LSA coexistence
CBRS model · Field trials

1 Introduction

One may observe that the concept of advanced spectrum usage through spectrum sharing, dynamic spectrum access or flexible spectrum management, has

The work has been funded by the EU H2020 project COHERENT (contract no. 671639). The work by Adrian Kliks was also supported by the Polish Ministry of Science and Higher Education funds for the status activity project "Cognitive and sustainable communication systems".

I. Moerman et al. (Eds.): CROWNCOM 2018, LNICST 261, pp. 119–132, 2019.
https://doi.org/10.1007/978-3-030-05490-8_12

become solid and mature in a broad sense [1,2]. It is nowadays well known that the static allocation of frequency resources among various stakeholders or technologies may lead to high resource underutilization, but at the same time, it seems to be the simplest and highly accurate way of protecting incumbent users from harmful interference. Therefore, exclusive use of spectrum bands is and will be still a dominant approach in the near future. Concurrently, unlicensed spectrum use such as Industrial, Scientific, and Medical (ISM) bands results to some extent in high spectrum utilization at the price of relatively high level of interference power observed in the allocated band. Flexible spectrum management is a tool that will try to solve the problem of ineffective spectrum usage while simultaneously lower the impact of interference phenomena. Moreover, it is now considered as a potential method or more effective approach for future applications by various stakeholders globally (such as Federal Communications Commission in USA (FCC), Conférence Eropéenne des administrations des Postes et des Télécommunications (CEPT) with European Telecommunications Standards Institute (ETSI) in Europe, Office of Communications (Ofcom) in UK, just to mention few).

Numerous researches, conducted experiments and even initial tests or trials in the field of spectrum sharing have paved the way for the currently observed trend in that domain [1,2]. Although it is currently not possible to guarantee accurately enough protection of the incumbent transmissions by relying on sole spectrum sensing and pure cognitive approach, the application of dedicated databases seems to be a pragmatic solution to this issue. It is widely suggested that such database-oriented solution should possess reasoning and learning capabilities on one hand side, and be supported by adjusted advanced monitoring and sensing functions on the other side [3–6] In this regard it is worth mentioning that ETSI is working on the implementation of the Licensed Shared Access (LSA) concept in the 2.3–2.4 GHz band [7,8]. Respectively, FCC created the foundations for dedicated solution for 3.5 GHz band, known as Citizen Broadband Radio Service (CBRS) [9]. Spectrum sharing has been also considered as an viable option for 5G networks [10–12], and from that perspective the application of LTE-A or New Radio (NR) base station operating in one of the two above mentioned regimes is of high interest.

LSA framework was introduced as a system allowing licensed and protected secondary use of spectrum for mobile network operators (MNO) by ETSI. The ETSI Reconfigurable Radio Systems, RRS, technical report [13] extends the concept by applying LSA for local and temporary licenses. The principal options for spectrum sharing between the operators and vertical sectors are the following: 1. first option - the spectrum users have different local or global priorities, 2. Second option, where the rule first-come-first-served is being applied, or 3. Last option - application of co-existence management, which tries to balance dynamically between demand and supply for spectrum.

In this demonstration we consider different priorities applied to coexisting operators (LSA licensees), which could be applied for example, when the mobile operator has a nation-wide license and it allows secondary use of the band locally by vertical sectors. The vertical sectors are private LTE operators in this demonstration. In short, in this paper we consider the implementation of the LSA model for simultaneous deployment of two LTE-A based networks operating in the frequency division duplexing (FDD) scheme, where one represents a national mobile operator and the other represents a local private LTE operator. To the extent of our knowledge, the proposed vertical sharing scheme where the coexistence of the LSA licensees is managed by the LSA Controller has not been demonstrated in the current literature related to LSA.

The paper is organized as follows. In Sect. 2 we briefly introduce the LSA and CBRS models. In Sect. 3, the system model and mechanisms to enable coexistence between the operators are described. Section 4 provides results of the field trials in a real LTE-A network. Section 5 concludes.

2   Foundations of LSA and CBRS Coexistence Model

So far, nearly all radio licenses for mobile broadband have been allocated with nationwide licenses. Mobile network operators have shared a specific frequency band in the frequency domain as block licenses. However, this approach makes it difficult for an operator to enter a new, possibly underutilized, area owned by another operator. This is especially difficult for smaller or virtual operators offering customized services for different use cases, who cannot compete in spectrum auctions with stronger operators. The high number of IMT bands and higher frequencies of the bands have initiated ideas of sharing mobile operator bands also geographically. The ideas include sub-leasing, neutral host operators, overlapping macro and small-cell networks, and local 5G licenses for industry verticals. In these proposals, two or more mobile operators potentially have adjacent geographical operating areas. In order to manage such a spectrum sharing schemes, two approaches are widely considered. These are briefly described for surveying purposes, as well as background introductory to the proposed modified LSA -based sharing system.

2.1   Licensed Shared Access - LSA

Licensed Shared Access (LSA) concept has been originally introduced by the Radio Spectrum Policy Group (RSPG) in its document [18] and was a response to the industry interests for new spectrum usage models. In principle, it aims at introducing new (additional) licensed users on spectrum bands currently assigned to other incumbent systems. By assumption, LSA concept assumes some level of volunteering, thus dedicated agreements between involved stakeholders are required. LSA model was a subject of intensive research, regulatory and standardization efforts, resulting in dedicated standards released by ETSI for 2.3–2.4 GHz band [7,8]. Ongoing regulatory activities are performed towards development of harmonized technical conditions, cross-border coordination, guidelines for the LSA sharing framework, incumbent usage, implementation examples, and technical sharing solutions specifically between the mobile broadband and incumbent PMSE service in the 2.3–2.4 GHz band [12]. As a result, a regulatory framework for LSA has been created, which assumes the presence of two dedicated entities operating on top of the existing network architectures. These are LSA Controller and LSA Repository (see Fig. 1). Whereas the former entity targets the assurance of the incumbent user protection (through calculation of the protection areas, analyzing from various perspectives various interference-related aspects etc.), the latter acts as the advanced repository for storage and updating the information about spectrum availability and usage. The summary of the spectrum sharing evolution towards LSA can be found in [19].

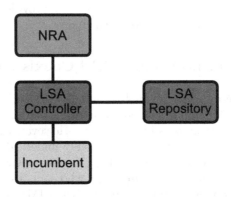

Fig. 1. LSA functional architecture

It is also worth mentioning that on February 2018 ETSI has released the feasibility study on temporary spectrum access for local high-quality wireless networks [13], which further strengthens the motivation for conducting the LSA-focused experiment with two coexisting MNOs operating in the 2.6 GHz. The considered scheme as well as the conducted experiment are described in the following sections.

2.2 Citizen Broadband Radio Service - CBRS

Citizen Broadband Radio Service (CBRS) with Spectrum Access System is the solution promoted recently by Federal Communications Commission (FCC) in the USA. It allows to utilize the contiguous 150 MHz width fragment of spectrum in the 3.5 GHz band, mainly between 3550 MHz and 3700 MHz. In general, this model foreseen simultaneous coexistence of multiple systems (also multiple wireless technologies) under specific circumstances, which guarantee the Quality-of-Service fulfilment of any protected user. In that context, three tiers solution has been created, which allows for hierarchical spectrum sharing (between the tiers) and vertical spectrum sharing (within the tier) [9,17].

In particular, the highest tier encompasses Incumbent Users (IU) which require full protection from harmful interference originated from lower layers (other systems coexisting in this band). The IUs include military and mete-orological radar systems, as well as grandfathered Fixed Satellite Service and grandfathered Wireless Broadband. These systems may operate in the entire band considered for CBRS systems. No additional permission (beside the one obtained from the regulator) is required, and the IUs may start transmission any time it is necessary. The second tier consists of so called Prioritized Access License (PAL) users, which may utilize up to 70 MHz of band within the 3550–3650 MHz band (the remaining 50 MHz band is excluded from PAL usage). Each PAL base station may send requests for multiplication of 10 MHz band to Spectrum Access System (SAS), and SAS should allocate only contiguous fragment of the spectrum. SAS can be treated as a dedicated entity for spectrum and interference management in the CBRS model, but designated to control the second tier of users (PALs). Finally, the General Authorized Access (GAA) users are considered to constitute the lowest, third layer of the CBRS system, which must protect the upper tier users and must accept possible interference generated towards them. GAA devices may operate in the entire band. Figure 2 depicts the three tier model.

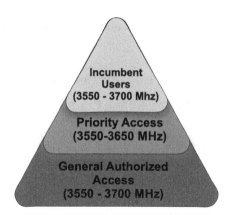

Fig. 2. Three tier CBRS model

Following the CBRS Alliance standard [16], a group of Citizens Broadband Radio Service Devices (CBSDs) may create a group (called Coexistence Group), where all the group members are abide to the same interference and spectrum managements policies. Dedicated logical entity, called Coexistence Manager will facilitate the operation of tier-3 users by management of all CBSDs within the group.

Although in this work we concentrate on the LSA applied to LTE networks with a similar coexistence functionality as introduced in the CBRS framework, let us note that major parts of the aforementioned CBRS model with a coexistence management has been tested recently on a real network in Poznan, Poland, described in [14].

3 LTE Coexistence - Vertical Spectrum Sharing Scheme for 2.6 GHz

An LSA sharing scenario is implemented where one eNodeB (eNB) acts as a primary mobile operator and has the highest priority, while the other eNB is a Private LTE operator and has a lower priority - see Fig. 3. The experiment has been conducted using OTE (one of the Greek network operators) premises and network equipment. All eNBs used in this experiment were part of the fully operational network with its own network management system deployed in Athens, Greece. The spectrum management system consisting of LSA Repository and Controller is implemented in Fairspectrum's server physically separated from the controlled LTE networks. Fairspectrum LSA Controllers can access the eNBs through remote access from a virtual machine located in OTE's facilities.

The 2.6 GHz FDD band 7 is considered with downlink frequencies 2620–2690 MHz and 10 MHz channel bandwidth (respectively, possible Evolved-UTRA Absolute Radio Frequency Numbers, EARFCN, for downlink transmission have been set to 2800–3400, and for uplink to 20800–21400). In the testbed in OTE premises, there are two 2.6 GHz FDD eNBs connected to core network. Although there are only two operators in the demonstration, the scheme can be generalized to account for multiple core networks and eNBs due to the distributed eNB Controllers.

3.1 Applied LSA Interference Protection Mechanism

In our demonstration, the LSA controller (C1 and C2) in Fig. 3 is a software implementation responsible of polling parameters from the eNBs, such as GPS coordinates, possible transmit power levels, current transmit channel, link status etc., committing the new operational parameters to the eNBs, and informing the Repository of the current parameters of each operator. Furthermore, the communication between LSA Repository and LSA Controller direction contains the operator priority class, used channel, transmit power, interference-to-noise-ratio criteria, bandwidth, noise figure, and adjacent channel leakage ratio (ACLR). These parameters are necessary for Controller to manage the coexistence.

The LSA Repository manages the timing of the necessary operations and assigns priority classes to the operators. The priority classes can be determined beforehand by the National Regulatory Authority (NRA) and input in the LSA Repository, or agreed through a mutual agreement between the operators. Furthermore, the Repository (LR) informs the operational parameters to the Controllers (LC) upon request.

The process flow consisting of information exchange and interference protection mechanisms is illustrated in Fig. 4, and described in the following:

1. Each Controller polls the parameter values from the eNBs every 60 s through a dedicated tool which is a part of the operator's Operations, administration and management system (OAM). The Controller chooses the best channel as

$$ch_{max} = \arg\max_{i} \{\mathbf{eirp}(i)\}, \qquad i = 1 \dots M$$

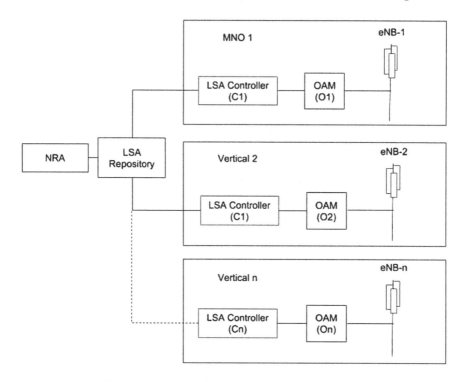

Fig. 3. Illustration of the experimentation system

where **eirp** is a vector containing the maximum EIRP values for each M 10 MHz channels for the eNB location, and the corresponding EIRP value, $eirp_{max} = \mathbf{eirp}(ch_{max})$. The EIRP values are based on path losses using the Extended Hata propagation [20] model between the interference source (eNB) and the protection contour of the other operator(s). Specifically, the EIRP value per channel is specified as:

$$\text{EIRP} \leq -174 + 10 \, log_{10}(BW) + NF + \frac{I}{N}$$
$$+ L_{eHata}(h_t, h_r, d, c) - G_t - G_r, \tag{1}$$

where BW is the channel bandwidth in Hz, NF is the noise figure, $\frac{I}{N}$ is the interference to noise ratio, $L_{eHata}(h_t, h_r, d, c)$ is the path loss with a distance d between the eNB transmit antenna and the protection contour of the protected mobile network, c is the clutter type (urban, suburban, open) at the receiver location, h_t, h_r are the transmitter and receiver heights, and G_r, G_t are the transmit and receive antenna gains, respectively. The protection contour limit, γ, can be for example specified as the limit where the useful signal level of -80 dBm/10 MHz is observed.

2. The Repository provides the available licensee data to the Controller (in general, Repository also contains incumbent data which, however, in this

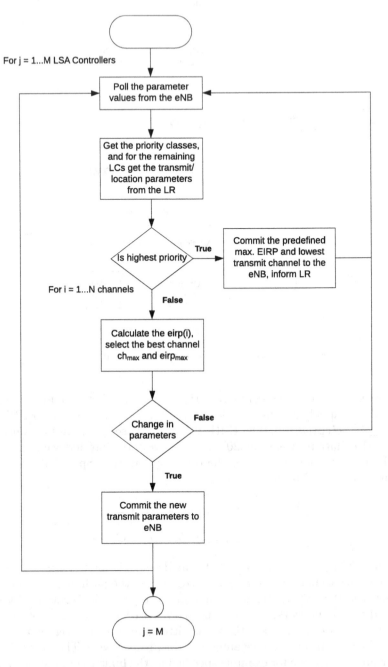

Fig. 4. Flow chart of the algorithm.

demonstration is not considerer). Since there are no other operators using the spectrum according to the provided data, the EIRP limit is set to predetermined maximum, i.e. 47 dBm for each channel. The controller then assigns the first available frequency (2620–2630 MHz) as the transmit channel with an appropriate EIRP for the eNB. The Controller commits the new transmit parameters to the eNB and informs this data also to the Repository.

3. Subsequently (or simultaneously), the Controller polls the values from the second eNB and synchronizes the licensees' data from the Repository. In this case, the protection contour of the first eNB is calculated and its transmit channel is taken into account in calculating the **eirp** vector if the priority class of the first operator is higher than that of the second operator. If the priority class of the second operator is higher than the priority class of the first operator the second Controller can assign the channel used by the lower priority operator to the higher priority operator. In this case, the second Controller bypasses all the lower priority protection contours in the calculation of the EIRP list for the second eNB. The controller then chooses the best channel for the second eNB, and notifies the Repository. The Repository further informs other Controller(s) to make a new calculation of the EIRP list based on the provided parameters and adjust their operational parameters.

4. Simultaneously, the Repository instructs each Controller to poll the parameter values from the eNBs every 60 s, and the process begins from the start (item 1 above). If there are no parameter changes, e.g. no priority class changes or location changes, or there are no new Controllers connected to the network, the system remains stable (no commits are made to the eNBs), and the eNBs continue to transmit on their current allocated channels and powers.

4   Field Trial Results

In the experiment, two LTE networks will operate dynamically within the 2.6 GHz band: the private network is of lower priority with regards to the MNO LTE network. The spectrum is monitored with Tektronix spectrum analyzer connected to a laptop. In the figures, 2600–2700 MHz band is shown (center frequency = 2650 MHz, span = 100 MHz, resolution bandwidth $rBW = 500$ KHz). The configuration parameters are presented in Table 1.

The demonstration begins by setting the lower priority Private LTE eNB on center frequency 2625 MHz with 10 MHz BW and transmit power P_t as 24 dBm (Fig. 5. The possible transmission power, P_t, for the eNBs are 17 to 24 dBm with one dB interval. The spectrum mask of the private LTE is shown on 2620–2630 MHz. On the right hand side of the spectrum at around 2670–2690 MHz band is unknown traffic not relevant to this demonstration. Next, as shown in Figs. 6 and 7, the higher priority MNO chooses the transmission channel currently operated by the private LTE. The private LTE is forced to choose another channel, and due to the adjacent channel leakage power the second best channel is at 2645 MHz (as shown in Fig. 8).

Table 1. Configuration parameters

Parameter	Value
N	$-104\,\text{dBm}$
NF	$4\,\text{dB}$
BW	$10\,\text{MHz}$
ACLR	$42\,\text{dB}$
h_t, h_r	$10\,\text{m}, 1.5\,\text{m}$
c	suburban
G_t	$10\,\text{dB}$
G_r	$0\,\text{dB}$
γ	$-80\,\text{dBm}/10\,\text{MHz}$
P_t	$[17...24]\,\text{dBm}$

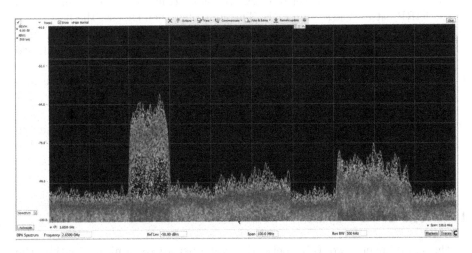

Fig. 5. Experimentation course, Phase 1 - private LTE network operates normally on $f_c = 2625$ MHz, the primary MNO has made a reservation on the same channel.

4.1   Lesson Learned

1. The delay of the Controller obtaining the configuration parameters of the other operator from the Repository depends on the selected polling interval, which in our tests was set to 60 s. However, since the commission of new parameters to the eNBs took nearly the same time, decreasing the interval does not drastically speed up the channel assignment. However, the commission time is device and network management system specific and cannot be generalized. Some eNBs and core network systems may response more rapidly and the polling interval would then offer more flexibility to control the response time. In total, the transmit channel change took around 3 min for the eNB to block the current transmission and switch to a different fre-

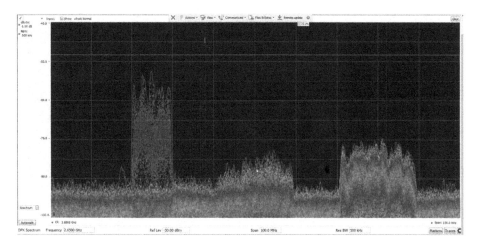

Fig. 6. Experimentation course, Phase 2 - private LTE network is forced to switch off the transmission and move to another channel.

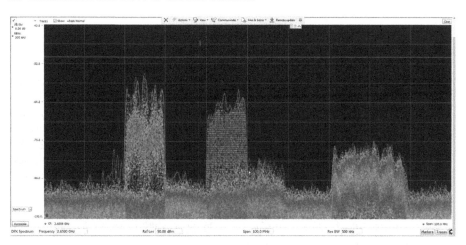

Fig. 7. Experimentation course, Phase 3 - private LTE starts transmission in the new channel.

quency band, which is adequate in a practical sharing scenario, where the channel reservation can be known hours or days beforehand.

2. Spectrum resources are scarce and expensive, thus spectrum sharing creates new opportunities for operators. Sharing decreases CAPEX and therefore it is beneficial from financial perspectives. It also provides the means to have a better utilization of the spectrum resources at periods of time with low network traffic. Furthermore, if operator decides to enter a new geographical area owned by another operator it will be much less costly to use the unused spectrum, while opening services to the end users can be started quickly. The

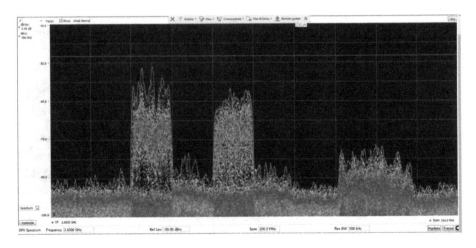

Fig. 8. Experimentation course, Phase 4 - both LTE networks operate simultaneously.

opportunities offered by spectrum sharing in a fashion demonstrated in this paper are based on CAPEX reduction, better resource utilization and low cost entry in a new band much quicker than waiting for regulatory license contests, which is an uncertain method of obtaining spectrum resources to many smaller, vertical or virtual operators.

3. To enable coexistence between the licensees the LSA framework could consider feedback from the LSA Controllers to the LSA Repositories (or a similar logical entity) regarding the licensees' network parameters, which in turn could provide the relevant information on network configuration parameters back to the Controllers. In our trials, we implemented successfully this information exchange, which enabled the Controllers to make the necessary protection calculations and assign the new frequency bands to the operators, thus avoiding interference conditions. It is clear that in order to implement this kind of feedback further studies would be needed, especially on the communication protocol, and exactly what parameters are possible to exchange in a large scale multi-operator environment. Moreover, in case that there are multiple vertical operators competing the primary licensees' spectrum, there should some kind of centralized reservation system where the vertical operators could make reservations of their spectrum use.

5 Conclusions

In this paper we presented briefly the LSA and CBRS systems, and proposed License Shared Access -based sharing scenario with a coexistence management between the licensees similar than that of the CBRS's. This allows the primary LSA license holder to lease the spectrum to the vertical operators when it is not used by the primary operator. We demonstrated the system successfully in a real network setting consisting of two LTE-A base stations, core network, LSA Repository and LSA Controller. Furthermore, we implemented the communication of the relevant network parameters between the LSA Controllers through the LSA Repository in order to enable coexistence without channel collision and harmful interference.

References

1. Tehrani, R.H., Vahid, S., Triantafyllopoulou, D., Lee, H., Moessner, K.: Licensed spectrum sharing schemes for mobile operators: a survey and outlook. IEEE Commun. Surv. Tutorials **18**(4), 2591–2623 (2016). https://doi.org/10.1109/COMST. 2016.2583499
2. Galiotto, C., Papageorgiou, G.K., Voulgaris, K., Butt, M.M., Marchetti, N., Papadias, C.B.: Unlocking the deployment of spectrum sharing with a policy enforcement framework. IEEE Access **6**, 11793–11803 (2018). https://doi.org/10.1109/ ACCESS.2018.2799244
3. Li, Y.: Grass-root based spectrum map database for self-organized cognitive radio and heterogeneous networks: spectrum measurement, data visualization, and user participating model. In: 2015 IEEE Wireless Communications and Networking Conference (WCNC), Istanbul, pp. 117–122 (2015) https://doi.org/10.1109/ WCNC.2015.7127455
4. Wang, N., Gao, Y., Evans, B.: Database-augmented spectrum sensing algorithm for cognitive radio. In: 2015 IEEE International Conference on Communications (ICC), London, pp. 7468–7473 (2015) https://doi.org/10.1109/ICC.2015.7249520
5. Sodagari, S.: A secure radio environment map database to share spectrum. IEEE J. Sel. Top. Sig. Process. **9**(7), 1298–1305 (2015). https://doi.org/10.1109/JSTSP. 2015.2426132
6. Caso, G., Nardis, L.D., Benedetto, M.G.D.: Toward context-aware dynamic spectrum management for 5G. IEEE Wirel. Commun. **24**(5), 38–43 (2017). https:// doi.org/10.1109/MWC.2017.1700090
7. ETSI: Reconfigurable Radio Systems (RRS); System architecture and high level procedures for operation of Licensed Shared Access (LSA) in the 2300 MHz – 2400 MHz band. TS 103 235 V1.1.1 (2015–10)
8. ETSI: Reconfigurable Radio Systems (RRS); System requirements for operation of Mobile Broadband Systems in the 2300 MHz – 2400 MHz band under Licensed Shared Access (LSA). ETSI TS 103 154 V1.1.1, October 2014
9. FCC: PART 96- CItizens Broadband Radio Service, Title 47 - Telecommunications, Chapter I, Subchapter D, Part 96. https://www.ecfr.gov. Accessed 19 Apr 2018
10. Radio Spectrum Policy Group, RSPG: Strategic roadmap towards 5G for Europe. Opinion on spectrum related aspects for next-generation wireless systems (5G). RSPG16-032 FINAL, Brussels, 09 November 2016. http://rspg-spectrum.eu/wp-content/uploads/2013/05/RPSG16-032-Opinion_5G.pdf. Accessed 19 Apr 2018
11. METIS-II project: Deliverable D3.2, Enablers to secure sufficient access to adequate spectrum for 5G. Deliverable of the Mobile and wireless communications Enablers for Twenty-twenty (2020) Information Society - II (METIS-II) project, under grant agreement 671680 (2017). https://metis-ii.5g-ppp.eu/wp-content/ uploads/deliverables/METIS-II_D3.2_V1.0.pdf. Accessed 19 Apr 2018
12. COHERENT project: Deliverable D4.2, Final report on flexible spectrum management (2017). http://www.ict-coherent.eu/coherent/wp-content/uploads/2018/03/ COHERENT_D4.2_v8.pdf. Accessed 19 Apr 2018

13. ETSI: Reconfigurable Radio Systems (RRS); Feasibility study on temporary spectrum access for local high-quality wireless networks. TR 103 588 V1.1.1, February 2018
14. Kliks, A., Kryszkiewicz, P., Kułacz, Ł., Kowalik, K., Kołodziejski, M., Kokkinen, H., Ojaniemi, J., Kivinen, A.: Application of the CBRS model for wireless systems coexistence in 3.6–3.8 GHz band. In: Marques, P., Radwan, A., Mumtaz, S., Noguet, D., Rodriguez, J., Gundlach, M. (eds.) CrownCom 2017. LNICST, vol. 228, pp. 100–111. Springer, Cham (2018). https://doi.org/10.1007/978-3-319-76207-4_9
15. Sohul, M.M., Yao, M., Yang, T., Reed, J.H.: Spectrum access system for the citizen broadband radio service. IEEE Commun. Mag. **53**(7), 18–25 (2015). https://doi.org/10.1109/MCOM.2015.7158261
16. CBRS Alliance: CBRS Coexistence Technical Specification, CBRSA-TS-2001, V1.0.0, 1 February 2018. https://docs.wixstatic.com/ugd/0c1418_6f589bffdfc34377a74c52453cd08656.pdf. Accessed 19 Apr 2018
17. Parvez, I., Sriyananda, M.G.S., Güvenç, İ., Bennis, M., Sarwat, A.: CBRS spectrum sharing between LTE-U and WiFi: a multiarmed bandit approach. Mobile Inf. Syst. **2016**, 12 (2016). https://doi.org/10.1155/2016/5909801
18. Radio Spectrum Policy Group, RSPG: Report on collective use of spectrum (CUS) and other spectrum sharing approaches, RSPG 11–392, November 2011
19. Mustonen, M., et al.: An evolution toward cognitive cellular systems: licensed shared access for network optimization. IEEE Commun. Mag. **53**(5), 68–74 (2015). https://doi.org/10.1109/MCOM.2015.7105643
20. NTIA: 3.5 GHz exclusion zone analyses and methodology. U.S. Department of commerce - National Telecommunications and Information Administration. Technical report 15–517 (2017)

Pricing Private LTE and 5G Radio Licenses on 3.5 GHz

Heikki Kokkinen[1]([✉]), Seppo Yrjölä[2], Jan Engelberg[3],
and Topias Kokkinen[1]

[1] Fairspectrum Oy, Otakaari 5, 02150 Espoo, Finland
info@fairspectrum.com
[2] Nokia, Oulu, Finland
seppo.yrjola@nokia.com
[3] Finnish Communications Regulatory Authority, Helsinki, Finland
jan.engelberg@ficora.fi

Abstract. The interest in private LTE and private 5G radio licenses is increasing along the IMT frequency bands, higher frequencies, new spectrum assignments, and demand for wireless industrial communication. This paper studies the private LTE and 5G license pricing using Finland as an example. The methods for pricing are the actual block license-based frequency fee pricing, Administrative Incentive Pricing (AIP), device based Private Mobile Radio pricing, and the device-based pricing of the Netherlands. The study shows that the selection of the pricing mechanism greatly impacts the license prices. Spectrum policy and regulation can be the trigger for novel private network ecosystem creation through creation of simple authorization processes to reduce the cost and minimize the complexity of use of spectrum for private LTE. In particular, provision of clear rules and guidance for spectrum valuation and pricing for the national regulator itself, as well as for the stakeholders wanting to supply and operate private LTE was found essential in reducing the cost and minimizing the complexity of private LTE spectrum use.

Keywords: Mobile communication market · Private networks
Spectrum pricing · Spectrum sharing · Regulation · 5G

1 Introduction

The increase of private LTE and 5G networks stem from the following changes in the society: explosion in number of IMT frequency bands, higher frequency ranges, new types of radio licensing for 3GPP technologies, and demand for wireless industrial communication. The private LTE concept is an enabler for industrial automation and it is realizable now. The roll out of private LTE and future 5G is constrained by an inability to access quality spectrum timely. Authorization of this spectrum is required on a localized basis in contrast to the national and exclusive basis that has applied for mobile network operators providing services to the public to date. The benchmark pricing of private LTE and 5G licenses is challenging, because the prices of nationwide

© ICST Institute for Computer Sciences, Social Informatics and Telecommunications Engineering 2019
Published by Springer Nature Switzerland AG 2019. All Rights Reserved
I. Moerman et al. (Eds.): CROWNCOM 2018, LNICST 261, pp. 133–142, 2019.
https://doi.org/10.1007/978-3-030-05490-8_13

mobile broadband radio licenses for public networks are considered to be very high and the radio licenses for private wireless networks very low.

The Evolved Universal Terrestrial Radio Access (E-UTRA) mobile broadband frequency bands have grown from 17 in 3GPP release 8 in 2007 to 60 in release 15 in 2017 [1, 2]. The difference in the number of frequency bands supported in eNodeBs and User Equipment (UE) globally and the number of frequency bands taken into use in an arbitrary country has grown even faster. It means that there are commercial off-the-shelf mobile devices and networks available for the frequency bands, which are not used by the mobile operator. Some of these bands could be potential for private LTE and 5G networks.

In 3GPP release 8 in 2007, the frequency bands reached at highest 2620 MHz [1], and in 2017 in release 15, the frequency bands went up to 5925 MHz [2]. For future 5G use, European Commission Radio Spectrum Policy Group (RSPG) recommends the 24.25–27.5 GHz as a pioneer band in Europe and considers that the band 40.5–43.5 GHz is a viable option for 5G in the longer term [3]. According to Global System Mobile Association (GSMA), the coverage bands are on the mobile broadband frequency bands 1.4 GHz and below [4]. The higher frequency bands are capacity band and their primary purpose is to provide capacity in densely populated areas. The capacity bands are potential for private LTE and private 5G due to limited coverage of the public mobile operator network and interference of private LTE and 5G networks only on a limited geographic area.

Practically, all deployed mobile broadband networks have block licenses. it means licensing of a block of spectrum on an area-defined basis [5]. The emerging licensing methods include license-exempt [6], Licensed Shared Access (LSA) evolution [7], and Citizen's Broadband Radio Service (CRBS) [8]. Spectrum assignments based on them lack coverage requirements, encourage for small mobile broadband networks, and decrease cost of spectrum access for private LTE and 5G networks. The most common alternative to the block licenses are device licenses. In the case of LTE or 5G networks, the price of the license is based on the number of the eNBs in the license.

The performance dimensions of 5G are: enhanced Mobile Broadband (eMBB), massive Machine Type Communications (mMTC), and Ultra-Reliable and Low Latency Communications (URLLC). They have been developed to support the requirements of vertical industries like factory automation. The main approach to satisfy the different Key Performance Indicators (KPI) of the various performance dimensions by a Mobile Network Operator (MNO) is to deploy network slicing [9]. Alternatively, the vertical industries may operate their 5G network using an own radio license, or a license traded or subleased from a MNO [10]. Key to the success of private network solutions is the ability to access suitable harmonized mobile spectrum in required locations in a timely way and on appropriate terms. This is likely to be challenging given the current approach to assignment of this spectrum, the lack of active secondary spectrum markets, and the very limited use of spectrum sharing in these bands.

The cost of getting and holding a radio license typically consists of a one-time auction price, a recurring frequency fee, or both of them. In Finland, the auction prices are market based and the auction payments go to general public treasury, whereas the frequency fees are used to cover the costs of the National Regulatory Authority (NRA).

As the regulator is a governmental non-profit organization, the frequency fee level is adjusted to the cost of administration, and not market based in 2018. The Finnish Information Society Code [11] added a possibility for Administrative Incentive Pricing (AIP) for the situations that a network license for telecommunications and television operations has been granted free of charge by the Government. The Finnish AIP is applicable in the cases where there is a lot of demand for the licenses and auctions or other market mechanisms have not been used in the spectrum assignment. In addition to AIP or auction, the spectrum holder also has to pay the frequency fee. The frequency fees in the UK, Sweden, Norway, Denmark, Ireland, Czech Republic were studied in [12].

In market economy, the price reflects supply and demand. When there is little liquidity due to limited supply or demand, the auctions do not work and price equilibrium between demand and supply is difficult to quantify [13]. Instead, different valuation methods are required. Valuation methods can be categorized into engineering value [14], Economic value [15], and strategic value [16]. The approaches for radio license pricing include: Direct benchmarking, Adjusted benchmarking, Econometrics, Avoided cost models, Full enterprise valuation, and Iterated cost models [5].

A larger scale of private LTE or private 5G network licensing is expected to begin in the band 3.4–3.8 GHz [17]. The reasons for that are: it has been selected as a 5G pioneer band [18], the LTE bands (42, 43, and 48) have been specified quite recently, and the equipment is appearing on the market. As a capacity band, the mobile operators will not deploy a large coverage network like in the coverage bands. Due to several incumbent governmental and commercial users in the band, it is difficult to clear the whole band for mobile broadband in most countries encouraging to local licensing. Local licensing regulation has been taken into use in the 3.5 GHz band in the Netherlands [19, 20], in Germany [21], and in Ireland [22]. It is about to come out in the US very soon [8] and it is considered e.g. in Finland.

Although, the spectrum decisions will have large impact on societies and key stakeholders' businesses, there is very little prior work on spectrum pricing in the context of private LTE or 5G networks. Therefore, this paper aims to study *how currently used pricing models fit to private LTE and private 5G radio licensing models*. The study calculates a radio license price for small, medium-size, large private LTE networks in various parts of Finland using the Finnish frequency fee, Finnish Private Mobile Radio (PMR) frequency fee, the AIP of the Finnish Information Society Code [11] applied to private LTE, and the Netherlands private LTE pricing [19].

License pricing is one of the tools, which the regulative authorities can use for spectrum management. The single most important target is efficient spectrum management, that leaves freedom for interpretation what efficient means. From the economy of the society perspective, the efficiency could be described as capability to create and provide communication services, the price level of the services, business activity, and employment [23]. More concretely, the spectrum pricing should encourage the license holder to invest in network infrastructure rather than speculate with the value increase of under-utilized spectrum. The pricing should allow the possibility to allocate the spectrum licenses to the user, who can create most value for the society with the spectrum resource. The pricing tools for the regulative authority to achieve efficient spectrum management include: auctions, Administrative Incentive Price (AIP), reselling rights of licenses, and technology and service independence of the licenses [23].

Our assumption is that the market of private LTE licenses, on large, does not have enough demand and supply from multiple stakeholders to make the auctions possible. The auctions are taken into account in this study as benchmark analysis and mapping the respective auction prices from liquid markets to frequency fee-type pricing. AIP pricing is derived from the Finnish AIP pricing of free-granted network licenses for telecommunications and television operations. These are compared to non-market-based frequency fee of block and device frequency licenses.

The rest of the paper is organized as follows. First, an overview of the pricing methods and data is presented. Then, the results of the pricing use cases are presented and discussed, followed by the conclusions in Sect. 4.

2 Pricing Methods and Data

In Finland [24], frequency fee is based on the availability, usability, and the frequency range. The frequency fee is calculated [25].

$$Fee = C_1 C_{inh} C_{6b} B_0 SP, \text{ where,} \tag{1}$$

C_1 is frequency band coefficient, C_{inh} is population coefficient, C_{6b} is system coefficient, B_0 is relative bandwidth, S is basic fee coefficient, and P is basic fee. The used coefficient values can be found in [24], and the numerical values are summarized in Table 1.

Table 1. The frequency fee coefficients for a private LTE or 5G network with a 10 MHz bandwidth in the 3.5 GHz band for one year

Coefficient	Block	Applied AIP	PMR
C_1	0.4	0.4	0.4
C_{inh}	Variable	Variable	0.01
C_{6b}	1	1	Variable
B_0	2000	2000	9.28
S	0.018	0.018	2.1
P	1295.5 €	9300 €	1295.5 €

The population coefficient is C_{inh} is obtained for block licenses by diving the inhabitant number living in the license area by population of Finland. C_{6b} system coefficient for device licenses is 0.25 x device number and the maximum value is 23.75, when there are 100 or more devices in the license. The minimum frequency fee is 18 €. According to the Finnish legislation, the frequency fee for mobile bands is calculated according to block license rules. The other options: applied AIP, PMR, auction and Netherlands pricing are just illustrative methods for comparison. The Netherlands license price is fixed 633 € per base station [19].

The auction price is based on the mean auction price in the 3.4 to 3.8 GHz bands in Slovakia, Romania, Hungary, Montenegro, Ireland, Czech Republic, Australia, UK, and Austria between May 2015 and March 2018. The mean sample value without the reserve prices in these auctions is 0.05 USD/MHz/pop for a 15-year period [26]. The annual amount of the auction price is calculated by multiplying one 15th of the average auction price with population density and the size of the license area.

The data for the study represents a random selection of a 2 km^2, 10 km^2, and 100 km^2 area in Finland. The location probability is weighted according to the population density in the location. This data selection means that each person living in Finland applies for a single private LTE license in their home municipality. The resulted distributions describe the price distribution of those applied private LTE licenses. For device-based license prices, we estimate 0.5 eNBs per km^2 in 2 km^2 area, 0.2 eNBs per km^2 in the 10 km^2 area, and 0.1 eNBs per km^2 in the 100 km^2 area. In all areas, we estimated 10 UEs per eNB. UE frequency fee is applicable only in PMR pricing. Ficora calculates the exact inhabitant number in the license area. In this study, we use the average inhabitant density for each municipality area.

In the data, for each municipality there is the same relative number of LTE private networks as there are inhabitants. In the smallest municipality, there is one reservation. The less populated areas of a municipality even out the most expensive urban areas in the same administrative area. As this method limits the maximum frequency fee price, we divide the largest city Helsinki in 9 different areas. We do not separate the cases where the municipality area is smaller than the license area. Compared to the real Ficora fees, this computation gives a little bit lower maximum fees and the distribution has visible steps representing the largest cities. Whereas the real Ficora fee distribution is smooth. In large areas, the real Ficora fees do not go quite as high as in this study, because there are no 100 km^2 areas with the highest population density.

3   Results

The license prices are calculated for 1 year with 10 MHz bandwidth in the 3.5 GHz mobile band. Three different license area sizes are studied: 2, 10, and 100 km^2 in Finland. The pricing is presented for Finnish block license, applied AIP, device licensing with the Finnish PMR method, device licensing with the method of the Netherlands, and an average European Union auction price on 3.4–3.8 GHz. The minimum, maximum, average, and median of the license prices in different municipalities in Finland are collected in Table 2.

The distributions of license prices covering an area of 2, 10, and 100 km^2 in different municipalities in Finland are presented in Figs. 1, 2, and 3, respectively. As the only difference between the applied AIP frequency fee, applied auction price, and the frequency fee is the basic fee, the form of the curves is similar. The Netherlands private LTE and Finnish PMR methods use device licensing. The price is not dependent on the population density, and they appear as step functions in the CDF graph. The number of base-stations per square kilometer is different in 2, 10, and 100 km^2 license areas. Consequently, the relative position of the step functions differs from the distribution curves in the respective graphs.

Table 2. Basic characterization of the studied license prices

Pricing	Min (€)	Max (€)	Average (€)	Median (€)
FIN Block 2 km²	18	41	18	18
FIN Block 10 km²	18	413	18	18
FIN Block 100 km²	18	4135	97	18
Applied AIP 2 km²	18	148	18	18
Applied AIP 10 km²	18	1484	35	18
Applied AIP 100 km²	18	14844	350	26
FIN PMR 2 km²	278	278	278	278
FIN PMR 10 km²	556	556	556	556
FIN PMR 100 km²	2652	2652	2652	2652
NL 2 km²	633	633	633	633
NL 10 km²	1266	1266	1266	1266
NL 100 km²	2652	2652	2652	2652
AUC 2 km²	18	164	18	18
AUC 10 km²	18	1645	39	18
AUC 100 km²	18	16446	388	29

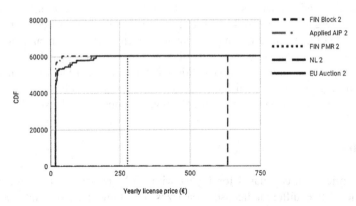

Fig. 1. Cumulative distribution of 2 km² license prices with different pricing methods.

The auction derived license pricing is the highest one among the population density depending license cases. The applied AIP price is very close to the auction price. The auction price is the most expensive one especially in the high-density areas. Depending on the device number per square kilometer, the device-based licenses are most expensive in sparsely populated areas and generally lowest cost in the areas of highest population density. The Netherlands device-based license is more expensive that the Finnish device license. The relative difference between Finnish and Dutch device licenses partially depends on the selected number of UEs per eNB. The impact of the number of the UEs becomes smaller in large areas as the PMR cost increases along the device number up to 100 devices.

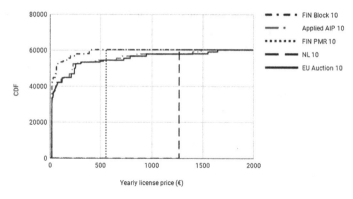

Fig. 2. Cumulative distribution of 10 km^2 license prices with different pricing methods.

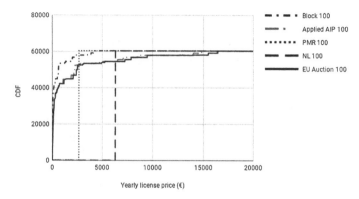

Fig. 3. Cumulative distribution of 100 km^2 license prices with different pricing methods.

4 Conclusions

There is ongoing development of private LTE and 5G network solutions for industrial automation. Timely access to harmonized mobile spectrum in required locations and with appropriate terms is key to the success of private LTE and private 5G solutions that are an enabler to industrial automation. Private LTE networks are, by their very nature, designed to be small-scale, sub-national and sometimes short-term. As a result, any licenses that are only available on national basis, with long license durations, and high upfront investment are not suitable, and are unaffordable for private LTE operators.

In this study, we compare different pricing methods for private LTE networks in the 3.5 GHz band using Finland as an example area. We compare on one hand AIP pricing to non-market priced licenses and on the other hand pricing based on device number to pricing based on population density. The selected cases partially represent the one-time payment (auction) and recurring payment (frequency fee). In many countries, these payment methods are bound to financing the operation of the radio administration.

A common situation is that the recurring frequency fees are used to cover radio administration costs, and the one-time auction payments fill the general government treasury. A mixture of these are AIP fees, which exceed the costs of radio administration, and which can either be dedicated to the communications authorities or grow the government treasury.

Two practical targets set in the introduction were: encouraging investments in the network infrastructure and allowing allocation of spectrum resources to the stakeholders who can create most value with the resource. When device and block licenses are compared, the device licenses decrease the interest to invest in the network infrastructure due to increasing cost, and they encourage to keep spectrum unused because it is possible to hold a lot of spectrum resources with minimal cost. Similarly, one-time payments can be considered as investment instruments by the license holder rather than as a resource to facilitate new business. Recurring payments force the license holder to continuously consider, if the value created with the spectrum resources is high enough to justify holding the license.

The auctions are an obvious tool to allocate spectrum to the stakeholder offering most for the resource on the markets where there are several buyers bidding for the spectrum. Unfortunately, it cannot generally be expected in the case of private LTE networks. An alternative to auctions is to keep frequency fee high enough to be selective in terms of buyers. The level of the frequency fee should in optimal case be derived from the market price for example by benchmarking from auction prices, known acceptable market price, or by deriving it from business models of the buyer. An observation of the relative position of the population density dependent distributions is that for the 3.5 GHz private LTE licenses the applied AIP price and auction benchmark prices are very well in-line.

The price should follow the demand. The areas and frequency ranges, which have a lot of demand should have higher prices than the ones with little demand. Generally, we can assume that the areas with high population density have high demand and the areas with low density have less demand. In the results section, we show that fixed device pricing does not follow the population density. It creates an obstacle to utilize the resource in the low demand areas and it does not create an incentive to guide the spectrum utilization to the high value users in the high demand areas.

The population density describes well the demand for traditional mobile network spectrum as the end customers are consumers. A significant customer group of private LTE are expected to be industrial estates like factories or ports. No one lives in factories or ports. The main research question to be studied further is how to quantify the demand of the industrial estates in private LTE pricing.

We could summarize the recommendations for private LTE pricing of spectrum licenses in 3.5 GHz band as follows: have a significant recurring payment, use block licenses, make the license price highly dependent on the population density, set the pricing for the lowest demand areas at nominal level, set the AIP fee level to the benchmark auction price, use benchmarking analysis to estimate the auction price, and use a factor to take into account the demand at industrial estates. Spectrum policy and regulation can be a trigger for novel private network ecosystem. Simple authorization processes reduce the cost and minimize the complexity of private LTE spectrum use.

References

1. 3GPP: Specification #36.101. Evolved Universal Terrestrial Radio Access (E-UTRA); User Equipment (UE) radio transmission and reception. Release 8 (2007)
2. 3GPP: Specification #36.101. Evolved Universal Terrestrial Radio Access (E-UTRA); User Equipment (UE) radio transmission and reception. Release 15 (2017)
3. European Commission: Opinion on spectrum related aspects for next-generation wireless systems (5G) (2016)
4. GSMA: Mobile Policy Handbook (2018)
5. Marks, P., Pearson, K., Williamson, B., Hansell, P., Burns, J.: Estimating the commercial trading value of spectrum. Report for Ofcom. Plum Consulting (2009)
6. MulteFire alliance. http://www.multefire.org/. Accessed 18 Apr 2018
7. Yrjölä, S., Kokkinen, H.: Licensed shared access evolution enables early access to 5G spectrum and novel use cases. EAI Endorsed Trans. Wirel. Spectr. **17**(12), e1 (2017)
8. FCC: 16-55 (2016) The Second Report and Order and Order on Reconsideration finalizes rules for innovative Citizens Broadband Radio Service in the 3.5 GHz Band (2016)
9. 3GPP: Study on management and orchestration of network slicing for next generation network. 3GPP TR 28.801 version 1.1.0. 3rd Generation Partnership Project (2017)
10. 5GPPP: 5G empowering vertical industries: Roadmap paper. The 5G Infrastructure Public Private Partnership, Brussels, February 2016
11. Act 917/2014 288: Market-based spectrum fee. https://www.finlex.fi/en/laki/kaannokset/2014/en20140917.pdf
12. Ministry of Transport and Communications Finland: Survey of Spectrum Fee Practices in Selected EU Countries (2009). http://julkaisut.valtioneuvosto.fi/bitstream/handle/10024/78247/Julkaisuja_35-2009.pdf?sequence=1. Accessed 18 Apr 2018
13. Tonmukayakul, A., Weiss, M.B.: A study of secondary spectrum use using agent-based computational economics. Netnomics **9**(2), 125–151 (2008)
14. Ahmed, A.A.W., Markendahl, J., Ghanbari, A.: Evaluation of spectrum access options for indoor mobile network deployment. In: Proceedings of 24th International Symposium on Personal, Indoor and Mobile Radio Communications (PIMRC Workshops), London, pp. 138–142 (2013)
15. Bazelon, C., McHenry, G.: Spectrum value. Telecommun. Policy **37**, 737–747 (2013)
16. Mölleryd, B.G., Markendahl, J., Mäkitalo, Ö., Werding, J.: Mobile broadband expansion calls for more spectrum or base stations-analysis of the value of spectrum and the role of spectrum aggregation. In: Proceedings of 21st European Regional ITS Conference, Copenhagen, Denmark (2010)
17. Kokkinen, T., Kokkinen, H., Yrjölä, S.: Spectrum broker service for micro-operator and CBRS priority access licenses. In: Marques, P., Radwan, A., Mumtaz, S., Noguet, D., Rodriguez, J., Gundlach, M. (eds.) CrownCom 2017. LNICST, vol. 228, pp. 237–246. Springer, Cham (2018). https://doi.org/10.1007/978-3-319-76207-4_20
18. European Commission: 5G for Europe: An Action Plan. Communication from the Commission to the European Parliament, the Council, the European Economic and Social Committee and the Committee of the Regions. COM (2016)588, Brussels (2016)
19. Radio Communications Agency Netherlands: Internetverbinding verbeteren. https://www.agentschaptelecom.nl/onderwerpen/internetverbinding-verbeteren. Accessed 18 Apr 2018
20. Ministry of Economic Affairs and Climate Policy Netherlands: Regeling vergoedingen Agentschap Telecom 2018 (2017). http://wetten.overheid.nl/BWBR0040138/2018-01-01. Accessed 18 Apr 2018

21. Bundesministerium für Verkehr und digitale Infrastruktur: 5G Strategy for Germany. https://www.bmvi.de/SharedDocs/DE/Publikationen/DG/098-dobrindt-5g-strategie.pdf?__blob=publicationFile. Accessed 18 Apr 2018
22. ComReg Document 16/71. 3.6 GHz Band Spectrum Award, Information Memorandum, 24 August 2016
23. Cave, M., Nicholls, R.: The use of spectrum auctions to attain multiple objectives: policy implications. Telecommun. Policy **41**(5–6), 367–378 (2017)
24. Finnish Ministry of Transport and Communications: Act 1028/2017. Liikenne- ja viestintäministeriön asetus hallinnollisista taajuusmaksuista ja Viestintäviraston taajuushallinnollisista suoritteista perittävistä muista maksuista. https://www.finlex.fi/fi/laki/alkup/2017/20171028. Accessed 18 Apr 2018
25. Finnish Ministry of Transport and Communications: Decree of the Ministry of Transport and Communications on the Frequency Fees and Other Fees the Finnish Communications Regulatory Authority Collects for Radio Administrative Services 1222/2010
26. Plum consulting. Access to spectrum and valuation of spectrum for private LTE, April 2018

LSA System Development with Sensing for Rapidly Deployable LTE Network

Kalle Lähetkangas[1][(✉)], Harri Posti[1], Harri Saarnisaari[1],
and Ari Hulkkonen[2]

[1] Centre for Wireless Communications, University of Oulu, 90014 Oulu, Finland
{Kalle.Lahetkangas,Harri.Posti,Harri.Saarnisaari}@oulu.fi
[2] Bittium Wireless Ltd., Ritaharjuntie 1, 90590 Oulu, Finland
Ari.Hulkkonen@bittium.com

Abstract. Public safety users require radio spectrum for their communication systems. In this study, sensors are proposed as a backup spectrum information source in a rapidly deployed public safety long term evolution (LTE) communication network with licensed shared access (LSA) system. While the LSA system has been well developed, the drawback measures have not been thoroughly investigated from the application point of view. Herein, a collaborative sensing method is suggested for detecting an incumbent spectrum user and for establishing a protection zone around it. Furthermore, methods are developed for combining information from sensors and from an LSA system in a rapidly deployable public safety LTE network. The information from the sensors can be used for verifying incumbent protection and also for finding available spectrum in critical scenarios. The proposed methods give wider spectrum knowledge than just by using repository information or local sensor information.

Keywords: Sharing arrangement · Commercial LTE network
Dynamic spectrum access

1 Introduction

Public safety (PS) actors today utilize closed communication networks, such as TETRA [11], as their primary communication systems. The advances in commercial networks have made them an attractive option for the PS actors who also want to benefit from the efficient technologies. The current standards for the long term evolution (LTE) networks are planned considering PS users as priority users [5–8]. This enables the commercial network providers to offer their services also to the PS actors, such as border control, police, first responders and military, whose effective communication capabilities are vital for the society. Moreover, the commercial LTE equipments are relatively inexpensive and the infrastructure is readily available.

© ICST Institute for Computer Sciences, Social Informatics and Telecommunications Engineering 2019
Published by Springer Nature Switzerland AG 2019. All Rights Reserved
I. Moerman et al. (Eds.): CROWNCOM 2018, LNICST 261, pp. 143–153, 2019.
https://doi.org/10.1007/978-3-030-05490-8_14

While commercial networks have advantages over the traditional closed PS networks, the PS actors can not yet completely rely their communication over the commercial networks. This is because the commercial networks might not be built in every required location and because the full functionality of the community infrastructure might not be available in the PS operations due to electrical breaks or infrastructure damages. A solution to counter these uncertainties is a local rapidly deployable LTE network [16] which can be carried with the PS actors to the point of action. In this network the PS actors have local and full control for guaranteed services.

These deployable networks require radio spectrum. The spectrum may be owned by the PS users, but that is inefficient use of scarce radio spectrum since most of the time the PS spectrum is unused. Another way is spectrum sharing. The spectrum sharing can be enabled with a political decision. Alternatively, the commercial network operators can have monetary incentives to offer complete communication solutions including secondary spectrum rights for their PS customers. Note that the shared spectrum usage should not generally disturb the commercial networks. This is true especially when the commercial networks also serve priority users such as public safety.

One way of obtaining and sharing spectrum with the commercial systems interference free is licensed shared access (LSA) [3,9,10]. Another spectrum sharing method is called spectrum access system, which is designed for centrally sharing the 3.5 GHz band in the United States [20,21,25].

This work concentrates in LSA, where the secondary spectrum user requests the spectrum from a central spectrum repository via internet. An overview of spectrum sharing principles with LSA for PS from the point of spectrum ownership has been given in [15].

However, the spectrum sharing system for rapidly deployed public safety networks must operate also in some problematic situations. One is prolonged internet connection loss that denies access to the repository. Moreover, the information in the repository might not be valid. This is for example a crisis situation when the primary spectrum users such as commercial networks are down. For these situations, spectrum sensing to detect vacant spectrum is needed. Note, that the fall-back measures in LSA specifications [10] are presented only on a high level, and do not include sensing.

Spectrum sensing has been extensively studied in wireless communications [13,26] and the sensing methods include, for example, energy detector [2,14,17], known signal correlation, cyclostationary, and radio identification based sensing methods. The spectrum sensing dimensions are frequency, space, time, power, directional information and polarization.

Sensor networks have been proposed to be used together with the LSA system in [19] to map the radio environment to a central data base together with the LSA repository. In that work, collaborative use of sensor networks enables efficient spectrum sharing between multiple LSA licensees. Spectrum sensing can also be done collaboratively. The collaborative sensing has been surveyed in [1,22,24]. Furthermore, multiple sensors can be used to mitigate the effect of shadowing and fading by sharing their information [12,18,23].

This work utilizes the already existing sensing and detecting methods in a new kind of manner and do not develop another decision making algorithm or update a central data base. Our point of view is to utilize additional available sensors in conjunction of LSA system. The proposed methods are planned to be used as a simple backup system for spectrum information on PS network utilizing LSA when these types of centralized repository systems might not be functional. For the first time we have a decision method for LSA to select the allowed resources with contradicting spectrum information sources. More specifically, when the repositories are fully functional and the commercial networks are working, the repository information is verified with sensors. Then, when the LSA system has problems, the sensors are utilized for obtaining the spectrum information.

We take the spatial perspective for the sensors. More specifically, this work utilizes distances from which a sensor can detect incumbents. A collaborative sensing method is proposed for ensuring the available spectrum when there are multiple sensors available. Other collaborative methods probabilistically increase the detection probability by sensing with multiple sensors. Compared to these methods our method obtains a higher detection probability by simply considering smaller spatial areas that are reliably detected by a single detector. Furthermore, by having multiple sensors at different locations the reliably detected area broadens.

The paper is organized as follows. Section 2 presents the network model. Section 3 introduces a collaborative sensing method for locating the possible incumbent and describes how to find a protection zone around it. Section 4 describes how the sensors and LSA repository can be used together to allow spectrum utilization. Here, the spectrum use agreements between the incumbent and the LSA licensee, i.e. sharing arrangements, determine wether the use is allowed or not. Section 5 describes how to control false and miss detections. Section 6 describes the practical use of the sensors, for when the LTE base stations of public safety can disturb with the sensing. Section 7 is the conclusion.

2   System Model

This work concentrates on a deployable closed PS Long Term Evolution (LTE) network, that acts as a secondary spectrum licensee in an LSA system. Figure 1 presents the network components and their connections. The left side of the figure is the considered deployable network. It is used for PS communication when the commercial network might be unavailable or drastically limited. The LTE access points use frequency division duplex. The LSA repository offers available spectrum information for the LTE access points via an Internet Protocol (IP) network connection. [1]The radio heads provide more spectrum information

---

[1] The commercial networks can be connected to this system for example with multi-radio access technologies such as a high antenna gain multioperator 3G/4G/LTE router lifted high above the ground level.

and are controlled with a sensor manager application. The distributed LSA controllers use the channel information from the repository and from the radio heads. The controllers control the use of carrier frequency of the LTE access points and synchronize their spectrum information. The light EPC before every access point is a light version of evolved packet core. It offers the necessary services for connecting the access points to the backhaul network and enables a connection between the LTE access points. The backhaul is formed with a private IP network, that can be either wired or wireless [4]. In our scenarios the private IP backhaul network is considered to be highly robust and self configuring. Note, that the number of access points, radio heads and routers can vary. This type of a network can be built for example with towable lifts or crane cars, that are equipped with the necessary equipment.

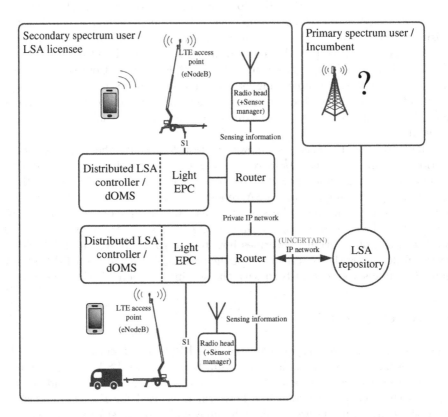

Fig. 1. LSA system for rapidly deployed LSA licensee network with LTE access points and radio heads for sensing. The primary spectrum users might be present, for which the sensing is used.

In order to analyze incumbent free areas with multiple sensors, the detection distances of a sensor in various conditions have to be defined. The distances depend on the specific sensing method, on transmitted signal power, on antenna gains, on attenuation, on random noise, on shadowing and this is not in the scope of this paper.

3   Collaborative Sensing Method

In this section, collaborative sensing is introduced for multiple sensors to sense if the channel is free or not and to calculate a protection zone for a possible incumbent user. The basic principle for collaboratively sensing the channel free is shown Figs. 2 and 3.

First, circles with radius d_f are drawn around the sensors that do not detect the incumbent. A distance d_f denotes the radius that is likely free of transmitters, given that there is no detection. Second, the union of these circles is taken. It is seen in Fig. 3 inside the solid thin red line. This area is free of the incumbent transmitter. Finally, the area within distance d_{inc} is removed from the boundary of the union. A distance d_{inc} is the maximum distance between the incumbent transmitter and the incumbent receiver. Removing this area, mitigates the hidden node problem. The remaining area is free of incumbent receivers. This area is seen in Fig. 3 inside the solid and rounded thick green line. Its complement is the protection zone, which is the area within which the incumbent receivers should not be subject to harmful interference caused by PS. The above method can also be utilized when there are multiple incumbent transmitters, but no detection. Note that multiple transmitters increase the distance from which the incumbent can be detected. Thus, the transmitter free distance calculated for a single incumbent d_f is free also in a multiple transmitter scenario.

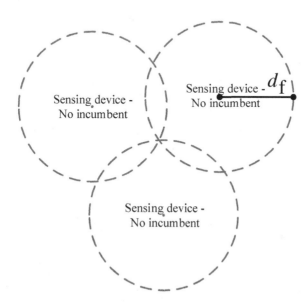

Fig. 2. Three sensors with no detection.

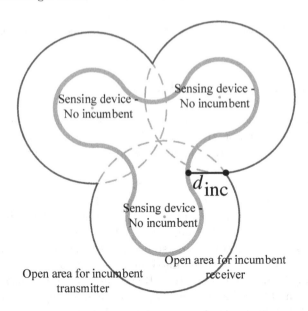

Fig. 3. Three sensors do not sense the incumbent. LSA controllers calculate an incumbent free zone for a possible incumbent, whose receiver is within distance d_{inc} from the transmitter. (Color figure online)

If there is only one incumbent transmitter, multiple sensors can be used to roughly locate it. The basic principle can be seen from Fig. 4. In this example, two sensors have sensed the incumbent and one sensor has not. First, circles with radius d_t are drawn around the sensors that detect the incumbent and an intersection between these circles is taken. A distance d_t denotes the radius within the detected LTE transmitter is with a close to one probability. Second, circles with radius d_f are drawn around all the sensors that do not detect the incumbent. Third, these circles are removed from the intersection. This is the area free of the incumbent transmitter. Finally, the area within distance d_{inc} from the boundary is added. The resulting area might have silent incumbent receivers. This area is seen in Fig. 4 inside the solid and rounded thick line. This is the area within which the incumbent receivers should not be subject to harmful interference caused by PS base stations. The transmission details have to be further agreed in the spectrum sharing arrangements.

4   Spectrum Sharing Arrangements for Combining Contradicting Spectrum Information

In this section, it is described how the distributed LSA controllers can use the protection zones described above for combining and verifying the spectrum information from different sources. The spectrum information sources are: the sensors, the LSA repository, and the other LSA controllers that synchronize spectrum

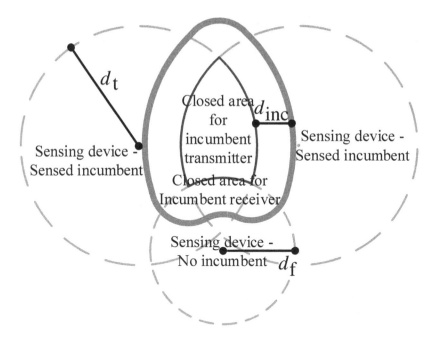

Fig. 4. Two sensors notice the same incumbent and LSA controllers calculate a closed protection zone for it, which is seen here as a green thick line. A detected transmitter is most probably closer to the sensor than d_t. Moreover, a distance d_f is likely free of transmitters, given that there is no detection.

use of their corresponding base stations. Moreover, a lack of commercial network services can indicate that there are unused spectrum resources.

The distributed LSA controllers determine if the channel use is allowed or not and share the allowed channels between each others while selecting the channel allocations and power levels. Then, the controllers have event based listeners for noticing changes in the spectrum information and in the availability of the channels. This listener initiates a channel change for the base stations if needed.

If the channel is allowed or not depends on the LSA sharing arrangement with the incumbents. The arrangements should be agreed separately for different location types. The types of locations can for example be areas with no known commercial networks and areas with broken commercial networks. Additionally, criticality of the missions has to be taken into account in the sharing arrangements.

In a highly critical scenario, where the commercial network is down, it is straightforward for the controllers only to select the least congested LSA channel from the nearest sensor. This channel is not likely used in this particular location. Furthermore, it has the least interference.

Tables 1 and 2 are two examples of sharing arrangements for what to do with contradicting and congruent spectrum information. Here, the tables show wether the spectrum use is allowed or not by the PS base stations. Similar sharing arrangements could also be made for borderline commercial network scenarios with insufficient commercial networks.

Table 1. A sharing arrangement for LSA licensee transmissions in areas with no known commercial networks.

Sensor(s) → LSA repository ↓	LSA channel in this area not detected free	LSA channel in this area detected free
LSA channel available	No	Allowed
LSA channel not available	No	No
Old LSA information with available channel	No	Allowed

Table 2. A sharing arrangement for LSA licensee transmissions in areas with broken commercial networks.

Sensor(s) → LSA repository ↓	LSA channel in this area not detected free	LSA channel in this area detected free
LSA channel available	Allowed	Allowed
LSA channel not available	No	Allowed
Old LSA information with available channel	No	Allowed

Note that the details of the allowed transmissions have to be further agreed. These include if the incumbent is allowed to transmit without informing the LSA repository. Moreover, the sharing arrangements resolve the transmission power and antenna height limitations, sensing methods and their detection probabilities and false and miss detection probabilities.

5   False and Miss Detections

While sensing, some amount of false and miss detections have to be tolerated. The values of these have to be agreed with the incumbent. The false detection probability per sensor can be decided first by selecting the detection threshold correspondingly. Then, in general, the maximum miss detection probability can be made smaller by considering a smaller radius, d_f, around the sensor. This radius is considered free of transmitters, given no detection. Here, the smaller detection radius d_f increases the received signal and thus increases the detection probability. Note that with a smaller d_f there might be a need for multiple sensors[2] to cover the required area. Another option for covering the area are sensors that are moving for example in the air.

6   Sensor Control in Practice

The use of multiple sensors needs an efficient tool for controlling all the information. This section describes methods for the PS network to use available sensors and to notice changes in the channel information.

The information from the sensors is analyzed at the distributed LSA controllers. The sensor specific information is used by the controllers to estimate the values for d_f and d_t. The sensor specific information includes at least the sensor antenna, height, location, gain and the environment of the sensor.

The PS network has a sensor manager application, that extracts the measurements of LSA licenseed channels from the available sensors. The sensor manager uses the unique commands for the corresponding sensors. Most spectrum sensors have programmable interfaces, using for example standard commands for programmable instruments (SCPI), C, or Python programming languages. The manager provides the measurements and sensor specific information for the distributed LSA controllers.

The LSA controllers access the sensing information when the PS transmissions do not disturb with sensing. For doing this, the channels are sensed before the PS base stations go on air. The information is saved for later use. However, if there are other nearby PS base stations on air, the LSA controller first waits for a communication break. Then it blocks the nearby base stations temporarily before accessing the sensed information. Moreover, the sensing can happen periodically during communication breaks. The periodical sensing is used to verify that the channel is still available. The time period should be agreed in the sharing arrangements.

7   Conclusion

We introduced a sensing method for PS to complement LSA spectrum information. This is done by determining reliable detection distances per sensor and by utilizing them according to the agreed sharing arrangements. A natural extension to this work is therefore to plan the required sensing network for more specific environments. The detection distances have to be further estimated for the specific sensors and for the specific incumbents.

Our scenario had a hidden assumption of simple and coarse detectors. It is also possible to consider more sophisticated sensing methods, such as power of arrival and angle of arrival techniques. These can be used for locating the detected incumbent users with a high accuracy. Then, the spectrum use could

---

[2] Moreover, with more detectors, false detections itself can be detected if multiple sensors give contradictory results.

be similarly allowed given that the detected incumbents can be located to be further than their reuse distance.

Acknowledgement. The authors would like to acknowledge CORNET project consortium. This research has been financially supported by Business Finland CORNET project and by Academy of Finland 6Genesis Flagship (grant 318927).

References

1. Akyildiz, I.F., Lo, B.F., Balakrishnan, R.: Cooperative spectrum sensing in cognitive radio networks: a survey. Phys. Commun. **4**(1), 40–62 (2011)
2. Benko, J.: A PHY/MAC proposal for IEEE 802.22 WRAN systems, part 1: The PHY. IEEE 802.22-06/0004r1, February 2006
3. Electronic Communications Committee: Licensed Shared Access (LSA). ECC Report 205, February 2014
4. Elektrobit: Enhancing the link network performance with EB tactical wireless IP network (TAC WIN). EB Defense Newsletter, December 2014. https://www.bittium.com/file.php?fid=785. Accessed Aug 2018
5. ETSI: LTE; mission critical video over LTE. ETSI TS 122 281 V15.1.0, July 2018
6. ETSI: LTE;mission critical data over LTE. ETSI TS 122 282 V15.1.0, July 2018
7. ETSI: Universal Mobile Telecommunications System (UMTS); LTE; mission critical push to talk (MCPTT) over LTE; stage 1. ETSI TS 122 179 V15.2.0, July 2018
8. ETSI: Universal Mobile Telecommunications System (UMTS); LTE; proximity-based services (ProSe); stage 2. ETSI TS 123 303 V15.1.0, July 2018
9. ETSI: Reconfigurable radio systems (RRS); system requirements for operation of mobile broadband systems in the 2 300 MHz–2 400 MHz band under licensed shared access (LSA). ETSI TS 103 154, V1.1.1, October 2014
10. ETSI: Reconfigurable radio systems (RRS); system architecture and high level procedures for operation of licensed shared access (LSA) in the 2 300 MHz–2 400 MHz band. ETSI TS 103 235 V1.1.1, October 2015
11. Etsi, E.N.: 300 392–1: Terrestrial trunked radio (TETRA); voice plus data (V+D); part 1: General network design. V1.4.1, January 2009
12. Ghasemi, A., Sousa, E.S.: Collaborative spectrum sensing for opportunistic access in fading environments. In: IEEE International Symposium on Dynamic Spectrum Access Networks, pp. 131–136, November 2005
13. Höyhtyä, M., et al.: Spectrum occupancy measurements: a survey and use of interference maps. IEEE Commun. Surv. Tutor. **18**(4), 2386–2414 (2016)
14. Kay, S.: Fundamentals of Statistical Signal Processing: Detection Theory, vol. 2. Prentice-Hall, Upper Saddle River (1998)
15. Lähetkangas, K., Saarnisaari, H., Hulkkonen, A.: Licensed shared access system possibilities for public safety. Mob. Inf. Syst. **2016**, 1–12 (2016)
16. Lähetkangas, K., Saarnisaari, H., Hulkkonen, A.: Licensed shared access system development for public safety. In: Proceedings of the European Wireless Conference, Oulu, Finland, May 2016
17. Lehtomäki, J.: Analysis of energy based signal detection. Ph.D. dissertation, Faculty of Technology, University of Oulu, Finland, December 2005
18. Mishra, S.M., Sahai, A., Brodersen, R.W.: Cooperative sensing among cognitive radios. In: IEEE International Conference on Communications, vol. 4, pp. 1658–1663 (2006)

19. Morgado, A., et al.: Dynamic LSA for 5G networks. In: European Conference on Networks and Communications, pp. 190–194, June 2015
20. Palola, M., et al.: The first end-to-end live trial of CBRS with carrier aggregation using 3.5 GHz LTE equipment. In: IEEE International Symposium on Dynamic Spectrum Access Networks, pp. 1–2, March 2017
21. Sohul, M.M., Yao, M., Yang, T., Reed, J.H.: Spectrum access system for the citizen broadband radio service. IEEE Commun. Mag. **53**(7), 18–25 (2015)
22. Subhedar, M., Birajdar, G.: Spectrum sensing techniques in cognitive radio networks: a survey. Int J. Next-Gener. Netw. **3**, 37–51 (2011)
23. Uchiyama, H., et al.: Study on cooperative sensing in cognitive radio based ad-hoc network. In: IEEE International Symposium on Personal, Indoor and Mobile Radio Communications, pp. 1–5, September 2007
24. Visotsky, E., Kuffner, S., Peterson, R.: On collaborative detection of TV transmissions in support of dynamic spectrum sharing. In: IEEE International Symposium on New Frontiers in Dynamic Spectrum Access Networks, pp. 338–345, November 2005
25. Wireless innovation forum: Signaling protocols and procedures for citizens broadband radio service (CBRS): Spectrum access system (SAS) - citizens broadband radio service device (CBSD) interface technical specification. WINNF-TS-0096 V 1.3.0, April 2018. https://workspace.winnforum.org/higherlogic/ws/public/download/6482/. Accessed Aug 2018
26. Yucek, T., Arslan, H.: A survey of spectrum sensing algorithms for cognitive radio applications. IEEE Commun. Surv. Tutor. **11**(1), 116–130 (2009)

Maxmin Strategy for a Dual Radar and Communication OFDM Waveforms System Facing Uncertainty About the Background Noise

Andrey Garnaev[1(✉)], Wade Trappe[1], and Athina Petropulu[2]

[1] WINLAB, Rutgers University, North Brunswick, USA
garnaev@yahoo.com, trappe@winlab.rutgers.edu
[2] Department of Electrical and Computer Engineering, Rutgers University, Piscataway, USA
athinap@rutgers.edu

Abstract. The paper considers the problem of designing the maxmin strategy for a dual-purpose communication and radar system that employs multicarrier OFDM style waveforms, but faces an uncertain level of background noise. As the payoff for the system, we consider the weighted sum of the communication throughput and the radar's SINR. The problem is formulated as a zero-sum game between the system and a rival, which may be thought of as the environment or nature. Since the payoff for such a system combines different type of metrics (SINR and throughput), this makes underlying problem associated with jamming such a systems different from the typical jamming problem arising in communication scenarios, where the payoff usually involves only one of these metrics. In this paper, the existence and uniqueness of the equilibrium strategies are proven as well as water-filling equations to design the equilibrium are derived. Finally, using Nash product the optimal value of weights are found to optimize tradeoff of radar and communication objectives.

Keywords: Dual-purpose communication and radar system
Maxmin · Background noise

1 Introduction

Recently, there has been interest in enabling radar and communication system to co-exist in the same frequency band to allow spectrum to be utilized more efficiently [21]. This has given rise to a significant amount of research on methods for spectrum sharing that minimize the interference between the two systems. One approach to achieve this is to formulate waveform design using OFDM signals and then optimally allocating subcarriers [11,25]. Radar waveform design for controlled interference is considered in [1,2]. For these aforementioned works,

© ICST Institute for Computer Sciences, Social Informatics and Telecommunications Engineering 2019
Published by Springer Nature Switzerland AG 2019. All Rights Reserved
I. Moerman et al. (Eds.): CROWNCOM 2018, LNICST 261, pp. 154–164, 2019.
https://doi.org/10.1007/978-3-030-05490-8_15

the design is performed for each system in isolation, and recently there has been work that explore the cooperative design of the two systems [3, 16].

In this paper, we consider a dual purpose communication-radar system that employs multicarrier OFDM style waveforms and explore *a complementary aspect* of its optimization that is motivated by the fact that these systems may or may not face interference, and thus will often have uncertainty about the background noise or interference in their operating scenarios.

To address this uncertainty, we look for a strategy that returns the maximal payoff for the system under the worst background condition which might arise. In order to explore this maxmin problem, we consider a weighted combination of communication throughput and radar's SINR as the utility, which reflects the coexistence performance of both communication and radar objectives. We show that the maxmin problem is equivalent to a zero-sum game between the system and an abstract rival, which maybe considered as 'the environment' or 'nature' and thus interpreted as a jammer. Since the payoff for such a system combines different type of metrics (SINR and throughput), this makes the jamming problem for such dual-purpose systems distinctly different from the jamming problems arising in typical communication or radar scenarios where the payoffs includes only one type of metric (only SINR or only throughput) (see, for example, [4, 5, 7, 9, 12, 13, 17, 18, 22, 23, 26]).

The organization of this paper is as follows: in Sect. 2, we present the model for the dual radar and communication system as zero sum game. In Sect. 3, the equilibrium strategies are found. In Sect. 4, the optimal value of weights are found to optimize tradeoff between the objectives. In Sect. 5, conclusions are given, while, in Appendix, the proofs of the obtained results are supplied.

2   Model

We begin our formulation by considering an operational scenario involving an RF transceiver that is attempting to support two different objectives: communication with a communication receiver that is distant and separate from the transmitter, while also supporting the tracking of a radar target through the reflections witnessed at the RF transmitter. In order to support these two different objectives, the transmitter uses a spectrum band that is modeled as consisting of n adjacent sub-channels, which may be associated with n different subcarriers. In this paper we employ a transmission scheme like OFDM, as considered in [8] for designing a bargaining strategy for a dual radar and communication system in the absence of hostile interference. With each of these n different subcarriers, two different (fading) channel gains are associated. Specifically, we let h_i^R correspond to the i-th radar channel gain associated with the round-trip effect of the transmitted signal, reflected off the radar target, and received at the RF transceiver. Similarly, we denote by h_i^C the i-th channel gain associated with the i-th communication subcarrier between the transmitter and the communication recipient. Since, although there are two different objectives, there is nonetheless a single transmitter responsible for deciding how to allocate power across the different subcarriers to best meet radar and communication tradeoffs, we consider a power vector $\boldsymbol{P} = (P_1, \ldots, P_n)$ as a strategy for such system, where P_i is the power assigned for transmitting on subcarrier i, and $\sum_{i=1}^n P_i = \overline{P}$ with $\overline{P}$ is the total power budget of the system. Let Π_S be the set of all feasible strategies for the system.

To model uncertainty about background noise we assume that the system knows the total noise resource $\overline{J}$ but does not know its allocation among the subcarriers $\boldsymbol{J} = (J_1, \ldots, J_n)$. Thus, the system knows only that $\sum_{i=1}^n J_i = \overline{J}$, but does not know each of J_i. We can say that this interference $\boldsymbol{J}$ is impelled by *nature*, if the interference was not caused by any artificial reason (such as by a jammer). We will use the common term *rival* to denote the source of this interference. Thus, we call $\boldsymbol{J}$ as the strategy for the rival Let Π_R be the set of all feasible strategies for the rival.

Let $T^C(\boldsymbol{P}, \boldsymbol{J}) = \sum_{i=1}^n \ln\left(1 + h_i^C P_i/(\sigma^2 + g_i^C J_i)\right)$, be the communication throughput, reflecting the communication objective, where σ_C^2 is known background noise, g_i^C is the ith (fading) sub-carrier gain associated with interference coming from a possible jamming source.

We note that radar detection and tracking are related to the associated SINR [20], and therefore the SINR at the radar, i.e., $\text{SNR}^R(\boldsymbol{P}, \boldsymbol{J}) = \sum_{i=1}^n h_i^R P_i/(\sigma^2 + g_i^R J_i)$, can be considered as the radar's objective, where g_i^R is the interference fading sub-carrier gains affecting the radar objective.

Then, we consider weighted sum of communication throughput and radar's SINR $v(\boldsymbol{P}, \boldsymbol{J}) = w^C T^C(\boldsymbol{P}, \boldsymbol{J}) + w^R \text{SNR}^R(\boldsymbol{P}, \boldsymbol{J})$ as the utility, reflecting the joint performance of both objectives.

We are looking for maxmin strategy, i.e., $\max_P \min_J v(\boldsymbol{P}, \boldsymbol{J})$. Since v is concave in $\boldsymbol{P}$ and convex in $\boldsymbol{J}$, $\max_P \min_J v(\boldsymbol{P}, \boldsymbol{J}) = \min_J \max_P v(\boldsymbol{P}, \boldsymbol{J})$. Moreover $(\boldsymbol{P}_*, \boldsymbol{J}_*)$ is a maxmin strategy if and only if the following inequalities hold [13]: $v(\boldsymbol{P}, \boldsymbol{J}_*) \le v(\boldsymbol{P}_*, \boldsymbol{J}_*) \le v(\boldsymbol{P}_*, \boldsymbol{J})$ for all $(\boldsymbol{P}, \boldsymbol{J})$. This allows one to interpret the problem of designing the maxmin strategy as a problem of finding equilibrium strategies in a zero-sum game between the system and the rival, where v is the payoff for the system while for the rival it is its cost function. Of course, since v is concave in $\boldsymbol{P}$ and convex in $\boldsymbol{J}$ there is at least one equilibrium [13].

3   Equilibrium

In this section we prove that rival's strategy is always unique, while multiple strategies might arise for the system only when $w^C = 0$. Additionally, we derive water-filling equations that allows one to find the equilibrium.

Theorem 1. *(I) Let $w^C > 0$. Then the equilibrium is unique and given as* $(\boldsymbol{P}, \boldsymbol{J}) = (\boldsymbol{P}(\omega, \nu), \boldsymbol{J}(\omega, \nu))$ *with*

(I-a) if $i \in I_{00}(\omega, \nu) := \{i : w^C h_i^C/\sigma^2 + w^R h_i^R/\sigma^2 \le \omega\}$ then $P_i(\omega, \nu) = 0$ and $J_i(\omega, \nu) = 0$,

(I-b) if $i \in I_{10}(\omega, \nu) := \{i : \omega_{+,i}(\nu) \leq \omega < w^C h_i^C / \sigma^2 + w^R h_i^R / \sigma^2\}$ then

$$P_i(\omega, \nu) = \frac{w^C}{\omega - w^R h_i^R / \sigma^2} - \frac{\sigma^2}{h_i^C} \text{ and } J_i(\omega, \nu) = 0, \tag{1}$$

where

$$\omega_{+,i}(\nu) = \frac{h_i^C}{2 g_i^C} \left(\frac{w^C g_i^C}{\sigma^2} - \nu - \frac{w^R g_i^R h_i^R}{h_i^C \sigma^2} \right.$$

$$\left. + \sqrt{\left(\frac{w^C g_i^C}{\sigma^2} - \nu - \frac{w^R g_i^R h_i^R}{h_i^C \sigma^2} \right)^2 + 4 \frac{w^C w^R h_i^R g_i^R g_i^C}{h_s^C \sigma^4}} \right) + \frac{w^R h_i^R}{\sigma^2}, \tag{2}$$

(I-c) if $i \in I_{11}(\omega, \nu) := \{i : \omega < \omega_{+,i}(\nu)\}$ then $J_i(\omega, \nu)$ is the unique root of the equation

$$\frac{w^C g_i^C}{\sigma^2 + g_i^C J_i(\omega, \nu)} + \frac{w^R h_i^R}{\sigma^2 + g_i^R J_i(\omega, \nu)} \frac{g_i^C}{h_i^C}$$

$$+ \frac{w^R h_i^R g_i^R}{(\sigma^2 + g_i^R J_i(\omega, \nu))^2} \left(\frac{w^C}{\omega - w^R h_i^R / (\sigma^2 + g_i^R J_i(\omega, \nu))} - \frac{\sigma^2 + g_i^C J_i}{h_i^C} \right) = \nu + \omega \frac{g_i^C}{h_i^C}, \tag{3}$$

$$P_i(\omega, \nu) = \frac{w^C}{\omega - w^R h_i^R / (\sigma^2 + g_i^R J_i(\omega, \nu))} - \frac{\sigma^2 + g_i^C J_i(\omega, \nu)}{h_i^C}. \tag{4}$$

Here $\omega > \underline{\omega} := w^R \max_i h_i^R / \sigma^2$ and $\nu > 0$ are given as the unique solution of the equations:

$$H_S(\omega, \nu) := \sum_{i=1}^n P_i(\omega, \nu) = \overline{P} \text{ and } H_J(\omega, \nu) := \sum_{i=1}^n J_i(\omega, \nu) = \overline{J}. \tag{5}$$

(II) Let $w^C = 0$. Then, the equilibrium rival strategy is unique and given as $\mathbf{J} = \mathbf{J}(\nu)$ with

$$J_i(\nu) = \lfloor (h_i^R / \nu - \sigma^2) / g_i^R \rfloor_+, \ i = 1, \ldots, n, \tag{6}$$

where ν is the unique positive root of the equation $H(\nu) := \sum_{i=1}^n J_i(\nu) = \overline{J}$,

(II-a) if there is no i such that $\nu = h_i^R \sigma^2$ then the system's strategy is unique and given as follows:

$$P_i = P_i(\nu) := \frac{\overline{P}}{D} \begin{cases} (\sigma^2 + g_i^C J_i(\nu))^2 / (h_i^C g_i^C), & i \in S(\nu), \\ 0, & i \notin S(\nu) \end{cases} \tag{7}$$

with $S(\nu) = \{i : J_i(\nu) > 0\}$ and $D = \sum_{j \in S(\nu)} (\sigma^2 + g_j^C J_j(\nu))^2 / (h_j^C g_j^C)$.

(II-b) if there is an i such that $\nu = h_i^R \sigma^2$, then the set $I(\nu) := \{i : nu = h_i^R \sigma^2\}$ is not empty, and thus the system has a continuum of equilibrium strategies given by:

$$P_i = P_i(\nu) := \frac{\overline{P}}{D_{\{\epsilon_j\}}} \begin{cases} (\sigma^2 + g_i^C J_i(\nu))^2/(h_i^C g_i^C), & i \in S(\nu) \backslash I(\nu), \\ \epsilon_i(\sigma^2 + g_i^C J_i(\nu))^2/(h_i^C g_i^C), & i \in I(\nu), \\ 0, & i \notin S(\nu), \end{cases} \tag{8}$$

where $\epsilon_i \in [0, 1]$ for $i \in I(\nu)$ and

$$D_{\{\epsilon_j\}} = 1 / \left(\sum_{j \in S(\nu) \backslash I(\nu)} (\sigma^2 + g_j^C J_j(\nu))^2/(h_j^C g_j^C) + \sum_{j \in I(\nu)} \epsilon_j(\sigma^2 + g_j^C J_j(\nu))^2/(h_j^C g_j^C) \right).$$

In case (II), since H is decreasing, to find ν, and the equilibrium, we have to solve the single waterfilling equation $H(\nu) = \overline{J}$ by applying bisection method. In case (I), $H_J(\omega, \nu)$ is decreasing on $\omega > \underline{\omega}$ and $\nu > 0$ while $H_S(\omega, \nu)$ is decreasing on ω and increasing on ν. Thus, to find ω and ν a superposition of two bisection methods to solve these water-filling equations has to be applied. Namely, *first*, for each fixed ν we find $\omega = \Omega(\nu)$ such that $H_J(\Omega(\nu), \nu) = \overline{J}$. This $\Omega(\nu)$ is continuous and decreasing on ν, and thus $H_S(\Omega(\nu), \nu)$ is also increasing on ν. *Second*, we can find ν as the unique root of the equation $H_S(\Omega(\nu), \nu) = \overline{P}$.

4   Optimal Value of Weights

First, we note that the functions v and $v/(w^R + w^C)$ achieve their optimum at the same point. Thus, by introducing new notation: $w^R := w^R/(w^R + w^C)$ and $w^C := w^C/(w^R + w^C)$, without loss of generality, we can assume that these weights are normalized, i.e., $w^R + w^C = 1$. Further, note that if $\overline{J} = 0$, i.e., there is no artificial noise introduced then the problem turns into a non-linear programming (NLP) problem for the system and it has a unique solution $\boldsymbol{P} = \boldsymbol{P}(\omega)$ where $P_i(\omega) = \lfloor w^C/(\omega - w^R h_i^R/\sigma^2) - \sigma^2/h_i^C \rfloor_+, i = 1, ..., n$, where ω is the unique root in $(\underline{\omega}, \infty)$ of the equation $\sum_{i=1}^n P_i(\omega) = \overline{P}$.

We now illustrate the results that we have obtained by providing an example. Let waveform consist of $n = 5$ subcarriers and fading channel gains are $h^C = (1, 2, 3, 4, 4.5)$, $h^R = (1, 0.95, 0.22, 0.15, 0.1)$. Thus, subcarrier 1 is the best one for the radar objective, while for the communication objective the subcarriers are arranged in decreasing order by their quality. Figures 1 and 2 illustrate the optimal strategy for the system in the absence $(\overline{J} = 0)$ and in the presence $(\overline{J} = 1)$ of the rival. Also presented are the corresponding rival strategies as functions of w^C while $w^R = 1 - w^C$ with $\overline{P} = 1$ and $\overline{P} = 10$. In the absence of the rival, for small w^C the system is focused on the radar objective, and its strategy coincides with the strategy that maximizes the radar's SINR, i.e., it applies the full power budget on the subcarrier 1. Since, for the communication objective, the subcarriers are arranged in increasing order, i.e., sub-carrier 5 is the best one while sub-carrier 1 is the worst one for communication, an increase in w^C makes the system utilize the power across the sub-carriers beginning with sub-carrier 5, then sub-carrier 4 and so on, while simultaneously reducing the amount of power devoted to subcarrier 1 (which was best for the radar objective). If power budget is not large enough (as it is for $\overline{P} = 1$) the system strategy can even not use subcarrier 1 if the weighting applied to the importance of the radar objective is small, while a large power budget (as it is for $\overline{P} = 10$) allows the strategy to keep all of the sub-carriers involved in equilibrium strategy. Also, for large $\overline{P}$ and w^C to be close to 1, the system strategy becomes close to a uniform power allocation, since it takes place in the high SNR regime in OFDM transmission. The presence of the rival makes the system choose to use more sub-carriers. In the case considered, for small w^C the system uses two sub-carriers (namely, sub-carrier 1 and sub-carrier 2). Of course, the rival jams only the sub-carriers employed by the system, and he does not jam the ones that are not used by the system. An increase in w^C changes the system's preference about which sub-carriers to use, while the rival, in his strategy, follows the system's strategy in determining how to allocate its effort.

We now introduce a curve Γ parameterized by w^C that of the pair of objective payoffs in the plane $(\mathrm{T}^C, \mathrm{SNR}^R)$: $\Gamma_{\overline{P},\overline{J}} = \{(\mathrm{T}^C_{\overline{P},\overline{J},w^C}, \mathrm{SNR}^R_{\overline{P},\overline{J},w^C}), w^C \in [0,1]\}$, where $\mathrm{T}^C_{\overline{P},\overline{J},w^C} = \mathrm{T}^C(\boldsymbol{P}_{\overline{P},\overline{J},w^C}, \boldsymbol{J}_{\overline{P},\overline{J},w^C})$, $\mathrm{SNR}^R_{\overline{P},\overline{J},w^C} = \mathrm{SNR}^R(\boldsymbol{P}_{\overline{P},\overline{J},w^C}, \boldsymbol{J}_{\overline{P},\overline{J},w^C})$, and $\boldsymbol{P}_{\overline{P},\overline{J},w^C}$ and $\boldsymbol{J}_{\overline{P},\overline{J},w^C}$ are equilibrium strategies for powers budgets $\overline{P}$ and $\overline{J}$ and $w^R = 1 - w^C$.

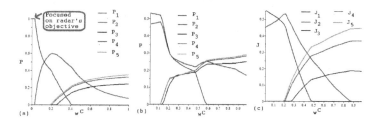

Fig. 1. (a) Optimal strategy of the system in the absence of the rival, (b) equilibrium strategy of the system in the presence of the rival, and (c) equilibrium strategy of the rival as functions of w^C with $w^R = 1 - w^C$ and $\overline{P} = \overline{J} = 1$.

Figure 3 first illustrates a pair of such curves in the absence $(\overline{J} = 0)$ and presence $(\overline{J} = 1)$ of the rival. This figure shows that an increase in w^C yields an increase in the communication payoff and also a decrease in the radar payoff. That is, while one objective gains the other objective decreases. Thus, a basic question arises as to how to find a trade-off value for w^C. One useful approach to defining such a trade-off is to use the Nash product (NP) function. As examples of designing Nash bargaining tradeoff, see, [6,10,15,19,24]. To define NP, we must introduce a disagreement point (DP) as follows: DP= $(\mathrm{T}^C_{\overline{P},\overline{J},0}, \mathrm{SNR}^R_{\overline{P},\overline{J},1})$. Then, the NP is given as follows: $\mathrm{NP}_{w^C} = (\mathrm{T}^C_{\overline{P},\overline{J},w^C} - \mathrm{T}^C_{\overline{P},\overline{J},0})(\mathrm{SNR}^R_{\overline{P},\overline{J},w^C} - \mathrm{SNR}^R_{\overline{P},\overline{J},1})$. The trade-off value for $w^C \in [0,1]$ is given as the one that maximizes NP_{w^C}. For

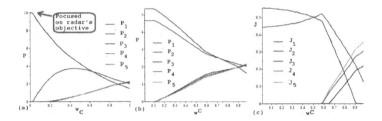

Fig. 2. (a) Optimal strategy of the system in the absence of the rival, (b) equilibrium strategy of the system in the presence of the rival, and (c) equilibrium strategy of the rival as functions of w^C with $w^R = 1 - w^C$ and $\overline{P} = 10$, $\overline{J} = 1$.

our model, since NP_{w^C} is a function of one real variable, the tradeoff value can be found, for example, by the Nelder-Mead simplex algorithm [14].

Figure 3 also illustrates disagreement points and trade-off values for the objectives. In the absence of the rival, the trade-off value for w^C is 0.28 with pay-offs $\text{SNR}^R = 0.664$ and $\text{T}^C = 1.98$, while in its presence the value w^C is reduced to 0.23 and the payoffs become $\text{SNR}^R = 0.488$ and $\text{T}^C = 1.59$. This figure also illustrates that the occurrence of jamming leads to a decrease in the trade-off payoffs for both objectives, as well as a decrease in the trade-off value for w^C. An increase in the system power budget yields an increase in the trade-off payoffs for both objectives as well as a decrease in the trade-off value of w^C. Such behavior for w^C can be explained by the fact that the radar payoff is a linear function of $\boldsymbol{P}$, while the communication's payoff is logarithmic, and the logarithm growth is slower any linear function. Thus, the radar payoff prevails over communication payoff when the system power budget becomes larger. Hence, to maintain the tradeoff between the two objectives w^C becomes larger to compensate for the growth of the radar objective's share in the joint system utility.

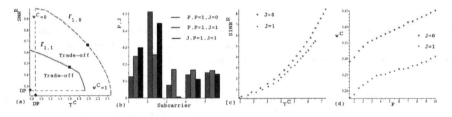

Fig. 3. (a) Curve for payoffs $\Gamma_{\overline{P},\overline{J}}$ when $\overline{P} = 1$ and $\overline{J} \in \{0, 1\}$, (b) equilibrium strategies corresponding to the trade-off value for w^C, (c) tradeoff payoffs in the plane $(\text{T}^C, \text{SNR}^R)$, and (d) the trade-off weight w^C parameterized by $\overline{P} = 0.5(0.5)10$.

5   Conclusions

The problem of designing the maxmin strategy for a dual-purpose communication and radar system facing an uncertain level of background noise is formulated and solved as a zero-sum game between the system and a noise with payoff combining SINR metric for the radar objective and throughput metric for the communication objective. Also, using Nash product the optimal value of weights are found to optimize tradeoff of radar and communication objectives.

Appendix: Proof of Theorem 1

Proof. (I) By definition, P and J are equilibrium strategies if and only if each of them is the best response to the other, i.e., they are solutions of the equations: $P = BR_S(J) := \text{argmax}\{v(P, J) : P \in \Pi_S\}$ and $J = BR_R(P) := \text{argmin}\{v(P, J) : J \in \Pi_R\}$. By the Karush-Kuhn-Tucker (KKT) theorem, since v is concave on P, $P \in \Pi_S$ is the best response strategy to J if and only if there is an ω (Lagrange multiplier) such that

$$w^C \frac{h_i^C}{\sigma^2 + h_i^C P_i + g_i^C J_i} + w^R \frac{h_i^R}{\sigma^2 + g_i^R J_i} \begin{cases} = \omega, & P_i > 0, \\ \leq \omega, & P_i = 0. \end{cases} \tag{9}$$

Similarly, since v is convex on J, $J \in \Pi_R$ is the best response strategy to P if and only if there is a ν (Lagrange multiplier) such that

$$w^C \frac{h_i^C g_i^C P_i}{(\sigma^2 + h_i^C P_i + g_i^C J_i)(\sigma^2 + g_i^C J_i)} + w^R \frac{h_i^R g_i^R P_i}{(\sigma^2 + g_i^R J_i)^2} \begin{cases} = \nu, & J_i > 0, \\ \leq \nu, & J_i = 0. \end{cases} \tag{10}$$

Then, (9) and (10) imply that ω and ν are positive. By (10) if $P_i = 0$ then $J_i = 0$. Thus, to find P and J we have to consider only three cases: (a) $P_i = 0, J_i = 0$, (b) $P_i = 0, J_i > 0$, and (c) $P_i > 0, J_i > 0$.

(a) Let $P_i = 0, J_i = 0$. Then, by (9) and (10), $w^C h_i^C / \sigma^2 + w^R h_i^R / \sigma^2 \leq \omega$. Thus, $i \in I_{00}(\omega, \nu)$, and (I-a) follows.

(b) Let $P_i > 0, J_i = 0$. Then, by (9) and (10), we have that

$$w^C h_i^C / (\sigma^2 + h_i^C P_i) + w^R h_i^R / \sigma^2 = \omega, \tag{11}$$

$$w^C h_i^C g_i^C P_i / ((\sigma^2 + h_i^C P_i)\sigma^2) + w^R h_i^R g_i^R P_i / (\sigma^2)^2 \leq \nu. \tag{12}$$

By (11), $P_i = P_i(\omega, \nu)$ is given by (1). Note that, P_i is decreasing with respect to ω. By (1), $P_i > 0$ (this holds by assumption of (b)) if and only if:

$$w^R h_i^R / \sigma^2 < \omega < w^C h_i^C / \sigma^2 + w^R h_i^R / \sigma^2. \tag{13}$$

Substituting (1) into (12) yields that

$$\frac{w^C g_i^C}{\sigma^2} + \frac{w^C w^R h_i^R g_i^R}{\sigma^4 (\omega - w^R h_i^R / \sigma^2)} \leq \nu + \frac{w^R h_i^R g_i^R}{\sigma^2 h_i^C} + \frac{g_i^C}{h_i^C}\left(\omega - \frac{w^R h_i^R}{\sigma^2}\right). \tag{14}$$

The left side of (14) is decreasing with respect to ω from infinity for $\omega = w^R h_i^R/\sigma^2$ to $A_L := w^C g_i^C/\sigma^2 + w^R h_i^R g_i^R/(\sigma^2 h_i^C)$ for $\omega = w^C h_i^C/\sigma^2 + w^R h_i^R/\sigma^2$.

The right side of (14) is increasing with respect to ω from $\nu + w^R h_i^R g_i^R/h_i^C$ for $\omega = w^R h_i^R/\sigma^2$ to $A_R := \nu + w^R h_i^R g_i^R/(\sigma^2 h_i^C) + w^C h g_i^C/\sigma^2 = \nu + A_L > A_L$ for $\omega = w^C h_i^C/\sigma^2 + w^R h_i^R/\sigma^2$. Thus, for any positive ν there is a unique $\omega = \omega_{+,i}(\nu)$ such that (13) holds, while (14) holds as equality. It is clear that $\omega_{+,i}(\nu)$ is decreasing on ν. Since this is a quadratic equation on ω, $\omega_{+,i}(\nu)$ can be found in closed form, by (2), and (II-b) follows.

(c) Let $P_i > 0, J_i > 0$. Then, by (9) and (10) we have that

$$w^C h_i^C/(\sigma^2 + h_i^C P_i + g_i^C J_i) + w^R h_i^R/(\sigma^2 + g_i^R J_i) = \omega, \tag{15}$$

$$w^C h_i^C g_i^C P_i/((\sigma^2 + h_i^C P_i + g_i^C J_i)(\sigma^2 + g_i^C J_i)) + w^R h_i^R g_i^R P_i/(\sigma^2 + g_i^R J_i)^2 = \nu. \tag{16}$$

By (15), we have that

$$P_i = w^C/(\omega - w^R h_i^R/(\sigma^2 + g_i^R J_i)) - (\sigma^2 + g_i^C J_i)/h_i^C. \tag{17}$$

By (17), P_i is decreasing with respect to J_i. Substituting (17) into (16) implies (3). The left side of (3) is decreasing with respect to J_i and tends to zero while J_i tends to infinity. Thus, for each ω and ν, (3) has a root (which is unique) if and only if:

$$\frac{w^C g_i^C}{\sigma^2} + \frac{w^C w^R h_i^R g_i^R}{\sigma^4 \left(\omega - w^R h_i^R/\sigma^2\right)} > \nu + \frac{w^R h_i^R g_i^R}{\sigma^2 h_i^C} + \frac{g_i^C}{h_i^C}\left(\omega - \frac{w^R h_i^R}{\sigma^2}\right). \tag{18}$$

By (14), the condition (18) is equivalent to $\omega < \omega_{+,i}(\nu)$. Denote this root by $J_i(\omega, \nu)$. Then, substituting this $J_i(\omega, \nu)$ into (17) we can uniquely define P_i denoted by $P_i(\omega, \nu)$, and (I-c) follows.

Note that, by (3), $J_i(\omega, \nu)$ is decreasing on ω and ν. The left side of (16) is increasing with respect to P_i and decreasing with respect to J_i. Thus, the fact that $J_i(\omega, \nu)$ is decreasing with respect to ω implies that $P_i(\omega, \nu)$ is also decreasing with respect to ω. Also, the left side of (15) is decreasing on P_i and on J_i. Thus, the fact that $J_i(\omega, \nu)$ is decreasing on ν implies that $P_i(\omega, \nu)$ is increasing on ν. Thus, $H_J(\omega, \nu)$ is continuous and decreasing on ω and ν, while $H_S(\omega, \nu)$ is continuous and decreasing on ω and increasing on ν. These monotonous properties yields that solution of (5) is the unique, and (I) follows.

(II) If $w^C = 0$ then (9) implies (6). Thus, $J_i(\nu)$ is defined uniquely. Substituting this $J_i(\nu)$ into (9) and taking into account that $\boldsymbol{P} \in \Pi_S$ implies the result.

References

1. Aubry, A., De Maio, A., Huang, Y., Piezzo, M., Farina, A.: A new radar waveform design algorithm with improved feasibility for spectral coexistence. IEEE Trans. Aerosp. Electron. Syst. **51**, 1029–1038 (2015)
2. Bica, M., Huang, K.W., Koivunen, V., Mitra, U.: Mutual information based radar waveform design for joint radar and cellular communication systems. In: IEEE International Conference on Acoustics, Speech and Signal Processing (ICASSP), pp. 3671–3675 (2016)
3. Bica, M., Koivunen, V.: Delay estimation method for coexisting radar and wireless communication systems. In: IEEE Radar Conference, pp. 1557–1561 (2017)
4. Garnaev, A., Liu, Y., Trappe, W.: Anti-jamming strategy versus a low-power jamming attack when intelligence of adversary's attack type is unknown. IEEE Trans. Sig. Inf. Process. Netw. **2**, 49–56 (2016)
5. Garnaev, A., Trappe, W.: To eavesdrop or jam, that is the question. In: Mellouk, A., Sherif, M.H., Li, J., Bellavista, P. (eds.) ADHOCNETS 2013. LNICST, vol. 129, pp. 146–161. Springer, Cham (2014). https://doi.org/10.1007/978-3-319-04105-6_10
6. Garnaev, A., Trappe, W.: Bargaining over the fair trade-off between secrecy and throughput in OFDM communications. IEEE Trans. Inf. Forensics Secur. **12**, 242–251 (2017)
7. Garnaev, A., Trappe, W.: The rival might be not smart: revising a CDMA jamming game. In: IEEE Wireless Communications and Networking Conference (WCNC). IEEE (2018)
8. Garnaev, A., Trappe, W., Petropulu, A.: Bargaining over fair performing dual radar and communication task. In: 50th Asilomar Conference on Signals, Systems, and Computers, Pacific Grove, CA, pp. 47–51, November 2016
9. Garnaev, A., Trappe, W., Petropulu, A.: Optimal design of a dual-purpose communication-radar system in the presence of a Jammer. In: IEEE 19th International Workshop on Signal Processing Advances in Wireless Communications (SPAWC), pp. 1–5 (2018)
10. Garnaev, A., Trappe, W.: Fair scheduling of two-hop transmission with energy harvesting. In: Zhou, Y., Kunz, T. (eds.) Ad Hoc Networks. LNICST, vol. 223, pp. 189–198. Springer, Cham (2018). https://doi.org/10.1007/978-3-319-74439-1_17
11. Gogineni, S., Rangaswamy, M., Nehorai, A.: Multi-modal OFDM waveform design. In: IEEE Radar Conference, pp. 1–5 (2013)
12. Gohary, R.H., Huang, Y., Luo, Z.-Q., Pang, J.-S.: A generalized iterative waterfilling algorithm for distributed power control in the presence of a Jammer. In: IEEE International Conference on Acoustics, Speech and Signal Processing (ICASSP), pp. 2373–2376 (2009)
13. Han, Z., Niyato, D., Saad, W., Basar, T., Hjrungnes, A.: Game Theory in Wireless and Communication Networks: Theory, Models, and Applications. Cambridge University Press, Cambridge (2012)
14. Lagarias, J.C., Reeds, J.A., Wright, M.H., Wright, P.E.: Convergence properties of the Nelder-Mead simplex method in low dimensions. SIAM J. Optim. **9**, 112–147 (1998)
15. Lan, T., Kao, D., Chiang, M., Sabharwal, A.: An axiomatic theory of fairness in network resource allocation. In: IEEE INFOCOM, pp. 1–9 (2010)
16. Li, B., Petropulu, A.P., Trappe, W.: Optimum co-design for spectrum sharing between matrix completion based MIMO radars and a MIMO communication system. IEEE Trans. Sig. Process. **64**, 4562–4575 (2016)

17. Liu, Y., Garnaev, A., Trappe, W.: Maintaining throughput network connectivity in ad hoc networks. In: 41st IEEE International Conference on Acoustics, Speech and Signal Processing (ICASSP), pp. 6380–6384 (2016)
18. Namvar, N., Saad, W., Bahadori, N., Kelleys, B.: Jamming in the Internet of Things: a game-theoretic perspective. In: IEEE Global Communications Conference (GLOBECOM), Washington, DC (2016)
19. Park, H., van der Schaar, M.: Bargaining strategies for networked multimedia resource management. IEEE Trans. Sig. Process. **55**, 3496–3511 (2007)
20. Poor, H.V.: An Introduction to Signal Detection and Estimation. Springer, New York (1994). https://doi.org/10.1007/978-1-4757-2341-0
21. Federal Communications Commission (FCC): FCC proposes innovative small cell use in 3.5 GHz band, December 2012. https://apps.fcc.gov/edocs_public/attachmatch/DOC-317911A1.pdf
22. Slimeni, F., Scheers, B., Le Nir, V., Chtourou, Z., Attia, R.: Closed form expression of the saddle point in cognitive radio and Jammer power allocation game. In: Noguet, D., Moessner, K., Palicot, J. (eds.) CrownCom 2016. LNICST, vol. 172, pp. 29–40. Springer, Cham (2016). https://doi.org/10.1007/978-3-319-40352-6_3
23. Song, T., Stark, W.E., Li, T., Tugnait, J.K.: Optimal multiband transmission under hostile jamming. IEEE Trans. Commun. **64**, 4013–4027 (2016)
24. Thomson, W.: Bargaining and the Theory of Cooperative Games: John Nash and Beyond. Edward Elgar Pub., Cheltenham (2010)
25. Turlapaty, A., Jin, Y.: A joint design of transmit waveforms for radar and communications systems in coexistence. In: IEEE Radar Conference, pp. 0315–0319 (2014)
26. Yang, D., Xue, G., Zhang, J., Richa, A., Fang, X.: Coping with a smart Jammer in wireless networks: a stackelberg game approach. IEEE Trans. Wirel. Commun. **12**, 4038–4047 (2013)

Using Deep Learning and Radio Virtualisation for Efficient Spectrum Sharing Among Coexisting Networks

Wei Liu[1]([✉]), Joao F. Santos[2], Xianjun Jiao[1], Francisco Paisana[2],
Luiz A. DaSilva[2], and Ingrid Moerman[1]

[1] IDLab University Ghent - IMEC, Technologiepark-Zwijnaarde 15, Ghent, Belgium
{wei.liu,xianjun.jiao,ingrid.moerman}@ugent.be
[2] Trinity College Dublin - CONNECT Centre, Dunlop Oriel House, Dublin, Ireland
{facocalj,paisanaf,dasilval}@tcd.ie

Abstract. This work leverages recent advances in machine learning for radio environment monitoring with context awareness, and uses the obtained information for creating radio slices that can optimally coexist with ongoing traffic in a given spectrum band. We instantiate radio slices as virtualised radios built on a software-defined radio platform. Then, we describe a proof-of-concept experiment that validates and demonstrates our proposed solution.

Keywords: Machine learning · Radio access technology classification
Radio virtualisation · Software-defined radio

1 Introduction

Increasingly, multiple Radio Access Technologies (RATs) must coexist in shared spectrum; this trend is only accelerating with the advent of 5G. In addition, the usage of flexible Radio Access Networks (RANs) with high reconfiguration capabilities presents new opportunities for interference coordination in shared spectrum scenarios. Radio Access Netowrks (RANs) may possess different degrees of compatibility, due to their unique waveforms, Medium Access Control (MAC) schemes, Radio Frequency (RF) parameters, or traffic requirements. In the context of network coexistence, it will be increasingly important for RANs to recognize the channels that exhibit transmission conditions that are favourable to their specific needs to optimize performance and, eventually, overall spectrum utilisation efficiency.

The project leading to this publication has received funding from the European Union's Horizon 2020 research and innovation program under grant agreement No. 732174 (ORCA project).

I. Moerman et al. (Eds.): CROWNCOM 2018, LNICST 261, pp. 165–174, 2019.
https://doi.org/10.1007/978-3-030-05490-8_16

Slicing is a concept used across Software-Defined Networks (SDNs), Network Function Virtualisation (NFV), and the 5G standard [1]. It involves sharing the underlying network infrastructure between multiple tenants, by assigning each tenant to a virtual network created with a portion of the network's resources, known as a network slice. This approach leads to an overall increase of network resource utilisation while offering greater flexibility, as each network slice can be used and managed independently [2,3]. Strategies similar to network slicing may be applied to optimize the utilisation of radio resources, which is referred to as radio slicing. More specifically, a radio slice in this work refers to a portion of the spectrum-time plane and the time share to utilize a radio interface assigned to a wireless link.

In general, network slicing requires some level of abstraction and virtualisation of physical devices and resources. Thus, network slicing and network virtualisation are closely tied [4]. The virtualisation of wired network components, e.g., links, routers and network interfaces, is a well-studied subject and is applied routinely, e.g., TCP/UDP ports and networking in virtual machines. In the wireless domain, virtualisation is still an active research topic [5]. In this paper, we combine deep learning, applied for spectrum awareness, and radio virtualisation for efficient spectrum sharing among coexisting networks.

It has been historically challenging to achieve such level of context awareness in scenarios where a wide variety of RATs coexist. However, with recent breakthroughs in the area of machine learning, it may be finally possible to bring these capabilities to existing RANs in a sufficiently flexible and cost-efficient manner. From the radio technology point of view, today's developers generally choose software-defined radio (SDR) solutions for their flexibility and fast development cycle. The adoption of SDR with high reconfiguration capabilities, together with breakthroughs in machine learning, brings the potential to use radio slicing as a means to optimize the coexistence among wireless networks and the utilisation of radio resources.

1.1   Spectrum Monitoring and Machine-Learning

The allocation of radio resources and configuration of RATs for supporting different types of services require the assessment and characterization of the underlying spectrum. Overall, spectrum monitoring can be used for enforcing spectrum policy, protecting incumbents in shared spectrum scenarios, supporting the coexistence between different RATs, and performing efficient radio resource management.

Contextual awareness is also key to radio and network slicing. The same RAT and its network slices may possess distinct protection requirements in terms of interference, and also employ different PHY parameters (e.g. subcarrier spacing), MAC schemes, and control structures.

Machine learning approaches have started to show promising results for spectrum monitoring and awareness, outperforming traditional solutions such as energy detection and expert feature detection [6]. These new approaches can collect features that go beyond simple waveform classification, e.g., frequency, bandwidth, and frame duration. Furthermore, such machine learning-based solutions achieve greater generality, as a single neural network can be trained to recognize multiple types of RATs, and evolvability, as the given neural network can be retrained to recognize new RATs.

1.2   Radio Virtualisation

Current commercial devices use dedicated chipsets that implement a specific wireless standard. This approach works well if the device only needs to support a single RAT. However, devices often must support multiple RATs. As a result, more and more chipsets are installed in one device, which inevitably increases the device's form factor, power consumption, and complexity.

In addition to the need for supporting multiple standards, it is often required to have multiple radio interfaces of the same technology on one device. For example, some commercial Wi-Fi Access Points (APs) support simultaneous operation on different channels, and according to multiple variants of the IEEE 802.11 standard. Behind the scenes, the AP is switching channels periodically. Before it switches to the next channel, it broadcasts the "unavailable period" to the associated stations in the current channel. In this way, the AP can act as virtual APs on multiple channels. However, this approach is not entirely transparent to the upper layers, as the AP services are interrupted during the times of switching between different channels.

From the radio virtualisation aspect, in this paper we demonstrate that: (i) a physical radio can be instantiated into multiple virtual radios, (ii) the virtualisation process is application-transparent, meaning that the virtual radio offers uninterrupted services from the upper layer perspective in a way that is indistinguishable from multiple physical radios.

2   Proposed Solution

A block diagram of our proposed solution is shown in Fig. 1. On the left side, a classifier uses a deep Convolutional Neural Network (CNN) trained for classifying different RATs. The input of the classifier is time domain IQ samples, captured from a finite number of channels (denoted by N) with equal bandwidth. The use of time domain IQ samples instead of a spectogram provides amplitude and phase information to the classifier: this additional information makes the classifier more robust in the classification and feature extraction of signals [7]. Figure 2 shows screenshots of the graphical display of the classifier: it illustrates the classification of different types of RATs, where we use the bounding boxes for extracting features from the RATs and calculating signal statistics. The output of the classifier indicates: the kind of signal present in a channel, measured by the signal intensity and bandwidth; and the type of traffic the signal carries, measured by the burst length, average channel duty cycle, and minimum Inter-Frame Interval (IFI).

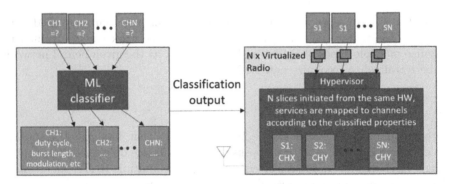

Fig. 1. A block diagram of the proposed solution: N virtual radios are instantiated according to service demands and context information provided by the machine learning (ML) classifier.

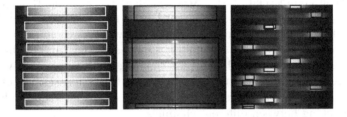

Fig. 2. Example of the RAT detection on three different channels over time. The different colours of the bounding boxes indicate different radio acccess technologies. (Color figure online)

The radio hypervisor handles N services from the host PC using a single SDR device. We identify data streams from different services by their TCP port. Our hypervisor collects the data from the N services, and then streams each of them to the SDR device with an appended "slice identifier". The slice identifier informs the SDR to send the data on a given channel and treat it with a given priority. Then, our hypervisor uses the output of the classifier to decide which channel will be used for a given service. This decision is based on the properties of the background traffic, described by the output of the classifier, and the demand of the traffic we want to serve.

For instance, a channel can appear highly occupied at first glance, but the classifier may identify that the background traffic on the channel is in fact composed of many short bursts. This kind of channel cannot sustain a service with high throughput requirements, but it can be suitable for a service with low throughput and low latency requirements, as there will be frequent transmission opportunities in between the bursts of background traffic. Moreover, the classifier also recommends the optimal coexistence settings for a slice, e.g., the transmission duration on a channel that can fit into the minimum IFI of the background traffic. In this way, the classifier's output is used to facilitate the resource mapping and optimization process on each virtual radio.

Zooming in towards the SDR side, the virtualisation comes down to using a single radio front-end and transceiver chain on multiple channels. Behind the scenes, the transceiver chain runs N times faster than the speed required for a single channel operation. On the transmission side, the baseband IQ samples for each channel are first up-sampled, and then shifted to the desired frequency offset, and finally combined with the baseband samples from the other channels and streamed to the Digital to Analog Converter (DAC), as detailed in [8]. The reverse process occurs on the receiver side. The concept of radio virtualisation does not depend on the exact architecture of the transceiver or other processing modules: it could happen at CPU level [9] or at the hardware level on the FPGA [10].

Our goal is to instantiate radio interfaces according to the required services, finding the best combination between a set of channels and services while taking into account the context information (such as existing background traffic) and the demand. Though this work focuses on frequency slicing, similar strategies can be applied to other types of resources, such as space or time.

3 Proof of Concept

3.1 Experiment Setup

We use an experiment to validate our solution, and its setup is shown in Fig. 3. We consider two 20 MHz channels: on each channel, we use a USRP N210 for generating the background traffic, referred to as the traffic generator, and another USRP N210 for capturing samples of the given channel, referred to as a channel probe. We stream the samples from the channel probes to the 'spectrum monitor', which is a laptop running a trained machine learning model on its Graphical Processing Unit (GPU) for classifying the radio environment on both channels. The Machine Learning (ML) model classifies the RAT of the background traffic present on each channel and extracts their contextual information in real time. This information will be used by a Base Station to select its optimal settings, including channel of operation.

A simple downlink scenario consisting of one Base Station (BS) and two User Equipments (UEs) is displayed in Fig. 3. The optimal setting from the ML classifier is transferred to a host PC that controls the BS. Each BS/UE consists of a host PC with an SDR device, which is further composed by a Xilinx Zynq 7000 ZC706 evaluation board [11] and an Analog Devices FMCOMMS2 front-end [12], referred to as the Zynq SDR hereafter.

On channel 1, the background traffic comprises relatively short bursts (on average 2 ms) interleaved by comparable IFI, while on channel 2, the individual frame is relatively longer (10 ms), with on average 60 ms IFI. We used an Anritsu MS2781B spectrum analyser for measuring the characteristics of the background traffic, and the results are illustrated in Fig. 4.

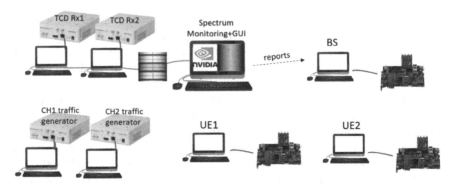

Fig. 3. The experimental setup: 2 N210 USRPs as background traffic generators, 2 USRP N210 as channel probes, 1 laptop as spectrum monitor, 1 BS which receives context information and serves the two UEs. Each BS/UE consists of a host and a Zynq SDR platform (Xilinx zc706+FMCOMMS2).

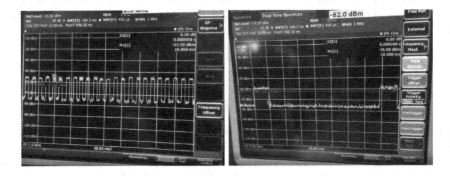

Fig. 4. The background traffic in the time domain: the traffic on channel 1, shown on the left side, has on average a 2 ms period and a duty cycle of roughly 50%; the channel 2 traffic, shown on the right side, has on average a 70 ms period and occupies the channel for about 13% of the time.

At the base station, the first question is which channel should be used to serve traffic for which UE. In this experiment, the traffic towards UE1 (referred to as T1) generates 5 frames at 100 bytes per second, and each frame must be delivered within 5 ms. This type of traffic is representative of traffic generated by a watchdog application in a factory environment, which reports regular "heartbeats" of a system, and can trigger critical safety procedures when needed. A large file transfer produces the traffic towards UE2 (referred to as T2). T2 only requires the link to sustain an average throughput in the order of Mbps. After combining the requirements of T1 and T2, and the context information regarding the background traffic, the BS makes its first decision: Channel 1 should be used to serve T1 for its more frequent transmission opportunities, and Channel 2 should be used to serve T2 for its overall lower occupation level.

We use a simple Listen Before Talk (LBT) module on the BS, which allows the BS to inject traffic only when a channel is idle. This process is shown on the left side of Fig. 5, where T2 shortly follows the background traffic on channel 2 with relatively lower signal strength.

The next question is how long the BS transmission can last on each channel, which is required to maximize the throughput for T2. The classifier collects different signal statistics, including the minimum IFI (1.35 ms), and provides them to the BS to optimize its transmission burst length. The application of this information results in a better usage efficiency for channel 2, as shown on the right side of Fig. 5.

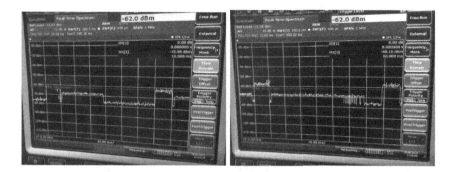

Fig. 5. The traffic injected by the BS on channel 2 under default (left hand side) and optimal (right hand side) transmission burst length settings.

3.2   Measurements and Results

We measure the latency of T1 and the throughput of T2 to indicate the quality of the desired services. Details of these measurements are given below.

Throughput of T2 is measured by capturing frames at the Ethernet interface on the host of UE2. The Wireshark IO statistic graph is shown in Fig. 6. The average throughput for default and optimal slice configurations are 912.7 kbps and 1908.9 kbps, respectively. We observe that the throughput doubles by applying the optimal setting. The standard deviation of the throughput under both conditions is around 150 kbps, which illustrates that the stability of the throughput is unaffected.

Latency can be measured at different levels. The time delay between the moment when a frame is being transmitted on the wireless medium and the moment when the receiver decodes a complete frame is the latency at the physical layer. In general, it is subject to the frame size, the specific wireless technology, and it is also PHY implementation dependent. However, these are not the

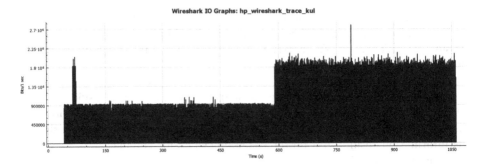

Fig. 6. Throughput of T2 shown by Wireshark IO statistics: an improvement is visible after applying the optimal setting recommended by the classifier.

focus of this work: we focus on the end-to-end delay, which includes the aforementioned physical layer delay, but additionally includes the time consumed by queuing in upper layer buffers, and processing delays at both transmitter and receiver sides in the SDR. For consistency, this measurement is conducted with fixed payload size, modulation and coding scheme.

The end-to-end latency of T1 is measured as follows: (i) Whenever the BS SDR receives a frame from the host, it triggers a TCP interrupt service routine (ISR), which toggles a General Purpose Input or Output (GPIO) pin within the same ISR. (ii) On the UE1 SDR side, whenever a frame pops out of the RX queue[1] before it is sent towards the host, the UE toggles a GPIO pin. (iii) Both the GPIO pins at the BS and UE are connected to a Saleae logic analyser. The logic analyser samples both pins at 6.25 Msps, ensuring the measurement precision at sub-microsecond level. A screenshot of the logic analyser's graphical user interface (GUI) is given in Fig. 7. The "sender" line shows the GPIO activity of the BS, while the "Receiver" line shows the GPIO activity of UE1. The latency is indicated by the distance between the two markers (i.e., A1, A2). For this particular case in the screenshot, it is 87.2 µs. The GUI also allows exporting the trace of the pin activity into a CSV file, which we later process using a simple Matlab script for generating the probability distribution of the latency measurements under various conditions.

Fig. 7. The interface of Saleae logical analyser.

---

[1] The physical layer receiver at the UE SDR decodes frames and inserts them into a queue, which is referred to as the RX queue.

The measurements are conducted under three conditions: (i) serving only T1 with no background traffic; (ii) serving T1 and T2 with no background traffic; (iii) serving T1 and T2 together with background traffic on both channels. The histograms of latency measurements under all conditions are given in Fig. 8. We observe that the latency for the first two conditions have similar distribution range, and they both have a high peak around 87 μs, which indicates that the latency of T1 is not negatively affected by serving T2. The virtual radio can hence operate in a way that is transparent to the user. The latency distribution for the 3rd case shows a high peak in the first interval, which corresponds to 87 μs— the best case scenario when the frame can be sent immediately without waiting for the background traffic, just as in the first two conditions. We also observe that probability is generally higher in $[0, 2000]$ μs range than the remaining part. This shows that the majority of the frames are sent after waiting for at most one complete frame of the background traffic, which lasts on average 2 ms. The worst case latency is around 3 ms: this can be explained by longer frames in the background traffic or missed detection of the transmission opportunities by the simple LBT module.

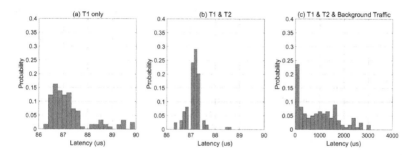

Fig. 8. The probability distribution of latency of T1 when: (a) serving only T1; (b) serving T1 and T2; (c) serving T1 and T2 with background traffic on both channels.

4   Conclusions

This work combines radio virtualisation for Software-Defined Radio platforms with deep learning technologies for optimizing spectrum utilisation, and the coexistence of wireless networks. We use a proof-of-concept experiment to show-case the combined application of: (i) radio virtualisation; and (ii) deep learning-based radio environment monitoring. Regarding radio virtualisation, it is demonstrated that a single radio device can be instantiated upon requests into multiple logical instances, each serving a different traffic flow with diverging requirements. Regarding radio environment monitoring, we showcase how decisions based on context awareness could improve coexistence and the quality of service experienced by each traffic flow.

References

1. 3rd Generation Partnership Project: 3GPP TR 28.801: study on management and orchestration of network slicing for next generation network. 3rd Generation Partnership Project, Technical report, May 2017
2. Rost, P., et al.: Network slicing to enable scalability and flexibility in 5G mobile networks. IEEE Commun. Mag. **55**(5), 72–79 (2017)
3. Khan, S.N., et al.: Virtualization of spectrum resources for 5G networks, In: 2017 European Conference on Networks and Communications (EuCNC), pp. 1–5 (2017)
4. van de Belt, J., et al.: Defining and surveying wireless link virtualization and wireless network virtualization. IEEE Commun. Surv. Tutor. **19**(3), 1603–1627 (2017)
5. Liang, C., et al.: Wireless network virtualization: a survey, some research issues and challenges. IEEE Commun. Surv. Tutor. **17**(1), 358–380 (2015)
6. Wunsch, F., et al.: DySPAN spectrum challenge: situational awareness and opportunistic spectrum access benchmarked. IEEE Trans. Cogn. Commun. Netw. **3**(3), 550–562 (2017)
7. Selim, A., et al.: Spectrum monitoring for radar bands using deep convolutional neural networks. IEEE Globecom (2017)
8. de Figueiredo, F.A.P., et al.: Radio hardware virtualization for software-defined wireless networks. Wirel. Pers. Commun. **100**(1), 113–126 (2018). https://doi.org/10.1007/s11277-018-5619-3
9. Mendes, J., et al.: Cellular access multi-tenancy through small cell virtualization and common RF front-end sharing. In: Workshop on Wireless Network Testbeds, Experimental evaluation and Characterization. ACM, pp. 35–42 (2017)
10. Jiao, X., Moerman, I., Liu, W., de Figueiredo, F.A.P.: Radio hardware virtualization for coping with dynamic heterogeneous wireless environments. In: Marques, P., Radwan, A., Mumtaz, S., Noguet, D., Rodriguez, J., Gundlach, M. (eds.) CrownCom 2017. LNICST, vol. 228, pp. 287–297. Springer, Cham (2018). https://doi.org/10.1007/978-3-319-76207-4_24
11. Zynq-7000 All Programmable SoC ZC706 evaluation kit, Xilinx (2015). https://www.xilinx.com/support/documentation/boards_and_kits/zc706/2015_4/ug961-zc706-GSG.pdf
12. AD-FMCOMMS2-EBZ User Guide, Analog Device (2018). https://wiki.analog.com/resources/eval/user-guides/ad-fmcomms2-ebz

PHY and Sensing

Evaluating Deep Neural Networks to Classify Modulated and Coded Radio Signals

Phui San Cheong[1], Miguel Camelo[2(✉)], and Steven Latré[2]

[1] University of Antwerp, Antwerp, Belgium
phuisan.cheong@student.uantwerpen.be
[2] IDLab Research Group, Department of Mathematics and Computer Science,
University of Antwerp - imec, Antwerp, Belgium
{miguel.camelo,steven.latre}@uantwerpen.be

Abstract. Cognitive Radio (CR) systems allow optimizing the use of the shared radio spectrum and enhancing the coexistence among different technologies by efficiently changing certain operating parameters of the radios such as transmit-power, carrier frequency, and modulation and coding scheme in real-time. Dynamic Spectrum Access (DSA), which allows radios to dynamically access and use the unused spectrum, is one of the tasks that are fundamental for a better use of the spectrum. In this paper, we extend the previous work on Automatic Modulation Classification (AMC) by using Deep Neural Network (DNNs) and evaluate the performance of these architectures on signals that are not only modulated but are also encoded. We call this the Automatic Modulation and Coding Scheme Classification problem, or AMC^2. In this problem, radio signals are classified according to the Modulation and Coding Scheme (MCS) used during their transmission. Evaluations on a data set of 802.11 radio signals, transmitted with different MCS and Signal to Noise Ratio (SNR), provide important results on the impact of some DNN hyperparameters, e.g. number of layers, batch size, etc., in the classification accuracy.

Keywords: Cognitive Radio · Dynamic Spectrum Access
Deep Neural Network · Convolutional Neural Network
Modulation and Coding Scheme

1 Introduction

Nowadays a large number of technologies are sharing the same radio spectrum and it has become a scarce commodity [1]. However, most of the spectrum is underutilized most of the time. In order to optimize the use of the radio spectrum, Cognitive Radio (CR) systems will play an important role due to their capabilities to communicate efficiently by changing certain operating parameters of the radio, such as transmit-power, carrier frequency, and modulation and

© ICST Institute for Computer Sciences, Social Informatics and Telecommunications Engineering 2019
Published by Springer Nature Switzerland AG 2019. All Rights Reserved
I. Moerman et al. (Eds.): CROWNCOM 2018, LNICST 261, pp. 177–188, 2019.
https://doi.org/10.1007/978-3-030-05490-8_17

coding scheme, in real-time [2]. One of the key features in CR is the Dynamic Spectrum Access (DSA), which allows radios to dynamically access and use the unused spectrum [1]. The decision-making process executed by DSA broadly falls in the fields of cross-layer optimization and is solved by using algorithms from mathematical optimization, e.g. evolutionary algorithms, and Artificial Intelligence, e.g. Machine Learning (ML). In general, DSA involves several tasks that a radio should execute with the aim of improving its performance. One of this task is the Automatic Modulation Classification (AMC), which is used to automatically determine the modulation type of the transmitted signal. One of the main challenges in AMC is to classify a received signal into a modulation type without (or limited) a prior information about the transmitted signal under dynamic channel conditions [3].

This problem has been mainly faced via either acLB and expert Feature-Based (FB) engineering combined with pattern recognition methods [23]. Note that while Likelihood-Based (LB) methods find optimal solutions by minimizing the probability of false classification at the cost of a high computational complexity, FB methods have lower complexity and their performance is (near-)optimal, when they are designed properly. However, these features are usually chosen by an expert and are based upon a certain set of assumptions, which most of the time, are not realistic [4]. In recent years, some of the limitations of such techniques have been partially solved by applying Deep Neural Networks (DNNs). DNNs are able to (1) automatically extract the important features on raw time-series data, and (2) perform the classification task [26] on the extracted features. A DNN consists of a set of interconnected computational nodes, which are called artificial neurons, that are hierarchically organized in different layers, namely input layer, hidden/intermediate layer(s) and an output layer. A set of weighted links connecting the nodes between the layers are constantly adjusted as the training continues, where neurons take the output of the linked neurons in the previous layer and compute a new output based on the activation function of each neuron. DNNs are Neural Networks (NNs) that surpass 3 layers (including input and output layers). Note that the greater the depth of the NN, the greater the ability of it to differentiate complex features on signals for tasks such as regression, classification, and clustering.

In this paper, we will extend the previous work on AMC by using DNNs and evaluating its performance on radio signals that are not only modulated but are also coded. We call this the Automatic Modulation and Coding Classification or AMC^2. In our approach, 802.11ac radio signals are classified using a DNN according to the Modulation and Coding Scheme (MCS) that was used during their transmissions and under different Signal to Noise Ratios (SNRs) of the communication channel. The main contributions of this paper are two-fold. Firstly, a DNN architecture is defined for the radio signal classification task based on raw In-phase and Quadrature (IQ) samples of the transmitted signal. Secondly, several experiments were performed and analyzed in order to determine the impact of some DNN hyperparameters (e.g. the number of layers, batch size, etc.) on the classification accuracy. The remainder of this paper will be structured as follows:

Sect. 2 introduces the related work on AMC using DNNs. In Sect. 3, the DNN architecture used to solve the AMC^2 problem on 802.11 signals is presented. Section 4 discusses the evaluations and the results of the proposed architecture. Finally Sect. 5 contains the conclusion and future extensions of the presented work.

2   Related Works

The task of AMC is to recognize the unknown modulation scheme of a received radio signal automatically. It plays an important role in intelligent communication systems like cognitive radios. In general, this task is hard due to the absence of a prior knowledge of the incoming signal, the effects of multi-path propagation, and the dynamics and uncertainty of the channel, among others. Two traditional methods to solve this problem are the LB and FB [23]. LB methods use a likelihood function of the received signal and try to maximize the likelihood radio given a threshold. These methods find optimal solutions by minimizing the probability of false classification but at the cost of a high computational complexity. FB methods [5] use several features of the received signals, e.g. instantaneous amplitude, phase and frequency, in order to recognize them based on their observed values. These features are usually chosen by an expert and used in combination with classifiers. In comparison to LB methods, FB ones have lower complexity and their performance is (near-)optimal when they are designed properly. Among classifiers, several ML methods for Pattern Recognition (PR) have been used for AMC such as NNs [6], clustering [7], Support Vector Machines (SVM) [8], Decision Trees (DT) [9], etc.

Several works have evaluated and compared the performance of different classifiers under a given set of expert features. NN-based classifiers have shown to overcome the performance of several ML methods for solving the AMC task [11,13,14,22]. Moreover, DNNs [21], NNs with more than one layer between the input and the output layers, have shown the best performance without explicitly requiring a FB method to extract radio signal features [10,12,15,17,18,26]. DNN architectures are capable of performing both the feature extraction and the classification of the radio signals using a unique NN. Authors in [17] showed that a DNN based on a Convolutional Neural Network (CNN), which are simply neural networks that use convolution in the place of general matrix multiplication in at least one of their layers [21], was able to outperform several expert FB methods using different classifiers. The CNN achieved a rough accuracy of 87%, across all the 11 types of modulated radio signals and SNRs on the test dataset, and using only raw IQ samples of the modulated radio signals as input. Similarly, Shengliang et al. [12] proposed a CNN classifier but on images that were generated after a data conversion from raw IQ samples to grey-colored images. Again, improvements and better classification accuracy were achieved over cumulant and ML-based modulation classification algorithms.

Instead of using CNN, authors in [10] proposed a deep learning architecture based on Extensible Neural Networks (ENN) for modulation classification in multi-path fading channel. The proposed DNN is based on energy natural logarithm model. The proposed ENN uses 3 smaller DNN, each one trained to recognize the amplitude, phase, and frequency of the radio signal. Results showed that the proposed ENN has higher Probability of Correct classification than traditional algorithms for modulation classification within the same training sequence and SNR. In [15], a CNN and Long Short-Term Memory (LSTM) are combined to create a Heterogeneous Deep Model Fusion (HDMF). A deep learning-based AMC method that employs Spectral Correlation Function (SCF) is introduced in [20]. In the proposed method, a Deep Belief Network (DBN) is applied for pattern recognition and classification with high accuracy even in the presence of environmental noise. Finally, the use of Sparse Autoencoders (SAE) DNN to solve the AMC problem was evaluated in [19] using different type of inputs. Three training inputs were IQ samples, the centroids of constellation points employing a fuzzy C-means algorithm to IQ diagrams, and the high-order cumulants of received samples. Each autoencoder layer was trained using the unsupervised training followed by the softmax classifier. The results showed that the accuracy of the proposed DNN architecture using an AWGN channel model with varying SNR outperformed AMC methods using Maximum likelihood classifier, cumulant based Genetic programming in combination with KNN classifiers and feed-forward neural network using cumulants and instantaneous power spectral density (PSD) as the features.

Based on the previous works, it is clear that DNN architectures solve the modulation of radio signals with high accuracy, even on pure raw data such as IQ samples and therefore removing the need of FB methods for prepossessing the received signal. However, and to the best of our knowledge, there is not a previous work to solve the problem of automatically classifying modulated radio signals that are also coded, which we have called the AMC^2 problem, using DNN.

3 Deep Architecture for AMC^2

Similar to the AMC task, AMC^2 can be defined as follows:

Definition 1. *The automatic modulation and coding scheme classification (AMC^2) is the task of recognizing the modulation and coding scheme used to transmit a received signal without the need of an a priori knowledge of such info.*

Note that most wireless systems, e.g. IEEE 802.11 and LTE, avoid this problem by including the MCS information in each signal frame so that the receivers are notified about the change in modulation scheme, and therefore, they would be able to react accordingly. However, this strategy affects the spectrum efficiency due to the extra modulation information in each signal frame. By automatically identifying the modulation type of the received signal, the receiver does not need to be notified about the MCS, the demodulation can still be successfully achieved and the spectrum efficiency is improved. For this reason, AMC^2 becomes a fundamental part of CR systems to solve this problem.

As it was shown in Sect. 2, DNN have been proved to be a powerful tool to solve the AMC problem in wireless communication systems even using only raw IQ samples. Traditionally, DNNs are usually built in a modular manner and, most of the cases, are inspired by architectures that have performed well on other problems. In this paper we will use a CNN [16,21] architecture based on the model described in [17]. Typically, a CNN comprises of convolutional layers, each followed by optional sub-sampling/regularization (pooling) layers and ending in fully-connected layers. These are hidden layers that are effectively chained functions that collectively transform the input data to the output.

The intermediate outputs from the hidden layers are not shown and are results of linear and non-linear processing of the input data. The linear processing of the input data involves multiplication of weight matrix and addition of bias vector, while the non-linear processing of the input data is triggered by the activation function. In this paper, the DNN architectures used for the AMC^2 is composed of 3 Convolutional layers, each of them followed by 3 Dense layers. A brief description of the individual layers and their function in the architecture are discussed below. The resulting architecture and size of each layer are shown in Fig. 4. Information about the size of the input layer and the properties of the input data is presented in Sect. 4 (Fig. 1).

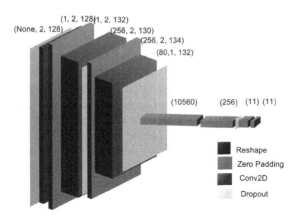

Fig. 1. 2-layered CNN accepting N × 2 × 128 inputs, where N is the batch size, and resolving to 11-class softmax output layer

3.1 Reshape and Zero-Padding Layer

A Reshape layer shapes the input data into the desired shape for the subsequent layers in the CNN. On the other hand, the Zero-Padding layer simply pads the border of the input data, to control the dimensionality of the output volumes. Together with input volume size, kernel size and stride zero-padding, this layer will ensure that the input fits nicely to the neurons in the Convolution layer.

3.2   Convolution Layer

A convolutional layer receives a 3D input vector and creates a 3D output vector that measures the filter responses at each input location, calculated as the sum of the element-wise product between filter and kernel size. This convolutional response encodes the input in terms of transformed intermediate outputs to systemically reduce input dimensionality as a part of feature learning.

3.3   Flatten and Dropout Layer

A flatten layer converts output from the previous layer from 3D to 1D vectors. This layer is necessary before Dense Layers, which accept only 1D vectors. The Dropout layer acts as a regularizing method used to avoid overfitting, i.e. the NN is able to classify objects that have not seen before. During training, neurons' weights and biases are adapted to detect specific features from the input dataset. The neuron weights would settle into their context within the network and could be too specific to the training data. When neurons are randomly dropped out of network during training, other neurons would be forced to handle representation required to predict missing neurons. This results in a neural network that would be capable to generalize new unseen data, in contrast to overfitting training data.

3.4   Dense Layer and Activation Function

A dense layer consists of neurons which have full connections to all activations in the previous layer. Their activations can be computed with a matrix multiplication. The activation function used in the Convolution and Fully-Connected/Dense Layers are Rectified Linear Unit (ReLu) and Softmax respectively. ReLu provides non-linear transformation to outputs of previous layers to learn the dataset. It is merely a two piecewise linear transformations that convert all outputs to positive values. This allows easy gradient optimization with good generalization capability. Softmax used in the last Dense Layer to represent a probability distribution over a discrete variable with n possible values, where n is the number of classes.

4   Experiments and Results

In this section, we will present the procedure and characteristics of the dataset generated and the main results of the evaluated architectures.

4.1   Dataset Generation

The dataset was created using the Matlab WLAN toolbox [25] and the technology selected for the radio signals with modulation and coding scheme is the IEEE 802.11ac. The radio signal was generated and represented in a 3-D vector with a shape of [N, IQ, P], where N is the number of samples of a signal with a given MCS and SNR, IQ is the real (In-phase) and imaginary (Quadrature) value representing the signal in a specific point in time, and the P is the number of consecutive points of that signal that are used as a single sample for training. For each MCS and SNR, $0 \leq SNR \leq 19$, a complex-valued time-series waveform is generated and a window with a width of 128 sample points is slid across the whole waveform 1000 times. Each IQ sample is normalized and stored separately resulting in [N, 2, 128] shape, where N is a factor (calculated by multiplication of the number of SNR types and number of MCS types) of 1000.

The simulation of the dataset begins with the creation of a Physical Service Data Unit (PSDU), which is then encoded to create a 4-packets waveform. Figure 2 shows an example of the waveform generated after transmitting 4 packets. The encoding is defined by the MCS. Only MCS 0–7 are used in the experiment. A 20-microsecond idle time is fixed between successive packets. The waveform is then passed through an evolving 802.11ac multipath fading channel (TGac). Additive White Gaussian Noise (AWGN) is added to the transmitted waveform to create the desired average SNR per sub-carrier. The 802.11ac transmitter is configured to use the very high throughput (VHT) format physical layer (PHY) packet, with a channel bandwidth of 80 Mhz, and a 1×1 MIMO array for one unique user. The Aggregate MAC Protocol Data Unit length is 1024. The transmission channel impairment is modeled to add channel and receiver noise, to produce a realistic modulated signal represented by $r(t) = s(t)*c+n(t)$, where $s(t)$ is time-series signal of a series of discrete bits modulated onto a sinusoid, c is path loss/gain constant on signal and $n(t)$ is additive Gaussian white noise.

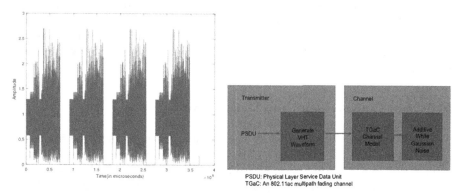

(a) Generated Waveform from four packets   (b) 802.11ac Signal Waveform Modeling
separated by 20-microsecond idle periods)

Fig. 2. Data set generation

After generating the data set, a preprocessing step is performed. The dataset generated are matrices of consisting IQ samples, SNR and label information for the different MCS schemes. Dataset is split into training, validation and test sets in ratio 60:20:20. The sample points for these sets are retrieved randomly from the dataset. After the splitting, it is further shuffled in place before being used in the CNN. During training, every training set is shuffled. The validation set that is used during training in order to measure the performance of the trained neural network on previously unseen data. The test data is used during prediction, where probabilities for each class is computed based on the test data's signal values. The maximum of the probabilities will be the 'winner'.

4.2   Prediction Accuracy

The confusion matrix for the proposed model, which is resulting from using the testing dataset for predictions, is presented in Fig. 3. It is possible to see that the average accuracy fluctuates among different SNR. It was found that the lowest obtained accuracy was 0.57, on average, and the highest prediction obtained for a given SNR, e.g. SNR = 19, was 0.8. It is clear that the higher the SNR, the higher the accuracy for predicting the correct MCS of the radio signal.

For our highest SNR case classification we show a confusion matrix in Fig. 3. At +19dB SNR, the diagonal in the confusion matrix is almost clear but some remaining discrepancies are that 64QAM with coding scheme 3/4 is misclassified as 64QAM with coding scheme 5/6. These can be explained due to the constellation 64QAM with coding scheme 5/6 is less resilient to noise and requires a higher SNR in order to be correctly identified.

4.3   Hyperparameters Results

Hyperparameters can be tuned and adjusted by the developer whereas parameters are set/automatically computed by models. While parameters are influenced by the number of filters, kernel size, and bias, the model hyperparameters are defined by the developer. The effects of the hyperparameters on the prediction accuracy of the CNN can be summarized as follow:

Additional Convolutional and Dense Layers. It is observed that the rule-of-thumb of adding convolutional layers with padding and dropout does not necessarily increase the accuracy of the classifications. In fact, the higher the number of neurons, which results from additional layers, increases the training time and the space requirements to store the data. The choice of the number of filters and its size have to be modest in order not to exceed the memory limits. From different model configurations, it can be concluded that 3-layered Convolutional with Padding and Dropout is optimized for the radio signal dataset of size [N, 2, 128] with N equal to 160000 (1000 × 8 MCS × 20 SNRs).

Dropout. The relationship of the dropout to the training/prediction accuracy is non-linear and varies for different CNNs architectures. For Model 1 as an example, it could learn and predict at only drop out rate of 0.0, 0.1 and 0.9, i.e. values close to 0 and 1. For 2-layered CNN, drop out rate 0.3 is the most optimal followed by 0.5 and 0.7.

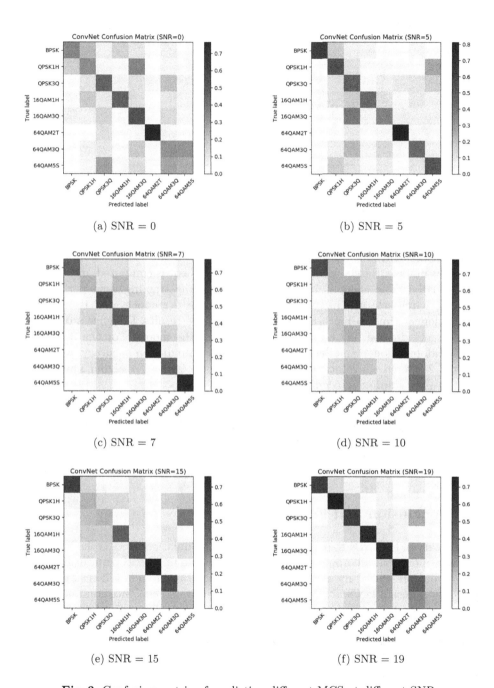

Fig. 3. Confusion matrix of predicting different MCS at different SNR

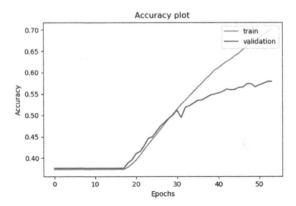

Fig. 4. Accuracy plot of the proposed architecture over the full datasetSNRs

Batch Size and No. of Epochs. Batch size of 2^5 and 2^{10} are chosen with the different models. Batch size defines how often gradient is computed and weights are updated. The effect is immediately seen in the training time per epoch. Smaller batch size will increase the training time per epoch, and it will also take a longer time to reach convergence. From the results, the effects of batch size largely depend on the number of layers of the model. For the 3-layered convolutional model, smaller batch size increases prediction accuracy, whereas, for the 2-layered convolutional model, the reverse is true. A higher number of epochs allow improving accuracy as it was expected.

Adam Optimizer. The default value in [24] is used throughout the evaluation, i.e. adam(lr $= 0.001$, $beta_1 = 0.9$, $beta_2 = 0.999$, epsilon $= 1e-8$, decay $= 0$) as it yields the highest training/prediction accuracy. It was detected that too high or too low learning rates could yield to homogeneous prediction and low accuracy.

5 Conclusion and Future Work

The ability of the CNN to detect different radio modulation types is the first step towards more real-life applications such as dynamic radio spectrum utilization. The paper presents some results that are intended to provide a heuristic guide in CNN to design DNN architectures for cognitive radio classification task using raw IQ data. Factors which influence training and prediction performance are identified and their impact on the CNN results are discussed. This acquired knowledge will be useful to create a new, optimized CNN specifically for radio classification tasks. As future work, we propose to evaluate the proposed DNN architectures on other waveforms, e.g. variations of the IEEE 802.11 standard or other technologies that also apply MCS to the transmitted signal, and exploring the possibility of using transfer learning on multiple radio technologies, each one with different physical layer, in order to reduce the training time.

References

1. Garhwal, A., Bhattacharya, P.P.: A survey on dynamic spectrum access techniques for cognitive radio. arXiv preprint arXiv:1201.1964 (2012)
2. Nolan, K.E., Doyle, L., O'Mahony, D., Mackenzie, P.: Modulation scheme recognition techniques for software radio on a general purpose processor platform. In: Proceedings of the First Joint IEI/IEE Symposium on Telecommunication Systems, Dublin (2001)
3. O'shea, T.J., Clancy, T.C., Ebeid, H.J.: Practical signal detection and classification in gnu radio. In: SDR Forum Technical Conference (SDR) (2007)
4. O'Shea, T., Hoydis, J.: An introduction to deep learning for the physical layer. IEEE Trans. Cogn. Commun. Netw. **3**(4), 563–575 (2017)
5. Hazza, A., Shoaib, M., Alshebeili, S.A., Fahad, A.: An overview of feature-based methods for digital modulation classification. In: 2013 1st International Conference on Communications, Signal Processing, and Their Applications (ICCSPA), pp. 1–6 (2013)
6. Azzouz, E.E., Nandi, A.K.: Modulation recognition using artificial neural networks. In: Azzouz, E.E., Nandi, A.K. (eds.) Automatic Modulation Recognition of Communication Signals, pp. 132–176. Springer, Boston (1996). https://doi.org/10.1007/978-1-4757-2469-1_5. ISBN 978-1-4757-2469-1
7. Swami, A., Sadler, B.: Modulation classification via hierarchical agglomerative cluster analysis. In: First IEEE Signal Processing Workshop on Signal Processing Advances in Wireless Communications. IEEE (1997)
8. Zhao, Z., Zhou, Y., Mei, F., Li, J.: Automatic modulation classification by support vector machines. In: Yin, F.-L., Wang, J., Guo, C. (eds.) ISNN 2004. LNCS, vol. 3173, pp. 654–659. Springer, Heidelberg (2004). https://doi.org/10.1007/978-3-540-28647-9_107. ISBN 978-3-540-28647-9
9. Kim, K., Polyodoros, A.: Digital modulation recognition: the BPSK versus QPSK case. In: MILCOM (1988)
10. Yang, G.Q.: Modulation classification based on extensible neural networks. Math. Prob. Eng. **2017**, 10 (2017). https://doi.org/10.1155/2017/6416019. Article ID 6416019
11. Nandi, A.K., Azzouz, E.E.: Algorithms for automatic modulation recognition of communication signals. IEEE Trans. Commun. **46**(4), 431–436 (1998)
12. Peng, S., et al.: Modulation classification based on signal constellation diagrams and deep learning. IEEE Trans. Neural Netw. Learn. Syst. **99**, 1–10 (2018)
13. Iversen, A.: The use of artificial neural networks for automatic modulation recognition, December 2003. http://www.macs.hw.ac.uk/cs/techreps/docs/files/HW-MACS-TR-0009.pdf
14. Ramakonar, V.S.: Modulation classification of digital communication signals (2002). http://ro.ecu.edu.au/theses/752
15. Zhang, D., et al.: Automatic modulation classification based on deep learning for unmanned aerial vehicles. Sensors **18**(3), 924 (2018)
16. O'Shea, K., Nash, R.: An introduction to convolutional neural networks (2015). https://arxiv.org/abs/1511.08458
17. O'Shea, T.J., Corgan, J., Clancy, T.C.: Convolutional radio modulation recognition networks. https://arxiv.org/abs/1602.04105
18. Kulin, M., et al.: End-to-end learning from spectrum data: a deep learning approach for wireless signal identification in spectrum monitoring applications. IEEE Access **6**, 18484–18501 (2018)

19. Ali, A., Yangyu, F., Liu, S.: Automatic modulation classification of digital modulation signals with stacked autoencoders. Digit. Sig. Process. **71**, 108–116 (2017)
20. Mendis, G.J., Wei, J., Madanayake, A.: Deep: learning-based automated modulation classification for cognitive radio. In: 2016 IEEE International Conference on Communication Systems (ICCS), Shenzhen, pp. 1–6 (2016). https://doi.org/10.1109/ICCS.2016.7833571
21. Goodfellow, I., Bengio, Y., Courville, A.: Deep Learning. MIT Press, Cambridge (2016). ISBN 9780262035613
22. Louis, C., Sehier, P.: Automatic modulation recognition with a hierarchical neural network. In: Proceedings of MILCOM 1994, Fort Monmouth, NJ, USA, vol. 3, pp. 713–717 (1994)
23. Dobre, O.A., Abdi, A., Bar-Ness, Y., Su, W.: Survey of automatic modulation classification techniques: classical approaches and new trends. IET Commun. **1**(2), 137–156 (2007). https://doi.org/10.1049/iet-com:20050176
24. Kingma, D.P., Ba, J.L.: Adam: a method for stochastic optimization. Published as a Conference Paper at ICLR 2015, July 2015. https://arxiv.org/pdf/1412.6980v8.pdf
25. Mathworks Documentation. WLAN System Toolbox. https://nl.mathworks.com/help/wlan/
26. Liu, X., Yang, D., El Gamal, A.: Deep neural network architectures for modulation classification. arXiv preprint arXiv:1712.00443 (2017)

Improving Spectrum Efficiency in Heterogeneous Networks Using Granular Identification

Rohit Singh[1(✉)] and Douglas Sicker[1,2]

[1] Engineering and Public Policy, Carnegie Mellon University, Pittsburgh, USA
rohits1@andrew.cmu.edu, sicker@cmu.edu
[2] School of Computer Science, Carnegie Mellon University, Pittsburgh, USA

Abstract. Given the ever-increasing demand for wireless services and the pending explosion of the Internet of Things (IoT), demand for radio spectrum will only become more acute. Setting aside (but not ignoring) the need for additional allocations of spectrum, the existing spectrum needs to be used more efficiently so that it can meet the demand. Other than providing more spectrum there are other factors (like, transmit power, antenna angles, QoS, bandwidth, and others) that can be adjusted to cater to the demand and at the same time increase the spectrum efficiency. With heterogeneity and densification these factors are so varied it becomes necessary that we have some tool to monitor these factors so as to optimize our outcome. Here we propose a PHY layer granular identification that monitors the physical and logical parameters associated with a device/antenna. Through a simple optimization problem, we show how the proposed identification mechanism can further the cause of spectrum efficiency and ease coordination among devices in a heterogeneous network (HetNet) to assign resources more optimally. Compared to received signal strength (RSS) way of assigning resources the proposed approach shows a 138% to 220% increase (depending on the requested QoS) in spectrum efficiency. Ultimately, this research is aimed at assisting the regulators in addressing future spectrum related efficiency and enforcement issues.

Keywords: Spectrum efficiency · Identification
Heterogeneous networks · Spectrum sharing · Optimization
Radio resource management

1 Introduction

The Cisco VNI report [1] suggests there will be a global increase in the devices and connection per capita to 3.5 Billion by the year 2021, which will take a

We would like to note Dr. John Chapin's contributions in his discussions on this concept with the authors. We would like to thank Prof. Dennis Roberson for sharing spectrum data from his Spectrum Observatory in Chicago as shown in Fig. 1.

I. Moerman et al. (Eds.): CROWNCOM 2018, LNICST 261, pp. 189–199, 2019.
https://doi.org/10.1007/978-3-030-05490-8_18

toll on the demand for spectrum. This impending demand for wireless services, and eventually requiring more spectrum, will drive fierce regulatory battles. As deployments become denser, we will likely face increasing issues of harmful interference and a rising noise floor, compounding the already difficult task of enforcement and efficiency for regulators. Furthermore, as devices become more densely deployed, it is likely that current methods for radio spectrum management will fall short, demanding novel radio access methods.

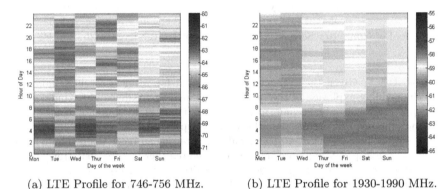

(a) LTE Profile for 746-756 MHz.   (b) LTE Profile for 1930-1990 MHz.

Fig. 1. Average aggregated spectrum occupancy waterfall chart for Chicago downtown measured by the received signal strength in dBm for year 2015–2017 (Color figure online)

It has been argued that we have faced a spectrum crunch [2] scenario for the last few decades. There has always been a notion that we need to get more spectrum to cater to this increasing demand for spectrum. However, most of the prime frequencies in the sub-6GHz spectrum are already occupied by government and/or licensed owners. The rapidly increasing demand for spectrum requires that the user equipments (UEs) are provided with more easy access to spectrum either through reassignment, reallocation, or access to higher spectrum through millimeter waves and most recently terahertz frequency [3]. However, these methods are often cumbersome and face deadlock due to huge cost, slow pace of technological advancement or political agenda.

Nevertheless, the demand for spectrum is bursty in nature and is a function of the time of day or day of the week. We performed a spectrum occupancy analysis based on time and days of the week as shown in Fig. 1a and b on a color scale of blue to red, where red signifies most activity. These are the popular LTE downlink frequencies, which highlights the fact that even in a highly populated city like Chicago, the cellular bands are not being utilized to the fullest. The spectrum data was collected by a directional antenna with a direct line-of-sight (LOS) from downtown Chicago [4]. The LTE Profile seems to have particular peak time of usage depending on the demand of the UEs. Not surprisingly, the pattern repeats at particular hours of the day (mostly 10am-8pm) and particular days of the week (mostly weekdays). Thus, instead of providing more spectrum through above-mentioned methods it will be benefiting that we use the existing resources (the frequency band) to the optimal level. Therefore, it will be valuable to combine applications/devices to operate cooperatively and utilize the same frequency by reducing the frequency reuse, so as to improve efficiency. Heterogeneous Networks (HetNets) have proved to be the best example where the spectrum efficiency can be increased by adjusting other technical parameters of the devices, like transmit power, antenna angles (azimuthal and vertical), Quality of Service (QoS), bandwidth, modulation schemes and others, to use spectrum more opportunistically.

In this paper, we propose a methodology to monitor these resources at a granular level through an identification (ID) structure. Today's cognitive radios are capable of causing or mitigating interference by adjusting the technical parameters associated with the device(s)/antenna(s). Thus, this makes it necessary that we identify these devices not only physically, but also logically by their operating parameters (i.e., the different technical parameters associated with that device) and provide it in a way that other devices and networks can recognize. However, while trying to cover more users in the process, we might risk causing harmful interference, which can quickly enter into a vicious cycle of demand for more spectrum. With ID structure, device(s)/antenna(s) can be informed about an impending interference and try to avoid it or may try to ease the enforcement process, which follows an interference scenario.

It reasons that knowing the IDs of other devices (particularly from HetNet systems) could be useful in optimizing resource use; nonetheless, it is necessary to show how such an ID could be used. Therefore, we use a granular layer monitoring of resources to show an increase in efficiency without adding additional spectrum or causing unwanted harmful interference. In the next sections, we will explore the need for going beyond the existing IDs and try to identify devices not only to find its owner, but also to unearth the mode of its operation to increase spectrum efficiency.

2   Related Work

One way of addressing the demand for spectrum is to increase spectrum efficiency through such methods as adaptive phase array antenna, beamforming and improved coding schemes. Recent 5G field tests [5] on advanced modulation schemes like sparse code multiple access (SCMA) and polar coding have shown improvement in spectrum efficiency. There is even a proposal for changes in hardware by using high-speed switches to make communication full duplex [6], where a transceiver can transmit and receive data at the same time and frequency. Still, complex interference issues like overload and spill-over can result in as a roadblock to these advancements if we do not monitor the devices' operations.

Generally, the notion for the service providers to cater to the demand has been to increase infrastructure, like buying more spectrum, deploying more small cells, adding a directional antenna, investing in multi-input-multi-output

(MIMO) antennas. However, by increasing the infrastructure we also increase the chances of harmful interference and uncertainty for the coexistence of devices for spectrum sharing. Thus, the spectral efficiency apparently decreases after a certain inflection point [7] for each new addition of infrastructure. The issue is that even if we have a lot of infrastructures we do not use it optimally. A solution is to keep track of the detailed parameters of an antenna so that they can be optimally allocated, e.g., through Radio Resource Management (RRM). Our proposed ID structure keeps track of the device(s)/antenna(s) physical and logical parameters.

There exists some research in HetNets that aim at controlling the parameters to improve the system efficiency, like a centralized greedy solution to optimize the transmit power in a HetNet [8]. In [9] it proposed power control strategies in femto cells depending on the demanded QoS of the users and the environment. While calculating the efficiency they proposed that the users should be provided with the minimum data rate so that they can still use the web applications. However, with 5G at the doorstep, the users are becoming more data-savvy than ever, which power control alone will not be able to cater to this need.

Moreover, with densification and the existing conservative strategies it perhaps may become difficult to even reach the bare minimum data rate in some cases. In [10] the authors proposed a similar argument where they used fractional frequency reuse coupled with transmit power control to coordinate interference between the APs in a HetNet. Moreover, with coordinated multipoint (CoMP) [11] steadily taking pace in the 5G deployment strategies, it shows that through coordination of technical parameters it is possible to further the process of efficiency. However, coordination has its own tradeoff like increased control message and scheduling. In CoMP joint processing, multiple antennas are involved to form an array of virtual antennas coordinated by APs to improve the signal strength. This makes the enforcement process much more complicated as there is now an array of virtual antennas that can cause unwanted harmful interference. ID can be used in this scenario to identify these virtual antennas.

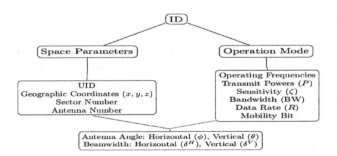

Fig. 2. Proposed ID structure

3   Identification Structure

Some radio communications traditionally made use of explicit methods for ID of participating entities, like call signs in amateur radios (e.g., AD0VT). However, identifiers have mostly been used for "name claim" to associate a device with its owner. Presently there exist many types of IDs in wireless networks, including IP addresses, Ethernet addresses, subscriber ids (in cellular networks), catalog numbers (in satellite systems), or International Mobile Equipment Identity (IMEI). Currently, there are devices in the market that can co-exist in more than one services and might have more than one of these IDs. With more heterogeneous devices assessing common frequency bands (due to advancement in technology and/or promotion of spectrum sharing) it may be useful (e.g., for enforcement purposes) to know more about the devices using these bands. By explicitly providing granular IDs in the physical layer, we allow a common ground for these heterogeneous devices to perform ex-post enforcement either in a centralized or a distributed fashion, potentially leading to improving network/spectrum efficiency. Similar benefits might be reaped by the homogeneous device operations, such as considering less conservative device level constraints to mitigate harmful interference.

As pointed in the earlier sections that there is a need for monitoring technical parameters and identifying these devices/antennas uniquely, we propose a detailed ID to identify device(s)/antenna(s) based on their space and operation mode as shown in Fig. 2. The space parameter consists of information like geographical coordinates of the device, and detailed placement of the antenna based on the sector and antenna numbers (if any). The space parameter will also have a Unique ID (UID) so as to keep track of redundancy when the device is mobile. On the other hand, the operation mode should consist of technical parameters, which can be adjusted dynamically, like operating frequencies, transmit power or receiver sensitivity based on the antenna type, bandwidth (for carrier aggregation), requested data rate based on user subscription/application. We assume that the receivers will use their corresponding transmitter to communicate its ID structure. Moreover, space for an RF radio is also dependent on the antenna angles and placement, so the parameters, like horizontal and vertical angles and beamwidth should also be included. Since these parameters can also be adjusted for methods like beamforming, it is considered as a part of both branches. This proposed ID structure will not only help allocate resources more optimally, but also ease the process of interference resolution and enforcement.

Generally, a device will try to sense the ID structure so that it can get knowledge about its neighbors and their respective operating parameters. However, due to the hidden node and the exposed node issues devices might not be able to sense the ID properly. Therefore, the devices can use a backbone Internet or relay system to avoid these issues. The method for transmission of ID will be dependent on the system and the tolerance level of the system for increased network load. For example, a mobility bit is present in the operation mode, which will check if a device is mobile or not, this can be used as a factor for how frequently the device(s) need to broadcast its ID. Another effort to reduce the network load for distributed systems would be to have a cluster head number in the operation mode branch. The cluster nodes will be responsible for multiple transmission of IDs if required, as in the case of LTE, access points (APs) can be cluster heads for the UEs.

4   Spectrum Efficiency Model

In this section we propose a spectrum efficiency model, which will use the information provided through the ID structure, as communicated by the device(s)/antenna(s) in the system. Efficiency can be defined in many ways in terms of technical, economical and spectral application as defined in [12]. However, here we define spectrum efficiency η at a given time instance as, $\eta = \frac{UC^R}{BW*S_f}$, which is the number of users covered UC^R per spectrum resource available in $Erlang/MHz/Km^2$, where the spectrum resource signifies the bandwidth BW and the coverage area S_f. Generally, the BW remains constant for a system, other than systems that use carrier aggregation to increase bandwidth dynamically. The user coverage and the coverage area changes very frequently and is dependent on multiple factors. We say a user is covered if it is satisfied with a QoS of R, which is specific to a users' plan and its surrounding neighbors. Let the cumulative coverage area for the APs operating in the same frequency be S_f. The geographical space covered by a particular frequency band f is dependent on several factors, like transmit power, antenna type, and antenna angles. With ID, devices can access the above-mentioned information and adjust it to maximize their individual/system spectrum efficiency.

Let the set of transmitters and receivers be TX and RX respectively. Let Ω be the cartesian combination of all resource options available to a transmitter. The number of independent channels available F_r can also affect the user coverage. Thus, the APs operating in the same frequency after assignment be Ψ_f, where $|\Psi_f| = N_f$. For $i \in TX$, $j \in RX$ and $k \in \Omega$ we construct the optimization problem as shown in Eq. 1 and constrained by Conditions 2–4.

$$\max \frac{1}{F_r} \sum_{f=1}^{F_r} \sum_{i=1}^{N_f} \frac{\eta_{if}}{N_f} \tag{1}$$

subjected to,

$$R_{jk} \geq R_j^* \forall j \in RX, \exists k \in \Omega \tag{2}$$

$$\sum_{j \in RX, k \in \Omega} a_{ijk} P_{ij} \leq \alpha P_i^{max} \forall i \in TX \tag{3}$$

$$\sum_{i \in TX} a_{ijk} c_{jik} \leq \zeta_j \forall j \in RX, \exists k \in \Omega \tag{4}$$

Condition 2 checks the user coverage based on the requested data rate R_j^* extracted from the ID structure. Let a_{ijk} be an integer variable, which is 1 if a transmitter and receiver pair is assigned a resource k and 0 otherwise. Condition

3 caps the APs from crossing the allocated transmit power αP_i^{max} for a transmitter i, where α is the fraction of power available for the transmitter. While trying to cover more users we might risk causing harmful interference to other users thus affecting the total system efficiency. Therefore, condition 4 makes sure that the aggregated system interference c_{ijk} for a transmitter-receiver pair for a particular resource combination k be less than the receivers' sensitivity ζ_j.

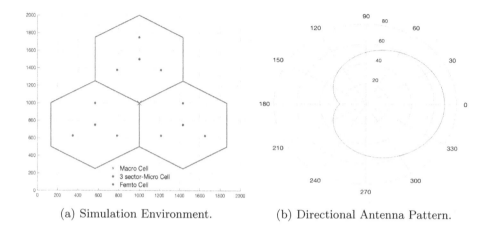

(a) Simulation Environment.   (b) Directional Antenna Pattern.

Fig. 3. Simulation environment

5   Evaluation

In this section we evaluate our spectrum efficiency model coupled with the proposed ID structure, to conduct discrete event simulations.

5.1   Environment Setting

To evaluate the benefit of a heterogeneous ID structure, we consider a HetNet setting with cell configuration shown in Fig. 3a. The environment is a 2 km × 2 km square area consisting of micro and femto cells, with a macro cell at the center, which is responsible for relaying data to the micro and femto cells, representing an umbrella cell. A list of radio parameters is shown in Table 1 [13]. We consider specific path loss PL models for the AP as shown in Table 1 [14, 15]. We consider operating frequency of 2000 MHz with a bandwidth of 10 MHz.

The microcell is further divided into 3 sectors. These sectors are made by changing the horizontal beam-width with the main lobe of the antenna within the beam-width as shown in Fig. 3b [16]. We have considered a single-input-single-output (SISO) antenna structure with directional antennas for the femto cell. This allows the antennas to change their coverage by adjusting ϕ & θ, and fit the capacity of the users in that area. We assume the beamwidth horizontal δ^H and vertical δ^V to be fixed at 60° and 2.7° respectively [13] for the directional antennas; however, these parameters can also be altered to fit the user coverage.

The user arrival rate follows a Poison distribution with a mean arrival rate ranging from 50 to 400 UEs per second. We assume a random-way point model for the UEs for the direction and the speed of the users ranging from $0, 1.4, 9, 15$ m/s. Detailed radio characteristics for UE are shown in [13].

Since the information in the ID structure is used to update the variables in the optimization problem shown in Sect. 4, the ID distribution factors into the efficiency of the approach. As explained in Sect. 3 that the distribution of the ID structure will be system and application dependent, which can either be centralized, maybe through Centralized Radio Access Network (C-RAN), or be completely distributed. The communication of the ID can either be through a backbone internet or control channels or even use of ledgers. Here we assume that the devices can communicate the ID through a control channel like architecture.

Table 1. Radio parameters

Parameters	Macro cell	Micro cell	Femto cell
P_i^{max}	46 dBm	33 dBm	23 dBm
G_i^{Atype}	16 dBi		5 dBi
Antenna type	Omni-directional	3 sector directional	Directional
Ht_{MAX}	40 m	15 m	5 m
PL	$10\alpha log(d_{ij}) + \beta + 10\gamma log(f_c) + \chi_\sigma$		$20log(f_c) + Nlog(d_{ij}) + Lf(n_w) - 28$

5.2 Discussion

To measure the improvement in spectrum efficiency for our proposed ID structure method, we compare it to the classical RSS method of resource assignment. Let the ID approach be Scenario I and the RSS method be Scenario II. As explained in Sect. 4 that efficiency η is directly dependent on the user coverage; however, there is a tradeoff between coverage and throughput, so we define coverage for 2 sub-cases, RI: $R_j^* > 5$ Mbps and RII: $R_j^* > 12$ Mbps. Different data rates signify different services, like web, voice, video stream. With two extremes cases of data rate demand, we try to estimate the worst-case bounds coverage for a 5G kind setup. The coverage area S_f is calculated dynamically based on the parameters selected. For Scenario I the frequency allocation is dynamic, while for Scenario II the frequency is allocated individually to avoid excess co-channel interference.

As explained in Sect. 2 that increasing infrastructure/spectrum does not necessarily guarantee more user coverage as there are other factors, which needs to be monitored. We compare the average spectrum efficiency results to F_r values of 6 and 3. When $F_r = 3$ we consider it is a constrained resource scenario. We show in Fig. 4 that even reducing the frequency reuse from 6 to 3 our proposed ID structure is able to maintain spectrum efficiency by adjusting the other parameters; however, RSS is not able to do so.

When we compare Fig. 4a and b we observe that though there is an overall increase in the average efficiency for $F_r = 3$ the trend for the respective methods remains the same, with RI as the best case efficiency. The overall increase in efficiency in the constrained resource scenario is due to the APs getting compelled to reuse the channel for the same user demands. However, the Scenario II does not show an optimal way of resource allocation and thus falls short compared to Scenario I. Moreover, we see that for both Scenarios I and II, the gap between the RI and RII data distribution increases as we keep on constraining F_r. This shows that for a constrained resource scenario covering users with higher QoS demand will become more difficult. However, Scenario I maintains an overall increase in average spectrum efficiency. In Fig. 4b, Scenario I is able to show a 2.4 to 3.2 times improvement compared to Scenario II for RI and RII respectively.

The trend for Scenario I seems to have some variations with respect to arrival rate, while Scenario II shows a steady trend. Scenario I shows a variation of 0.02–$0.5\,\mathrm{E/MHz/km^2}$, which is due to the dynamic allocation of resources (like, frequency, transmit power and antenna angles) and UE locations, so that these resources are assigned more optimally. We see that in Scenario II, which assigns resources based on the strongest received signal, the efficiency decreases as it does not monitor the unwanted aggregated harmful interference, which is caused due to the assignment. Thus, the trend remain quite stable as the assignment criterion remains the same even with the increase of arrival rate.

We acknowledge that this method of identification comes with some open-ended challenges, including: where such IDs make sense and where they might not be necessary; what is the best method to communicate the IDs to other devices; and the benefits and costs of extending traditional ID requirements, particularly to shared or lightly-licensed spectrum bands. Additionally, this method of service/device/operation specific ID might be challenging to implement in terms of: (1) regulators updating policy, (2) carriers modifying operations, (3) user participation and cooperation, (4) manufacturers designing and implementing the devices, and (5) standards being created. However, with collaborative

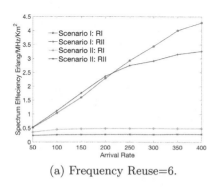

(a) Frequency Reuse=6.

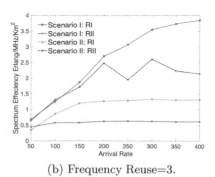

(b) Frequency Reuse=3.

Fig. 4. Average spectrum efficiency for different UE arrival rates and frequency reuse factors (with each point representing average of 100 simulations)

push from regulators and manufacturers this ID structure could be implemented and useful.

6   Conclusion

In this paper, we showed that with a granular level ID structure, of identifying device(s)/antenna(s) based on their space and operation parameters, we can further the cause of using resources more optimally. This ID structure will ease the ex-post enforcement process for the regulators to monitor for unwanted harmful interference mostly in the shared and lightly licensed bands. Complex interference issues like overload and spill-over can be resolved by just monitoring the ID parameters. Moreover, with heterogeneity and densification of APs and UEs this ID structure will allow a common ground for the devices to identify their operation modes uniquely in the system. Similar benefits can be reaped by homogeneous networks as well. Additionally, we showed that spectrum efficiency or user coverage per spectrum resource can be increased without adding additional spectrum. The ID structure comes with some tradeoffs and open-ended challenges; however, these could be resolved with coordination between the regulators and the industry to achieve the goal of an improved spectrum efficiency.

References

1. Cisco Visual Network Index: Global Mobile Traffic Forecast Update 2016–2021. Technical report, Cisco, USA (2017)
2. Connecting America: The National Broadband Plan. Technical report, Federal Communications Commission (2010)
3. Song, H.J., Nagatsuma, T.: Present and future of terahertz communications. IEEE Trans. Terahertz Sci. Technol. **1**(1), 256–263 (2011). https://doi.org/10.1109/TTHZ.2011.2159552
4. McHenry, M.A., McCloskey, D., Roberson, D.A., MacDonald, J.T.: Spectrum occupancy measurements, Chicago, Illinois, 16–18 November 2005. Technical report, Shared Spectrum Company Report (2005)
5. Wang, J., et al.: Spectral efficiency improvement with 5G technologies: results from field tests. IEEE J. Sel. Areas Commun. **35**(8), 1867–1875 (2017). https://doi.org/10.1109/JSAC.2017.2713498
6. Debaillie, B., et. al.: In-band full-duplex transceiver technology for 5G mobile networks. In: 41st IEEE European Solid-State Circuits Conference (ESSCIRC), Graz, Austria, pp. 84–87, (2015). https://doi.org/10.1109/ESSCIRC.2015.7313834
7. Ding, M., Perez, D.L.: Performance impact of base station antenna heights in dense cellular networks. IEEE Trans. Wirel. Commun. **16**(12), 8147–8161 (2017). https://doi.org/10.1109/TWC.2017.2757924
8. Sung, D.H., Baras, J.S., Zhu, C.: coordinated scheduling and power control for downlink cross-tier interference mitigation in heterogeneous cellular networks. In IEEE Global Communications Conference (GLOBECOM 2013), Atlanta, GA, USA, pp. 3809–3813 (2013). https://doi.org/10.1109/GLOCOM.2013.6831666

9. Xu, X., Kutrolli, G., Mathar, R.: Dynamic downlink power control strategies for LTE femtocells. In: 7th International Conference on Next Generation Mobile Apps, Services and Technologies, Prague, Czech Republic, pp. 181–186 (2013)
10. Li, Q., Hu, R.Q., Xu, Y., Qian, Y.: Optimal fractional frequency reuse and power control in the heterogeneous wireless networks. IEEE Trans. Wirel. Commun. **12**(6), 2658–2668 (2013)
11. Nam, W., Bai, D., Lee, J., Kang, I.: Advanced interference management for 5G cellular networks. IEEE Commun. Mag. 5G Wirel. Commun. Syst.: Prospect. Challenges **52**(5), 52–60 (2014)
12. Report of the Spectrum Efficiency Working Group. Technical report, Federal Communications Commission Spectrum Policy Task Force (2002)
13. Singh, R., et. al.: A method for evaluating coexistence of LTE and radar altimeters in the 4.2–4.4 GHz band. In: 17th Wireless Telecommunications Symposium (WTS), Chicago, IL, USA, pp. 1–9 (2017)
14. Propagation Data and Prediction Models for the Planning of Indoor Radiocommunication Systems and Radio Local Area Networks in the Frequency Range 900 MHz to 100 GHz. Technical report, International Telecommunication Union (ITU), RRecommendation ITU-R P.1238 (1997)
15. Sun, S., et. al.: Propagation path loss models for 5G urban micro- and macro-cellular scenarios. In: 83rd IEEE Vehicular Technology Conference (VTC 2016-Spring), Nanjing, China, pp. 1–6 (2016). https://doi.org/10.1109/VTCSpring.2016.7504435
16. Reference Radiation Patterns of Omnidirectional, Sectoral and Other Antennas for the Fixed and Mobile Services for Use in Sharing Studies in the Frequency Range from 400 MHz to about 70 GHz. Technical report, International Telecommunication Union (ITU), Recommendation ITU-R F.1336-4 (2014)

Interference Rejection Combining for Black-Space Cognitive Radio Communications

Sudharsan Srinivasan[✉] and Markku Renfors

Laboratory of Electronics and Communications Engineering,
Tampere University of Technology, Tampere, Finland
{sudharsan.srinivasan,markku.renfors}@tut.fi

Abstract. This paper focuses on multi-antenna interference rejection combing (IRC) based black-space cognitive radio (BS-CR) operation. The idea of BS-CR is to transmit secondary user (SU) signal in the same frequency band with the primary user (PU) such that SU's power spectral density is clearly below that of the PU, and no significant interference is inflicted on the PU receivers. We develop a novel blind IRC technique which allows such operation mode for effective reuse of the PU spectrum for relatively short-distance CR communication. We assume that both the PU system and the BS-CR use orthogonal frequency division multiplexing (OFDM) waveforms with common frame structure. In this case the PU interference on the BS-CR signal is strictly flat-fading at subcarrier level. Sample covariance matrix based IRC adaptation is applied during silent gaps in CR operation. During CR transmission, the target signal detection and channel estimation utilize multiple outputs from the IRC process obtained with linearly independent steering vectors. The performance of the proposed IRC scheme is tested considering terrestrial digital TV broadcasting (DVB-T) as the primary service. The resulting interference suppression capability is evaluated with different PU interference power levels, silent gap durations, and CR device mobilities.

Keywords: Black-space cognitive radio · Underlay CR · Interference rejection combining · IRC · Receiver diversity · OFDM · DVB-T

1 Introduction

Cognitive radios (CRs) are designed to operate in radio environments with a high level of interference and, at the same time, produce negligible interference to the primary users (PUs) [1–3]. CRs have been widely studied in recent years, with main focus on opportunistic white-space operation, i.e., dynamically identifying unused spectral resources for CR operation. Also underlay CR operation has received some attention. Here the idea is to transmit in wide frequency band with low power-spectral density, typically using spread-spectrum techniques [4]. Black space CR (BS-CR), where a CR deliberately transmits simultaneously along the primary signal in the same time-frequency resources without causing objectionable interference has received limited attention [5–8]. In general, BS-CR can operate without need for spectrum sensing and

© ICST Institute for Computer Sciences, Social Informatics and Telecommunications Engineering 2019
Published by Springer Nature Switzerland AG 2019. All Rights Reserved
I. Moerman et al. (Eds.): CROWNCOM 2018, LNICST 261, pp. 200–210, 2019.
https://doi.org/10.1007/978-3-030-05490-8_19

requires only limited spectral resources. BS-CR can make very effective reuse of spectrum over short distances.

One of the major requirements for CR operation is to minimize the interference to the primary transmission system. In BS-CR this is reached by setting the CR transmission power at a small-enough level. The most important factor that enables such a radio system is that stronger interference is easier to deal with as compared to weaker interference [9], if proper interference cancellation techniques are utilized. Previous studies from information theory provide theoretically achievable bounds for such cognitive radios [10].

The use of multiple antennas allows for spatio-temporal signal processing, which improves the detection capability of the receiver under fading multipath channel and interference. Various methods of interference cancellation can be found in [11–16] and the references therein. For a detector to be optimum under interference, it has to be a multi-user detector [11].

Interference rejection combining (IRC) receivers do not need detailed information about the interfering signals, such as modulation order and radio channel propagation characteristics. Therefore, IRC receivers are simple compared to optimum detectors, making them desirable for CR scenarios.

IRC techniques are widely applied for mitigating co-channel interference, e.g., cellular mobile radio systems like LTE-A [17]. The use of multiple antennas in CRs has been studied earlier, e.g., in [16]. Our initial study on this topic in highly simplified scenario with suboptimal algorithms was in [18], but to the best of our knowledge, IRC has not been applied to BS-CR (or underlay CR) elsewhere. The novel elements of the scheme proposed in this paper include the following:

- The spatial channel of the interfering PU signal does not need to be explicitly estimated, while an initial IRC solution is found by calculating the sample covariance matrix during a silent gap in CR transmission.
- The channel of the target CR transmission is estimated for the maximum number of linearly independent signals from which the PU interference has been suppressed.
- The IRC weights are obtained from the channel estimates and initial IRC solution through maximum ratio combining (MRC) of the linearly independent signal set.

In this paper we consider BS-CR operation in the terrestrial TV frequency band, utilizing a channel with an on-going relatively strong TV transmission. The PU is assumed to be active continuously. If the TV channel becomes inactive, this can be easily detected by each of the CR stations in the reception mode. Then the CR system may, for example, continue operation as a spectrum sensing based CR system. In our case study, we focus on the basic scenario of IRC based multi-antenna CR receiver with co-channel interference generated by a single PU transmitter. The performance of such a system under different interference levels, timing offsets, and modulation orders is studied. Also, the effect of silent period length and CR device mobility on the performance is evaluated. The rest of the paper is organized as follows: In Sect. 2, the BS-SC scenario and proposed IRC scheme are explained. The system model and IRC solution are formulated in Sect. 3. Section 4 presents the simulation setup and performance evaluation results. Finally, concluding remarks are presented Sect. 5.

2 IRC-Based Black-Space Cognitive Radio Scenario

In our basic scenario, illustrated in Fig. 1, we consider a CR receiver using multiple antennas to receive data from a single-antenna cognitive transmitter. The CR operates within the frequency band of the PU, and the PU power spectral density (PSD) is very high in comparison to that of the CR. The primary transmission is assumed to be always present when the CR system is operating. The primary transmitter generates a lot of interference to the CR transmission, which operates closer to the noise floor of the primary receiver, and due to this, the primary communication link is protected. We consider frequency reuse over relatively small distances, such as an indoor CR system. The multi-antenna configuration studied here is that of single-input multiple output (SIMO). Other configurations, involving also transmit diversity in the CR link are also possible, but they are left as a topic for future studies.

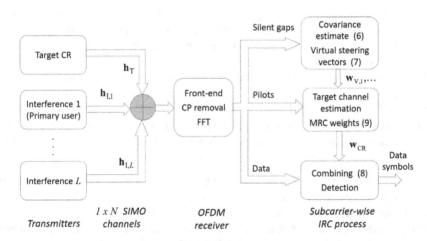

Fig. 1. Blackspace CR system model.

Here the PU is a cyclic prefix orthogonal frequency division multiplexing (CP-OFDM) based DVB-T system [19]. The CR system is also an OFDM based multi-carrier system using the same subcarrier spacing and CP length as the primary system. Thus, it has the same overall symbol duration. The CR system is assumed to be synchronized to the primary system in frequency and in quasi-synchronous manner also in time. The CP length is assumed to be sufficient to absorb the channel delay spread together with the residual offsets between the two systems observed at the CR receiver. Consequently, the subcarrier-level flat-fading circular convolution model for spatio-temporal channel effects applies to the target CR signal and to the PU interference signal as well. Then the IRC process can be applied individually for each subcarrier. Since the CR receiver observes the PU signal at very high SINR level, synchronization task is not particularly difficult and low-complexity algorithms can be utilized. Considering short-range CR scenarios, the delay spread of the CR channel has a minor effect on the overall channel delay spread to be handled in the time alignment of the two systems. Basically, if all CR stations are synchronized to the PU, they are also synchronized with each other.

Both the primary and the CR systems use QAM subcarrier modulation, but usually with different modulation orders. The received CR signal consists of contributions from both the desired CR communication signal and the primary transmission signal, the latter one constituting a strong interference. Our proposed scheme includes two phases in the CR system operation:

1. During the first phase, the CR transmission is stopped (silent gap) and the IRC process is adapted blindly to minimize the energy of combined signal during the silent period. This is done individually for each subcarrier. Since the target channel is not available during this stage, IRC solutions are found for the maximum number of linearly independent (virtual) steering vectors. During the CR reception phase, the corresponding IRC output signals are used for channel estimation and data detection. They are referred to as partial IRC signals.
2. During the second phase, the CR system is operating. The CR channel coefficients are estimated for each partial IRC signal using training symbols (containing reference symbols in all subcarriers). For data symbols, the partial IRC signals are combined using maximum ratio combining (MRC) based on the estimated channel coefficients.

This two-phase process is straightforward to implement and it is able to track the channel fading with relatively low mobility. In future work, it is worth to consider adaptation of the IRC process without silent gaps after the first one required for the initial solution. This would help to reduce the related overhead in throughput.

No explicit channel estimation of the PU channel is required in this approach. The CR channel is estimated from the partial IRC signals, from which the PU interference has been effectively suppressed.

3   IRC for Black-Space Cognitive Radio

Following the quasi-synchronous OFDM system model explained in the previous section, the detection process at the CR receiver can be formulated at OFDM subcarrier symbol level as a flat-fading process. For the $1 \times N$ SIMO antenna configuration of the CR transmission link and L interfering signals, the received signal can be expressed as

$$\mathbf{r} = \mathbf{h}_\mathrm{T} x_\mathrm{T} + \sum_{l=1}^{L} \mathbf{h}_{\mathrm{I},l} x_{\mathrm{I},l} + \boldsymbol{\eta}. \tag{1}$$

Here $\mathbf{h}_\mathrm{T} \in \mathbb{C}^{N \times 1}$ is the channel gain vector for the target CR transmission, $\mathbf{h}_{\mathrm{I},l} \in \mathbb{C}^{N \times 1}$ is the spatial channel from the lth interferer to the CR receiver, x_T and $x_{\mathrm{I},l}$ are the corresponding transmitted subcarrier symbols, and $\boldsymbol{\eta} \in \mathbb{C}^{N \times 1}$ is spatially white additive white Gaussian noise (AWGN). Naturally, during silent gaps of CR operation, the first term of (1) is missing. For detection, the signals from different antennas are weighted and combined using a linear combiner. This can be expressed as the inner product

$$y = \mathbf{w}^{\mathrm{H}}\mathbf{r}, \tag{2}$$

where $\mathbf{w} \in \mathbb{C}^{N \times 1}$ is the combiner weight vector, and H stands for Hermitian (complex-conjugate transpose). Finding the optimum weight vector is an optimization problem. Generally, the linear minimum mean-squared error (LMMSE) solution minimizes the mean-squared error in the target signal x_{T},

$$J = E\left[\left|x_{\mathrm{T}} - \mathbf{w}^{\mathrm{H}}\mathbf{r}\right|^2\right]. \tag{3}$$

In interference rejection combining (IRC) we assume knowledge of the covariance matrix of the interferences. If the channels from the interferers to the CR receiver antenna array are known, the noise plus interference covariance matrix can be expressed as

$$\mathbf{\Sigma}_{\mathrm{NI}} = \sum\nolimits_{l=1}^{L} P_l \mathbf{h}_{\mathrm{I},l} \mathbf{h}_{\mathrm{I},l}^{\mathrm{H}} + P_{\mathrm{N}}\mathbf{I}. \tag{4}$$

Here $P_{\mathrm{I},l}$ is the power of interferer l, P_{N} is the noise power, and $\mathbf{I}$ is the identity matrix of size N. Then the well-known LMMSE solution [20] is

$$\mathbf{w} = \mathbf{\Sigma}_{\mathrm{NI}}^{-1}\mathbf{h}_{\mathrm{T}}\left(\mathbf{h}_{\mathrm{T}}^{\mathrm{H}}\mathbf{\Sigma}_{\mathrm{NI}}^{-1}\mathbf{h}_{\mathrm{T}} + 1/P_{\mathrm{T}}\right)^{-1}, \tag{5}$$

where P_{T} is the target CR signal power.

Estimating the interferer channel vector would increase the complexity of the CR receiver, even in the single interferer case of our basic scenario. In case of multiple interferers, e.g., from other BS-CR systems operating nearby, this would be quite challenging. Therefore, we use the sample covariance matrix of the received signal,

$$\bar{\mathbf{\Sigma}}_{\mathrm{NI}} = \sum\nolimits_{m=1}^{M} \mathbf{r}(m)\mathbf{r}(m)^{\mathrm{H}} \tag{6}$$

during the silent gap of the CR transmission as the estimate of $\mathbf{\Sigma}_{\mathrm{NI}}$. Here m is the OFDM symbol index and M is the length of the estimation period (i.e., silent gap length) in OFDM symbols.

In the proposed scheme it is not possible to estimate the CR channel before the interference cancellation stage. Therefore, during CR operation phase 1, we carry out the IRC adaptation process for N orthogonal virtual steering vectors, resulting in N weight vectors $\mathbf{w}_{\mathrm{V},1}, \mathbf{w}_{\mathrm{V},2}, \ldots, \mathbf{w}_{\mathrm{V},N}$. We use the unit vectors $\mathbf{h}_{\mathrm{V},1} = [1, 0, 0, \ldots, 0]^{\mathrm{T}}$, $\mathbf{h}_{\mathrm{V},2} = [0, 1, 0, \ldots, 0]^{\mathrm{T}}, \ldots, \mathbf{h}_{\mathrm{V},N} = [0, 0, 0, \ldots, 1]^{\mathrm{T}}$ as the virtual steering vectors for simplicity. Furthermore, instead of the scaling of (5), the weight vectors are scaled to have unit Euclidean norm,

$$\mathbf{w}_{\mathrm{V},n} = \bar{\mathbf{\Sigma}}_{\mathrm{NI}}^{-1}\mathbf{h}_{\mathrm{V},n} \Big/ \left\|\bar{\mathbf{\Sigma}}_{\mathrm{NI}}^{-1}\mathbf{h}_{\mathrm{V},n}\right\|. \tag{7}$$

This results in unit noise variance for the corresponding weighted output signals $y_n = \mathbf{w}_{V,n}^H \mathbf{r}$, $n = 1, 2, \ldots, N$, which is essential for the following maximum ratio combining (MRC) stage. The outputs y_n are different observations of the target signal, for which the interference cancellation has been applied. When the number of receiver antennas is higher than the number of interference sources, there is diversity in these observations, and diversity combining can be used for enhancing the performance. Among the linear combination methods, MRC maximizes the signal to interference-plus-noise ratio of the combined signal.

During the second CR operation phase, data symbols are transmitted, along with training symbols at regular intervals. For each training symbol (containing reference symbols in all active subcarriers), the N channel coefficients $\hat{h}_{V,1}$, $\hat{h}_{V,2}$, $\ldots$, $\hat{h}_{V,N}$ are first estimated for each of the effective channels corresponding to the N observations as $\hat{h}_{V,n} = \mathbf{w}_{V,n}^H \cdot \mathbf{r}/p$, where p is the transmitted pilot symbol value. Then the data symbol estimate is obtained by maximum ratio combining the N samples obtained by applying the virtual steering vectors,

$$\hat{d} = \mathbf{w}_{\mathrm{MRC}}^H \cdot \left[\mathbf{w}_{V,1} \ \mathbf{w}_{V,2} \ \cdots \ \mathbf{w}_{V,N} \right]^H \cdot \mathbf{r}, \tag{8}$$

where the MRC weights are given by

$$\mathbf{w}_{\mathrm{MRC}} = [\hat{h}_{V,1} \, \hat{h}_{V,2} \ldots \hat{h}_{V,N}]^T \bigg/ \sqrt{\sum_{k=1}^{N} |\hat{h}_{V,k}|^2}. \tag{9}$$

The effective weight vector becomes

$$\mathbf{w}_{\mathrm{CR}} = \left[\mathbf{w}_{V,1} \ \mathbf{w}_{V,2} \ \cdots \ \mathbf{w}_{V,N} \right] \cdot \mathbf{w}_{\mathrm{MRC}}$$
$$= \sum_{n=1}^{N} \hat{h}_{V,n} \mathbf{w}_{V,n} \bigg/ \sqrt{\sum_{k=1}^{N} |\hat{h}_{V,k}|^2}. \tag{10}$$

We can see that for data symbol detection with stationary channels, we just need to calculate and use this weight vector, instead of applying the MRC weights on the samples obtained by the weight vectors $\mathbf{w}_{V,n}$.

This model indicates various options for dealing with channel fading. Generally, the PU channel should not vary significantly between the silent periods. The most critical scenario in this respect is a moving CR receiver, which causes also the PU channel to be time varying. Due to the strong PU interference, the interference cancellation process is sensitive to the resulting errors in the channel covariance estimate. For slowly-fading CR channels, it is enough to calculate the effective weights for each training symbol and use the same weights until the next training symbol. With higher mobility, the effective weights can be interpolated between consecutive training symbols. The effect of mobility is investigated through simulations in the following section.

4 Performance Evaluation

The simulations are carried out for the system setup explained in Sect. 2. The carrier frequencies of CR and PU are the same and it is here set to 700 MHz, which is close to the upper edge of the terrestrial TV frequency band. The modulation order used by CR varies between 4QAM, 16QAM, and 64QAM. The pilot symbols are binary and have the same power level as the data symbols. The primary transmitter signal follows the DVB-T model with 16QAM modulation, 8 MHz bandwidth, and CP length of 1/8 times the useful symbol duration, i.e., 28 μs. The IFFT/FFT length is 2048 for both systems. The DVB-T and CR systems use 1705 and 1200 active subcarriers, respectively. ITU-R Vehicular A channel model (about 2.5 μs delay spread) is used for the CR system and Hilly Terrain channel model (about 18 μs delay spread) for PU transmission. The CR receiver is assumed to have four antennas, and uncorrelated 1×4 SIMO configurations are used for both the primary signal and the CR signal.

The number of spatial channel realizations simulated in these experiments is 500. The ratio of CR and PU signal power levels at the CR receiver (referred to as the signal to interference ratio, SIR) is varied. The lengths of the OFDM symbol frame and silent gap for interference covariance matrix estimation are also varied (expressed in terms of CP-OFDM symbol durations). The training symbol spacing is 8 OFDM symbols, and the frame length is selected in such a way that training symbols appear as the first and last symbol of each frame, along with other positions. Channel estimation uses linear interpolation between the training symbols.

Figure 2 shows a basic bit error-rate (BER) vs. SNR simulation result with 4QAM (QPSK) and 64QAM modulations and SIR values of −10, −20, and −30 dB. Also the interference-free baseline case (SIR = 100 dB) is included. The CR block length is 41 OFDM symbols (6 training symbols and 35 data symbols), and the interference covariance estimation is based on a silent gap of 32 OFDM symbols. In this case, the interference covariance estimate is very good, and IRC performs very well. The effect of the interference power is relatively small: reducing the SIR from −10 dB to −30 dB, the performace loss at 1% BER level is about 0.6 dB for QPSK and about 1.7 dB for 64QAM. When comparing the BS-CR performance with the interference-free case, the loss is about 3.5 dB for both QPSK and 64QAM at 1% BER level and −30 dB SIR.

Next we consider the performance with slowly-fading channels. It was found also experimentally that the case where the CR transmitter is moving but CR receiver is stationary is much easier to handle, because the interference covariance matrix is stationary as long as the PU and CR receiver are stationary. Therefore, we focus on the case where the CR receiver is moving, while the CR transmitter is stationary, and both the target CR channel and the interference are fading with the same mobility, 3 km/h. Figures 3 and 4 show both the effect of the silent gap length and the OFDM frame length on the performance. We can notice that by placing the silent gap in the middle of the frame and using the interference covariance estimate for detecting both the preceding and following OFDM symbols, the CR frame length could be doubled without performance loss. However, this is not assumed in Figs. 3 and 4, because it would require extensive data buffering on the receiver side. In this simulation set-up, the best length for the silent gap is about 32 OFDM symbols. Generally, while acceptable CR link performance can still be achieved, significant performance loss is observed with respect to the stationary case. Also the feasible CR frame length is rather limited, leading to relatively high overhead due to the silent gaps. The performace loss with 3 km/h mobility is about 4.7 dB and 10 dB with the the frame lengths of 17 and 41 OFDM symbols, respectively, compared to the stationary case.

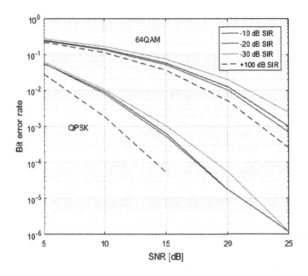

Fig. 2. Performance QPSK and 64QAM systems with stationary channel, silent gap duration of 32 symbols, and OFDM frame length of 41 symbols.

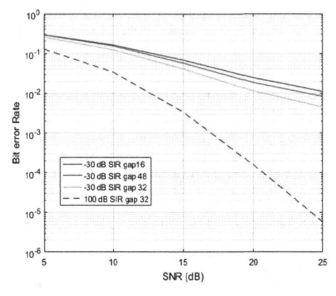

Fig. 3. Performance of a 16QAM system with 3 km/h mobility, 700 MHz carrier frequency, OFDM frame length of 17 symbols, with various gaps and SIR = −30 dB.

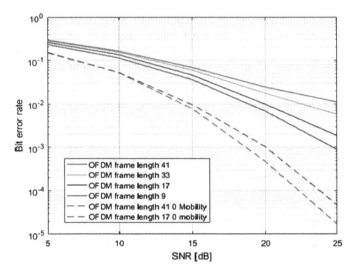

Fig. 4. Performance for a 16QAM system with 3 km/h mobility, 700 MHz carrier frequency, silent gap of 32 symbols, and SIR = −30 dB.

5   Conclusion

The performance of cognitive transmission links in the presence of strong interferences in the black-space CR scenario was investigated. The interference rejection capability of IRC using multiple receive antennas for various modulation orders was studied. It was found that the IRC performs very well in the basic SIMO-type BS-CR scenario when stationary channel model is applicable, e.g., in fixed wireless broadband scenarios. However, the scheme is rather sensitive to the fading of the PU channel. Due to the strong interference level, the interference cancellation process is affected by relatively small errors in the covariance matrix estimate. For covariance estimation, the silent gap length should be in the order of 32 OFDM symbols, and the CR OFDM frame length should be of the same order or less, even with 3 km/h mobility. This leads to high overhead due to the silent gaps.

In future work, it is worth to consider adaptation of the IRC process without silent gaps after the first one required for the initial solution. This would help to reduce the related overhead in throughput. One possible approach is to do this in a decision-directed manner: first estimating the covariance matrix in the presence of the target signal and then cancelling its effect based on detected symbols and estimated target channel.

In the basic TV black-space scenario, there is only one strong TV signal present in the channel, in agreement with our assumption about the primary interference sources. DVB-T system allows also single-frequency network (SFN) operation and the use of repeaters to improve local coverage. In both cases, the primary transmissions can be seen as a single transmission, with a spatial channel that depends on the specific transmission scenario, and the proposed scheme is still applicable.

The scheme can also be extended to scenarios where multiple CR systems are operating in the same region. If all CR systems are time-synchronized to the PU and they are at a relatively small distance from each other, they are also synchronized with each other, and could be handled by the IRC process as an additional interference source following the model of Eq. (1). In future studies, also the effect of antenna correlation will be taken into consideration. The complexity reduction of the IRC receiver with larger number of antennas is also an interesting topic for further studies.

References

1. Yucek, T., Arslan, H.: A survey of spectrum sensing algorithms for cognitive radio applications. IEEE Commun. Surv. Tutor. **11**(1), 116–129 (2009)
2. Liang, Y.C., Hoang, A.T., Zeng, Y., Zhang, R.: A review on spectrum sensing for cognitive radio: challenges and solutions. In: EURASIP J. Adv. Signal Process., 1–15 (2010)
3. Dikmese, S., Srinivasan, S., Shaat, M., Bader, F., Renfors, M.: Spectrum sensing and resource allocation for multicarrier cognitive radio systems under interference and power constraints. EURASIP J. Adv. Signal Process. **2014**, 68 (2014)
4. Wyglinski, A.M., et al.: Cognitive Radio Communications and Networks: Principles and Practice. Academic Press, Cambridge (2010)
5. Selén, Y., Baldemair, R., Sachs, J.: A short feasibility study of a cognitive TV black space system. In: Proceedings of IEEE PIMRC, Toronto, ON, pp. 520–524 (2011)
6. Rico-Alvariño, A., Mosquera, C.: Overlay spectrum reuse in a broadcast network: covering the whole grayscale of spaces. In: Proceedings of IEEE DySPAN 2012, WA, pp. 479–488 (2012)
7. Wei, Z., Feng, Z., Zhang, Q., Li, W.: Three regions for space-time spectrum sensing and access in cognitive radio networks. IEEE Trans. Veh. Technol. **64**(6), 2448–2462 (2015)
8. Beyene, Y., Ruttik, K., Jantti, R.: Effect of secondary transmission on primary pilot carriers in overlay cognitive radios. In: Proceedings of CROWNCOM 2013, Washington, DC, pp. 111–116 (2013)
9. Carleial, A.B.: A case where interference does not reduce capacity. IEEE Trans. Inf. Theory **21**, 569–570 (1975)
10. Devroye, N., Mitran, P., Tarokh, V.: Achievable rates in cognitive radio channels. IEEE Trans. Inf. Theory **52**, 1813–1827 (2006)
11. Verdu, S.: Multiuser Detection. Cambridge University Press, Cambridge (1998)
12. Winters, J.: Optimum combining in digital mobile radio with cochannel interference. IEEE Trans. Veh. Technol. **2**(4), 539–583 (1984)
13. Liaster, J., Reed, J.: Interference rejection in digital wireless communication. IEEE Signal Process. Mag. **14**(3), 37–62 (1997)
14. Klang, G.: On interference rejection in wireless multichannel systems. Ph.D. thesis, KTH, Stockholm, Sweden (2003)
15. Beach, M.A., et al.: Study into the application of interference cancellation techniques. Roke Manor Research Report 72/06/R/036/U, April 2006
16. Bakr, O., Johnson, M., Mudumbai, R., Ramchandran, K.: Multi-antenna interference cancellation techniques for cognitive radio applications. In: Proceedings of IEEE WCNC (2009)
17. Cheng, C.C., Sezginer, S., Sari, H., Su, Y.T.: Linear interference suppression with covariance mismatches in MIMO-OFDM systems. IEEE Trans. Wirel. Commun. **13**, 7086–7097 (2014)

18. Srinivasan, S., Dikmese, S., Menegazzo, D., Renfors, M.: Multi-antenna interference cancellation for black space cognitive radio communications. In: IEEE Globecom Workshops, San Diego, CA, pp. 1–6 (2015)
19. Ladebusch, U., Liss, C.A.: Terrestrial DVB (DVB-T): a broadcast technology for stationary portable and mobile use. Proc. IEEE **94**(1), 183–193 (2006)
20. Haykin, S.: Adaptive Filter Theory, 4th edn. Prentice-Hall, Upper Saddle River (2001)

An Image Processing Approach
to Wideband Spectrum Sensing
of Heterogeneous Signals

Ha Q. Nguyen[✉], Ha P. K. Nguyen, and Binh T. Nguyen

Viettel Research and Development Institute, Hoa Lac High-tech Park,
Hanoi, Vietnam
nguyenquyha@gmail.com, khanhha318@gmail.com, thaibinhnx@gmail.com

Abstract. We introduce a simple yet efficient framework for the localization and tracking of fixed-frequency and frequency-hopping (FH) wireless signals that coexist in a wide radio-frequency band. In this spectrum sensing scheme, an energy detector is applied to each Short-time
Fourier Transform of the wideband signal to produce a binary spectrogram. Bounding boxes for narrowband signals are then identified by using
image processing techniques on a block of the spectrogram at a time.
These boxes are also tracked along the time axis and fused with the
newly detected boxes to provide an on-line system for spectrum sensing.
Fast and highly accurate detection is achieved in simulations for various
FF signals and FH signals with different hopping patterns and speeds.
In particular, for the SNR of 4 dB over a bandwidth of 50 MHz, 97.98%
of narrowband signals were detected with average deviations of about
0.02 ms in time and 2.15 KHz in frequency.

Keywords: Wideband spectrum sensing · Wireless signal detection
Frequency hopping · Time-frequency analysis · Spectrogram
Waterfall image · Image morphology · Blob extraction

1 Introduction

Spectrum sensing is the central task of any cognitive radio networks [6,8], since
it provides a continuing surveillance for better utilization of the radio spectrum. Various methods have been proposed for the narrowband spectrum sensing (NSS) [14], which detects the presence of wireless signals in each frequency
subband. However, the local spectrum information provided by the NSS is defi-
cient for the decision making of cognitive nodes in the network. Furthermore,
the division of the radio spectrum into subbands are often too coarse to precisely identify all narrowband signals. Because of these shortcomings of NSS,
considerable attention has recently been shifted to the wideband spectrum sensing (WSS) [10], which investigates the whole spectrum of interest at a time. The
main challenge of WSS lies at the extremely-high sampling frequency, which

© ICST Institute for Computer Sciences, Social Informatics and Telecommunications Engineering 2019
Published by Springer Nature Switzerland AG 2019. All Rights Reserved
I. Moerman et al. (Eds.): CROWNCOM 2018, LNICST 261, pp. 211–221, 2019.
https://doi.org/10.1007/978-3-030-05490-8_20

has to be greater or equal to the bandwidth of the wideband signal, according to Shannon's theory. To ease this burden for the Analog-to-Digital Converter (ADC), a large body of literature [1,2,7,12,15] has focused on the sub-Nyquist sampling (a.k.a. compressive sampling) techniques for WSS. Existing methods for *signal detection*–the core of WSS–often rely on the detection of irregularities in the Power Spectrum Density (PSD) [3,11–13]. This 1-D approach yields accurate localization of the frequency subbands in every single time slot but, unfortunately, does not keep track of the evolution of narrowband signals over time. Another drawback of the 1-D detection algorithms is that they need to be repeated for every (short) time slot, leading to heavy computation that prevents them from real-time implementations.

In this paper, we propose a 2-D approach to WSS in which the signal localization is obtained by applying image processing techniques to a *block* of *binary* spectrogram that is a concatenation of multiple thresholded PSDs. The thresholding of PSDs, or energy detection, is done via a noise floor estimation algorithm proposed in [9], which is also based on image processing. The detected signals are then tracked across a waterfall of time-frequency images and associated with bounding boxes on the spectrogram to form an on-line detection system. Most importantly, the proposed scheme is able to simultaneously handle fixed-frequency (FF) and frequency-hopping (FH) signals that might be transmitted at the same time over a wideband spectrum. These 2 types of signals differ mainly by the time duration: a single hop of an FH signal is typically much shorter than an FF signal. Therefore, it requires a sufficiently long observation to distinguish one type of signal from the other. The benefits of our framework are twofold. First, unlike 1-D detection methods, the proposed mechanism provides a dynamic localization of the narrowband signals in both time and frequency. Second, the computation can be made very fast by amortizing the processing of a binary image over a certain period of time. Our WSS system can also be linked to the time-frequency analysis methods that are widely used in speech and acoustics processing [5].

The outline of the rest of the paper is as follows: Sect. 2 describes the building blocks of our spectrum sensing system; Sect. 3 reports some detection results on simulated data; and Sect. 4 concludes the paper.

2   Architecture of the Proposed System

Notation: Throughout this section, images are denoted by bold letters. For image I, we use the notation $I(x, y)$ to refer to the pixel value at row y and column x.

As shown in Fig. 1, the proposed scheme consists of 3 main modules: Spectrogram Binarization, Signal Localization, and Signal Tracking. The input to the system is a wideband analog signal $s(t)$ that is a (noisy) superposition of multiple narrowband signals inside the frequency band $[0, B_{\text{wide}}]$. The output of the system is a list of bounding boxes that dynamically localize all narrowband signals appearing in the time-frequency *waterfall* image (or spectrogram) of the input signal. See Fig. 7 for a visualization of the desired result: FF and FH signals are tightly surrounded by red and green boxes, respectively. Each bounding box has 4 vertices lying on the *integer* grid of the time-frequency image and is represented by a tuple (x, y, w, h), where (x, y) are the coordinates of the upper-left corner and (w, h) are the width and height, respectively. The 4 characteristics of a narrowband signal, namely, starting time, stopping time, center frequency, and bandwidth, are computed from its bounding box (x, y, w, h) as

$$t_{\text{start}} = y \times L/B_{\text{wide}}, \quad t_{\text{stop}} = (y + h) \times L/B_{\text{wide}}, \tag{1}$$
$$f_{\text{center}} = (x + w/2) \times B_{\text{wide}}/L, \quad B_{\text{narrow}} = w \times B_{\text{wide}}/L, \tag{2}$$

where L is the size of the window used in computing the spectrogram. In the sequel, we discuss the 3 modules of the system in detail.

Fig. 1. Building blocks of the proposed system for wideband spectrum sensing.

2.1 Spectrogram Binarization

This module is illustrated in Fig. 2. The analog signal $s(t)$ is first sampled by the ADC (Analog-to-Digital Converter) at Nyquist's rate:

$$s[n] = s\left(n/B_{\text{wide}}\right), \quad n = 0, 1, 2, \ldots$$

Then, finite-length signals are obtained by sliding a window $w[n]$ of size L along $s[n]$. In particular, for $m \geq 0$, we define windowed signals s_m as

$$s_m[n] = w[n] \cdot s[mL + n], \quad \text{for } n = 0, \ldots, L - 1.$$

Next, the PSD (Power Spectrum Density) of each signal block is computed via the FFT (Fast Fourier Transform) as

$$P_m[k] = 10 \log_{10} \left| \sum_{n=0}^{L-1} s_m[n] e^{-\frac{j2\pi kn}{L}} \right|^2, \quad \text{for } k = 0, \ldots, L - 1.$$

This windowed Fourier transform is also known as Short-time Fourier Transform (STFT). Using the above PSD, a noise floor $F_m[k]$ is estimated by a morphology-based algorithm proposed in [9].[1]

---

[1] In practice, due to the slow variation of the noise with time, the noise floor estimation can be done once for multiple signal blocks.

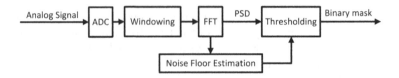

Fig. 2. Block diagram of the Spectrogram Binarization module.

The final step of the Spectrogram Binarization is to obtain binary masks $\{X_m\}_{m \geq 0}$ according to the thresholding

$$X_m[k] = \begin{cases} 1, & \text{if } P_m[k] > F_m[k] + T_{\text{offset}} \\ 0, & \text{otherwise}, \end{cases}$$

where T_{offset} (dB) is a hyper-parameter. Stacking these binary masks together yields a waterfall image of L columns and undefined number of rows. The horizontal and vertical axes of the image represent frequency and time, respectively.

2.2   Signal Localization

In this module, we extract M consecutive rows of the waterfall image obtained from the previous stage and identify the narrowband signal blobs inside it. As illustrated in Fig. 3, this function takes a binary image I of size $M \times L$ and outputs 2 box lists $\mathcal{F}$ and $\mathcal{H}$ for FF and FH signals, respectively. The main routines of the Signal Localization module are described below.

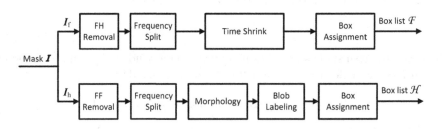

Fig. 3. Block diagram of the Signal Localization module.

Localization of FF Signals (Upper Branch)

1. *Initialize $I_f \leftarrow I$.*
2. *FH Removal:* This step erases FH signals out of the image I_f by setting

$$I_f(x, y) \leftarrow 0, \quad \text{if } \sum_y I_f(x, y) < T_{f,\text{col}} \times M,$$

where $T_{f,\text{col}} \in (0, 1)$ is a hyper-parameter. Interestingly, this step also helps reduce the noise, which are sporadically distributed in the spectrogram.

3. *Frequency Split:* This step provides a frequency localization for the FF signals. We divide I_f into N_f sub-images $\{I_f^{(k)}\}_{k=1}^{N_f}$—strips of columns of I_f that are separated by at least $T_{f,0}$ consecutive zero-columns. After this step, each sub-image supposedly contains a single FF signal. As the output of this step, we also store the indices of the first columns of these sub-images as $\{c_k\}_{k=1}^{N_f}$. Note that $T_{f,0}$ is a hyper-parameter of this routine.

4. *Time Shrink:* The time localization is then performed on each sub-image as

$$I_f^{(k)}(x,y) \leftarrow 0, \quad \text{if } \sum_x I_f^{(k)}(x,y) < T_{f,\text{row}} \times L_k,$$

where L_k is the number of columns in the kth sub-image and $T_{f,\text{row}} \in (0,1)$ is a hyper-parameter of this step.

5. *Box Assignment:* This step finally outputs a box list $\mathcal{F} = \{(x_k, y_k, w_k, h_k)\}_{k=1}^{N_f}$ where each box is given by

$$x_k = c_k, \quad w_k = L_k,$$
$$y_k = r + \min_{y:\sum_x I_f^{(k)}(x,y)>0} y,$$
$$h_k = \max_{y:\sum_x I_f^{(k)}(x,y)>0} y - \min_{y:\sum_x I_f^{(k)}(x,y)>0} y + 1.$$

In the above formulas, c_k is the index of the first column, L_k is the number of columns of the kth sub-image $I_f^{(k)}$, and r is the index of the first row of the whole input image I.

Localization of FH Signals (Lower Branch)

1. *Initialize* $I_h \leftarrow I$.
2. *FF Removal:* This step erases FF signals out of the image I_h by setting

$$I_h(x,y) \leftarrow 0, \quad \text{if } \sum_y I_h(x,y) > T_{h,\text{col}} \times M,$$

where $T_{h,\text{col}} \in (0,1)$ is a hyper-parameter.

3. *Frequency Split:* Similarly to the upper branch, we split I_h into K_h sub-images $\{I_h^{(k)}\}_{k=1}^{K_h}$ that are separated by at least $T_{h,0}$ consecutive zero-columns. However, unlike the Frequency Split for FF signals, each sub-image obtained from this step may contain multiple signal hops. The purpose of this step is actually to reduce the heavy computation incurred by the morphological operators in the next step.

4. *Morphology:* We then apply 2 morphological operators on each sub-image as

$$I_h^{(k)} \leftarrow \left(I_h^{(k)} \bullet E_1\right) \circ E_2,$$

where the symbols $\bullet$ and $\circ$ denote the closing and opening operators [4], respectively; E_1 and E_2 are the corresponding structuring elements. While the closing operator interpolates the holes in each hop, the opening operator plays the role of a denoiser. In experiments, we always choose E_1 and E_2 to be rectangle structuring elements of size $|E_1|$ and $|E_2|$, respectively, which are the hyper-parameters of this step. Figure 4 illustrates the effect of the Morphology procedure.

5. *Blob Labeling:* This step extracts the time-frequency hops by applying a connected-component labeling algorithm on each of the sub-images. The output of this step is a list of sets $\{S_k\}_{k=1}^{N_h}$ where each set S_k contains the coordinates (x, y) of 4-connected pixels of value 1.

6. *Box Assignment:* This step gives a box list $\mathcal{H} = \{(x_k, y_k, w_k, h_k)\}_{k=1}^{N_h}$ where

$$x_k = c_n + \min_{x \in S_k} x, \quad w_k = \max_{x \in S_k} x - \min_{x \in S_k} x + 1,$$

$$y_k = r + \min_{y \in S_k} y, \quad h_k = \max_{y \in S_k} y - \min_{y \in S_k} y + 1.$$

Here, c_n is the index of the first column of the nth sub-image $I_h^{(n)}$ that contains blob S_k, and r is the index of the first row of the whole image I.

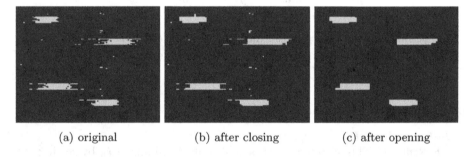

(a) original   (b) after closing   (c) after opening

Fig. 4. Morphological operators applied to part of the binary spectrogram containing several signal hops.

2.3   Signal Tracking

This module deals with the tracking of signals along the time axis. To that end, we divide the waterfall image into blocks $\{I_n\}_{n \geq 1}$ such that each block has M rows and every 2 consecutive blocks overlap by N_{overlap} rows. Each block I_n is then passed to the Signal Localization module to obtain 2 box lists $(\mathcal{F}_n, \mathcal{H}_n)$. These two lists are then combined with the previous lists to create 2 new lists $(\mathcal{F}'_n, \mathcal{H}'_n)$ that track all the narrowband signals up to time $t_n = n(M - N_{\text{overlap}}) + N_{\text{overlap}}$. The overall tracking procedure is diagrammed in Fig. 5. The 2 main routines of this module are discussed below.

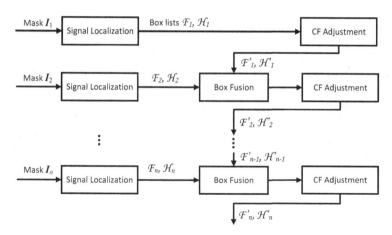

Fig. 5. Block diagram of the Signal Tracking.

1. *CF Adjustment:* In this routine, each bounding box of a narrowband signal is expanded such that the vertical center line (center frequency) of the box contains a significant number of nonzero pixels. Specifically, for a box (x, y, w, h) surrounding a signal, define image I to be the restriction of the spectrogram on the region inside this box. The (x, w) components of the box are then adjusted as

$$x_0 = \underset{x:\sum_y I(x,y)>T_{\text{center}} \times h}{\arg\min} |x - w/2|,$$

$$(x, w) \leftarrow \begin{cases} (x, 2x_0 + 1), & \text{if } x_0 > w/2 \\ (x + 2x_0 - w + 1, 2(w - x_0) - 1), & \text{if } x_0 < w/2. \end{cases}$$

Here, $T_{\text{center}} \in (0, 1)$ is a hyper-parameter of this step.

2. *Box Fusion:* This routine merges a newly detected box (x, y, w, h) with an existing box (x', y', w', h') in the previous list if the following conditions

$$y - (y' + h) > T_{\text{gap}},$$
$$\min\{x + w, x' + w'\} - \max\{x, x'\} > T_{\text{ratio}} \times \min\{w, w'\}$$

hold. We use different sets of hyper-parameters: $(T_{\text{f,gap}}, T_{\text{f,ratio}})$ for FF signals and $(T_{\text{h,gap}}, T_{\text{h,ratio}})$ for FH signals. The merged box is then defined as

$$w' \leftarrow \max\{x + w, w' + x'\} - \min\{x, x'\},$$
$$h' \leftarrow \max\{y + h, y' + h'\} - \min\{y, y'\},$$
$$x' \leftarrow \min\{x, x'\}, \quad y' \leftarrow \min\{y, y'\}.$$

The overall effect of the Signal Tracking module is illustrated in Fig. 6.

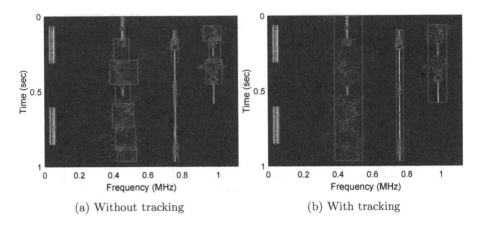

(a) Without tracking   (b) With tracking

Fig. 6. Signal Tracking with box fusion and center-frequency adjustment.

3 Numerical Results

The proposed sensing scheme was implemented in Matlab 2017b. We simulated 1 s of a 50 MHz-wideband signal in the spectrum $40 \div 90$ MHz, which produces 50×10^6 samples. This wideband signal contains 43 different narrowband FF signals using Frequency Modulation (FM), a collection of 200 FH signals hopping linearly at speed 200 hops/sec, and another collection of 500 FH signals hopping randomly at speed 500 hops/sec. That results in a total number of 743 signals. For computing the spectrogram, we used a rectangular window of size $L = 2^{14}$. The wideband signal was corrupted by Additive White Gaussian Noise with various levels of Signal-to-Noise Ratio (SNR).

Each binary image going through the Signal Localization module consists of $M = 500$ rows of the spectrogram and overlaps by $N_{\text{overlap}} = 50$ rows with the next image. The other hyper-parameters used in experiments are given in Table 1. The blob labeling was done via the built-in function **bwconncomp** of Matlab. Results are visualized in Fig. 7 with zoomed-in parts of the simulated frequency band. Out of the drawn bounding boxes, we assigned one to a narrowband signal if it overlaps significantly with the ground-truth bounding box. More precisely, the two boxes are matched if the ratio Intersection Over Union (IOU) between them is above 60%. A signal is called *detected* if it is assigned to a bounding box output by the spectrum sensing system. The detection rate and the Mean Absolute Error (MAE) of 4 characteristics of the detected signals, computed by (1) and (2), are reported in Table 2 for 5 different noise levels. It can be seen that the proposed scheme achieved both high detection rate and high accuracy across a relatively wide range of SNRs.

Table 1. Hyper-parameter values. 'SB' stands for Spectrogram Binarization.

Module	SB	Signal localization							Signal tracking				
Param	T_{offset}	$T_{\text{f,col}}$	$T_{\text{f,0}}$	$T_{\text{f,row}}$	$T_{\text{h,col}}$	$T_{\text{h,0}}$	$|E_1|$	$|E_2|$	T_{center}	$T_{\text{f,gap}}$	$T_{\text{f,ratio}}$	$T_{\text{h,gap}}$	$T_{\text{h,ratio}}$
Value	17	0.07	5	0.05	0.2	50	$(2,4)$	$(2,2)$	0.6	200	0.3	0	0.7

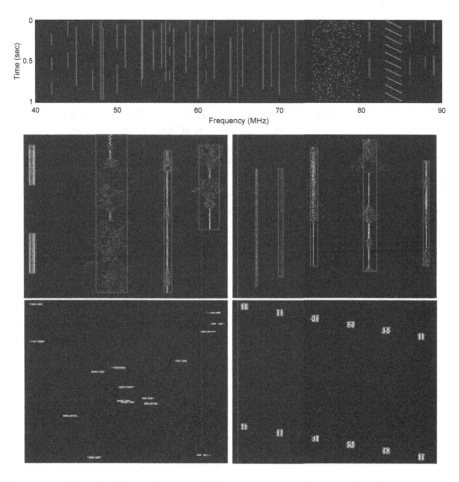

Fig. 7. Top: bounding boxes for FF and FH signals are drawn in red and green, respectively, on binary spectrogram over a bandwidth of 50 MHz and a duration of 1 s with SNR = −4 dB. Bottom 4 figures: Zoomed-in subbands. (Color figure online)

Table 2. Detection rate and mean absolute error of 4 characteristics of the detected signals with respect to different SNR levels of the wideband signal.

SNR	Detection rate	Mean absolute error			
		Starting time	Stopping time	Center frequency	Bandwidth
−4 dB	60.43%	0.0882 ms	0.0655 ms	2.4808 KHz	6.8783 KHz
−2 dB	85.87%	0.0649 ms	0.0334 ms	2.3223 KHz	6.2996 KHz
0 dB	94.21%	0.0411 ms	0.0201 ms	2.2278 KHz	5.2229 KHz
2 dB	96.10%	0.0315 ms	0.0155 ms	2.3593 KHz	3.5903 KHz
4 dB	97.98%	0.0272 ms	0.0169 ms	2.3307 KHz	1.9618 KHz

4 Conclusion

We have presented in this paper a novel method for on-line wideband spectrum sensing that relies on the processing and fusion of binary time-frequency images. These images are obtained by combining a simple energy detector with a noise floor estimator on the STFTs of the wideband signal. The signal localization and tracking are both performed on binary images, allowing fast algorithms. As simulations suggested, this method is effective for both fixed-frequency and frequency-hopping signals, which are likely to simultaneously appear in a wide spectrum. We believe that the proposed method can be implemented into a real system for automatic spectrum monitoring, an essential step towards the realization of cognitive radio networks.

References

1. Ariananda, D.D., Leus, G.: Cooperative compressive wideband power spectrum sensing. In: Proceedings of IEEE ASILOMAR, pp. 303–307. Pacific Groove, CA, July 2012
2. Cohen, D., Eldar, Y.C.: Sub-Nyquist sampling for power spectrum sensing in cognitive radios: a unified approach. IEEE Trans. Signal Process. **62**(15), 3897–3910 (2014)
3. Farhang-Boroujeny, B.: Filter bank spectrum sensing for cognitive radios. IEEE Trans. Signal Process. **56**(5), 1801–1811 (2008)
4. Gonzalez, R.C., Woods, R.E.: Digital Image Processing, 3rd edn. Prentice-Hall, Upper Saddle River (2006)
5. Lampert, T.A., O'keefe, S.E.M.: A survey of spectrogram track detection algorithms. Appl. Acoustics **71**(2), 87–100 (2010)
6. Liang, Y.C., Chen, K.C., Li, G.Y., Mahonen, P.: Cognitive radio networking and communications: an overview. IEEE Trans. Veh. Technol. **60**(7), 3386–3407 (2011)
7. Mishali, M., Eldar, Y.C.: Blind multiband signal reconstruction: compressive sensing for analog signals. IEEE Trans. Signal Process. **57**(3), 993–1009 (2009)
8. Mitola, J., Maguire, G.Q.: Cognitive radio: making software radios more personal. IEEE Pers. Commun. **6**(4), 13–18 (1999)
9. Ready, M.J., Downey, M.L., Corbalis, L.J.: Automatic noise floor spectrum estimation in the presence of signals. In: Proceedings of IEEE ASILOMAR, pp. 877–881 (1997)

10. Sun, H., Nallanathan, A., Wang, C.X.: Wideband spectrum sensing for cognitive radio networks: a survey. IEEE Wirel. Commun. **20**(2), 74–81 (2013)
11. Tian, Z., Giannakis, G.B.: A wavelet approach to wideband spectrum sensing for cognitive radios. In: Proceeding of IEEE CROWNCOM, pp. 1–5, Mykonos Island, Greece, 08–10 July 2006
12. Tian, Z., Tafesse, Y., Sadler, B.M.: Cyclic feature detection with sub-Nyquist sampling for wideband spectrum sensing. IEEE J. Sel. Top. Signal Process. **6**(1), 58–69 (2012)
13. Watson, C.M.: Signal detection and digital modulation classification-based spectrum sensing for cognitive radio. Ph.D. thesis, Northeastern University, Boston, MA, USA (2013)
14. Yucek, T., Arslan, H.: A survey of spectrum sensing algorithms for cognitive radio applications. IEEE Commun. Surv. Tutor. **11**(1), 116–130 (2009)
15. Zeng, F., Li, C., Tian, Z.: Distributed compressive spectrum sensing in cooperative multihop cognitive networks. IEEE J. Sel. Top. Signal Process. **5**(1), 37–48 (2011)

Author Index

Printed in the United States
By Bookmasters